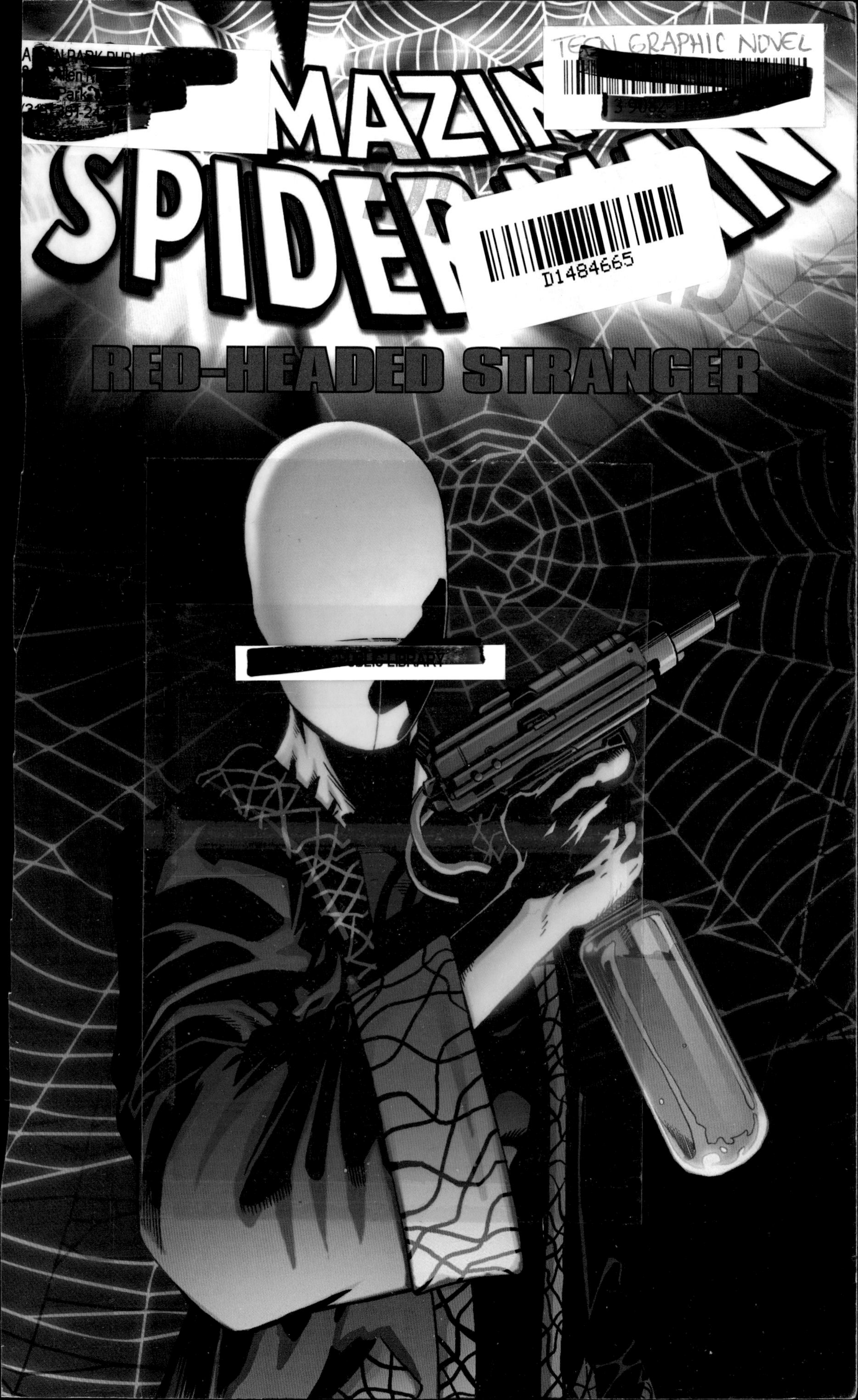

RED-HEADED STRANGER

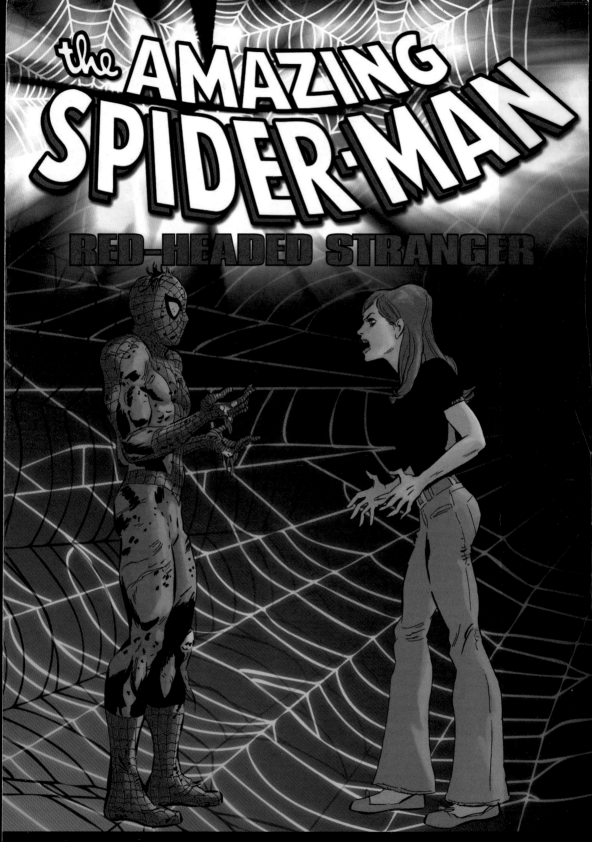

the AMAZING SPIDER-MAN

RED-HEADED STRANGER

SPIDER-MAN: RED-HEADED STRANGER. Contains material originally published in magazine form as AMAZING SPIDER-MAN #602-605. First printing 2009. Hardcover ISBN# 978-0-7851-4158-7. Softcover ISBN# 978-0-7851-3869-3. Published by MARVEL PUBLISHING, INC., a subsidiary of MARVEL ENTERTAINMENT, INC. OFFICE OF PUBLICATION: 417 5th Avenue, New York, NY 10016. Copyright © 2009 Marvel Characters, Inc. All rights reserved. Hardcover: $19.99 per copy in the U.S. (GST #R127032852). Softcover: $14.99 per copy in the U.S. (GST #R127032852). Canadian Agreement #40668537. All characters featured in this issue and the distinctive names and likenesses thereof, and all related indicia are trademarks of Marvel Characters, Inc. No similarity between any of the names, characters, persons, and/or institutions in this magazine with those of any living or dead person or institution is intended, and any such similarity which may exist is purely coincidental. **Printed in the U.S.A.** ALAN FINE, EVP - Office Of The Chief Executive Marvel Entertainment, Inc. & CMO Marvel Characters B.V.; DAN BUCKLEY, Chief Executive Officer and Publisher - Print, Animation & Digital Media; JIM SOKOLOWSKI, Chief Operating Officer; DAVID GABRIEL, SVP of Publishing Sales & Circulation; DAVID BOGART, SVP of Business Affairs & Talent Management; MICHAEL PASCIULLO, VP Merchandising & Communications; JIM O'KEEFE, VP of Operations & Logistics; DAN CARR, Executive Director of Publishing Technology; JUSTIN F. GABRIE, Director of Publishing & Editorial Operations; SUSAN CRESPI, Editorial Operations Manager; ALEX MORALES, Publishing Operations Manager; STAN LEE, Chairman Emeritus. For information regarding advertising in Marvel Comics or on Marvel.com, please contact Mitch Dane, Advertising Director, at mdane@marvel.com. For Marvel subscription inquiries, please call 800-217-9158. **Manufactured between** 10/26/09 and 11/25/09 (hardcover), and 10/26/09 and 4/28/10 (softcover), by R.R. DONNELLEY, INC., SALEM, VA, USA.

10 9 8 7 6 5 4 3 2 1

Writers: **FRED VAN LENTE**
WITH **BRIAN REED (ISSUE #605, CHAPTER 3)**
Pencilers: **BARRY KITSON, ROBERT ATKINS,
JAVIER PULIDO, LUKE ROSS**
& **YANICK PAQUETTE**
Inkers: **RICK KETCHAM, BARRY KITSON,
VICTOR OLAZABA, JOE RUBINSTEIN,
JAVIER PULIDO, RICK MAGYAR**
& **MARK FARMER**
Colorists: **JEROMY COX, ANTONIO FABELA,
JAVIER RODRIGUEZ, ROB SCHWAGER**
& **NATHAN FAIRBAIRN**
Letterer: **VC'S JOE CARAMAGNA**
Cover Artists: **ADI GRANOV, STEPHANE ROUX,
LEINIL YU** & **MIKE MAYHEW**
Assistant Editor: **TOM BRENNAN**
Editor: **STEPHEN WACKER**
Executive Editor: **TOM BREVOORT**
Web-Heads: **BOB GALE, MARC GUGGENHEIM,
JOE KELLY, DAN SLOTT, FRED VAN LENTE,
MARK WAID** & **ZEB WELLS**

Collection Editor: **JENNIFER GRÜNWALD**
Assistant Editors: **ALEX STARBUCK** & **JOHN DENNING**
Editor, Special Projects: **MARK. D. BEAZLEY**
Senior Editor, Special Projects: **JEFF YOUNGQUIST**
Senior Vice President of Sales: **DAVID GABRIEL**

Editor in Chief: **JOE QUESADA**
Publisher: **DAN BUCKLEY**
Executive Producer: **ALAN FINE**

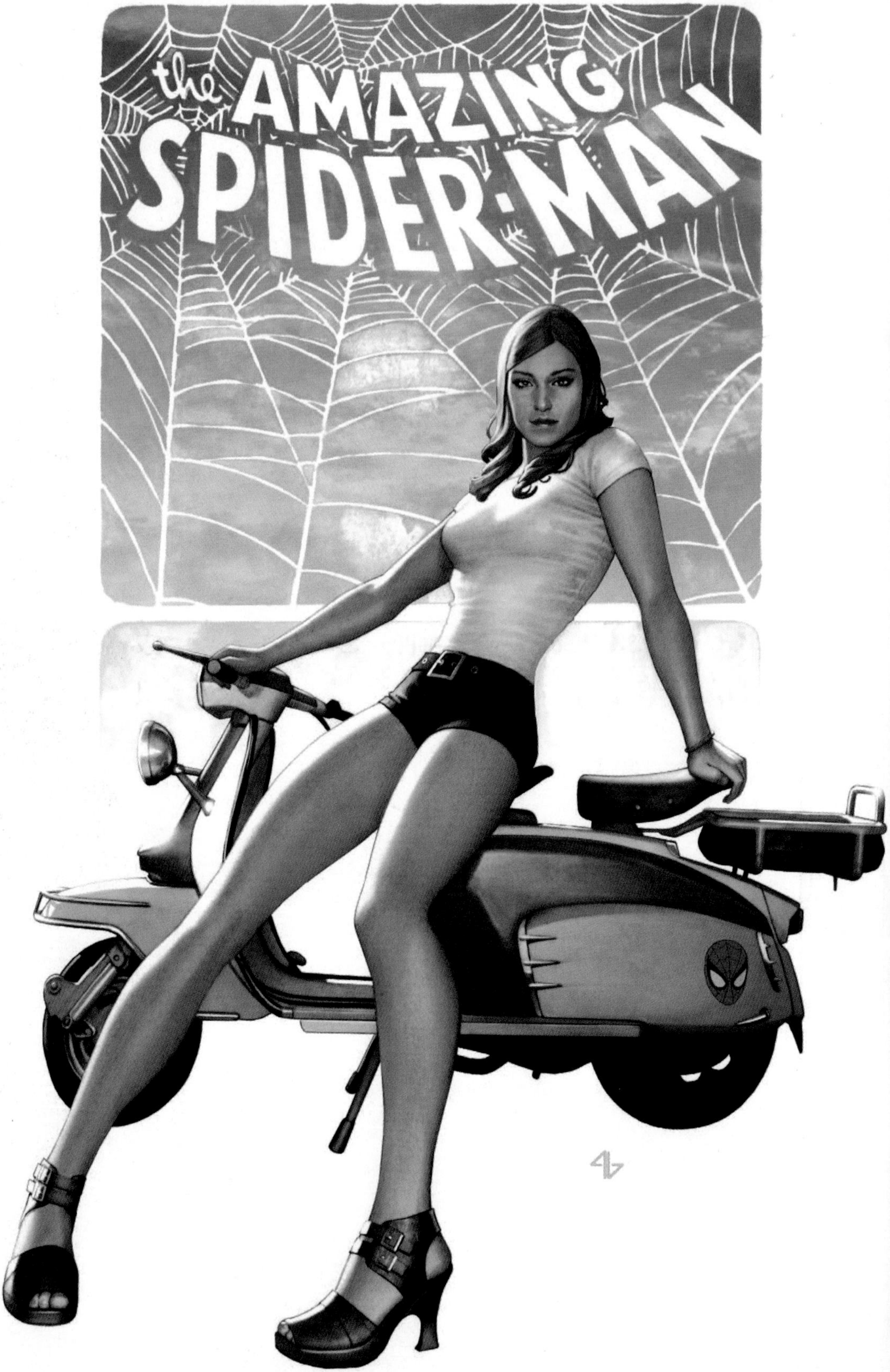
the AMAZING SPIDER-MAN

the AMAZING SPIDER-MAN

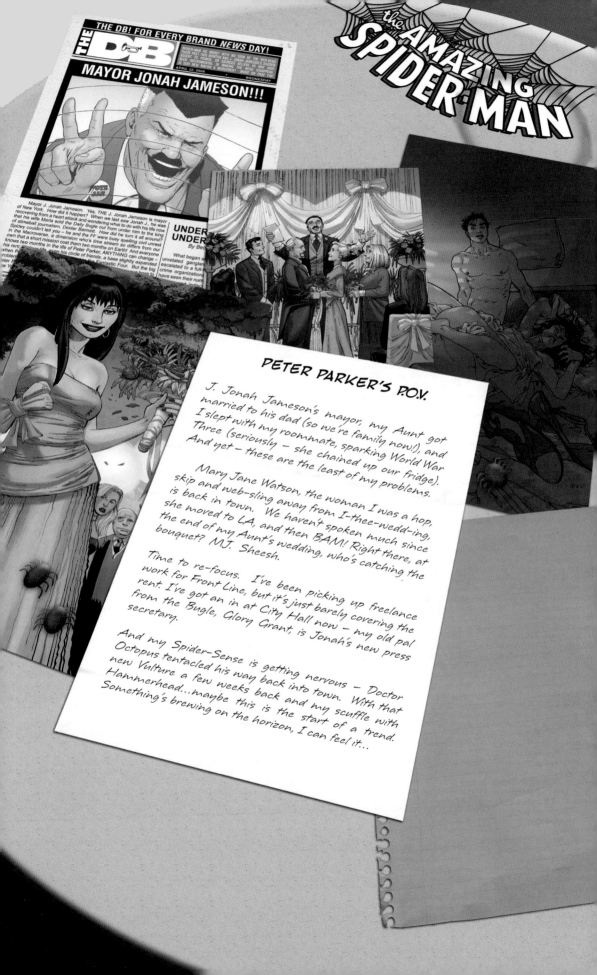

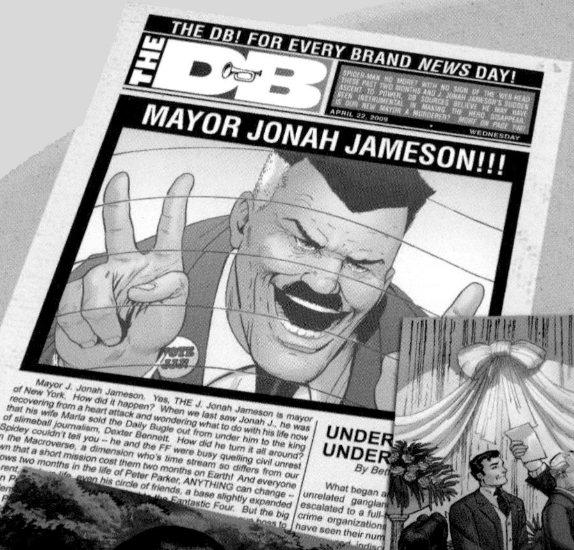
THE DB! FOR EVERY BRAND NEWS DAY!
THE DB
SPIDER-MAN NO MORE? WITH NO SIGN OF THE WEB-HEAD THESE PAST TWO MONTHS AND J. JONAH JAMESON'S SUDDEN ASCENT TO POWER, DB SOURCES BELIEVE HE MAY HAVE BEEN INSTRUMENTAL IN MAKING THE HERO DISAPPEAR. IS OUR NEW MAYOR A MURDERER? MORE ON PAGE 7A!
APRIL 22, 2009
WEDNESDAY
MAYOR JONAH JAMESON!!!
Mayor J. Jonah Jameson. Yes, THE J. Jonah Jameson is mayor of New York. How did it happen? When we last saw Jonah J., he was recovering from a heart attack and wondering what to do with his life now that his wife Marla sold the Daily Bugle out from under him to the king of slimeball journalism, Dexter Bennett. How did he turn it all around? Spidey couldn't tell you -- he and the FF were busy quelling civil unrest in the Macroverse, a dimension who's time stream so differs from our own that a short mission cost them two months on Earth! And everyone knows two months in the life of Peter Parker, ANYTHING can change --
UNDER
UNDER
What began a
unrelated ganglan
escalated to a full-
crime organizations
have seen their num

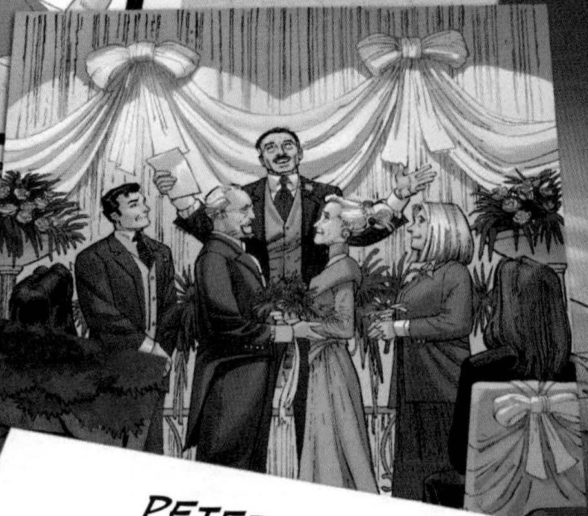

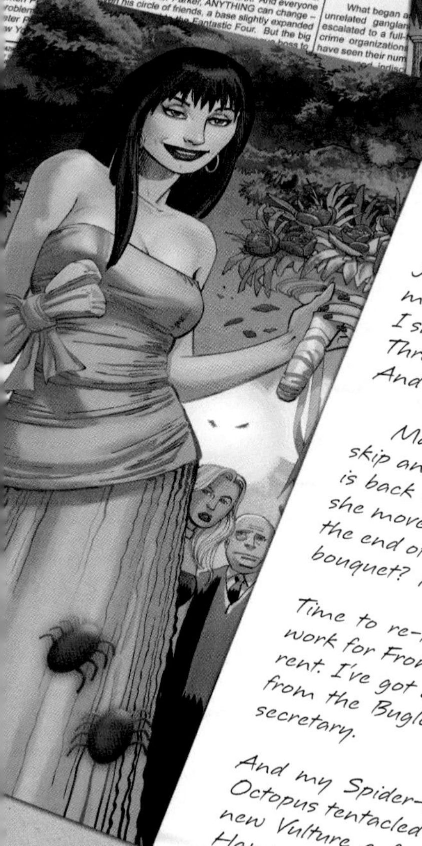

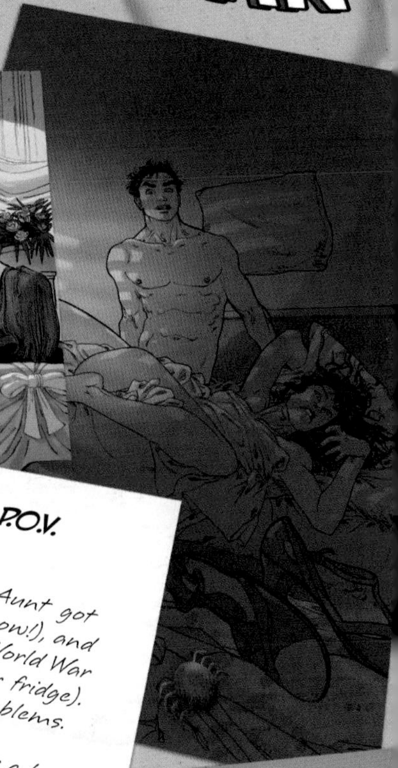

PETER PARKER'S P.O.V.

J. Jonah Jameson's mayor, my Aunt got married to his dad (so we're family now!), and I slept with my roommate, sparking World War Three (seriously – she chained up our fridge). And yet – these are the least of my problems.

Mary Jane Watson, the woman I was a hop, skip and web-sling away from I-thee-wedd-ing, is back in town. We haven't spoken much since she moved to LA, and then BAM! Right there, at the end of my Aunt's wedding, who's catching the bouquet? MJ. Sheesh.

Time to re-focus. I've been picking up freelance work for Front Line, but it's just barely covering the rent. I've got an in at City Hall now – my old pal from the Bugle, Glory Grant, is Jonah's new press secretary.

And my Spider-Sense is getting nervous – Doctor Octopus tentacled his way back into town. With that new Vulture a few weeks back and my scuffle with Hammerhead...maybe this is the start of a trend. Something's brewing on the horizon, I can feel it...

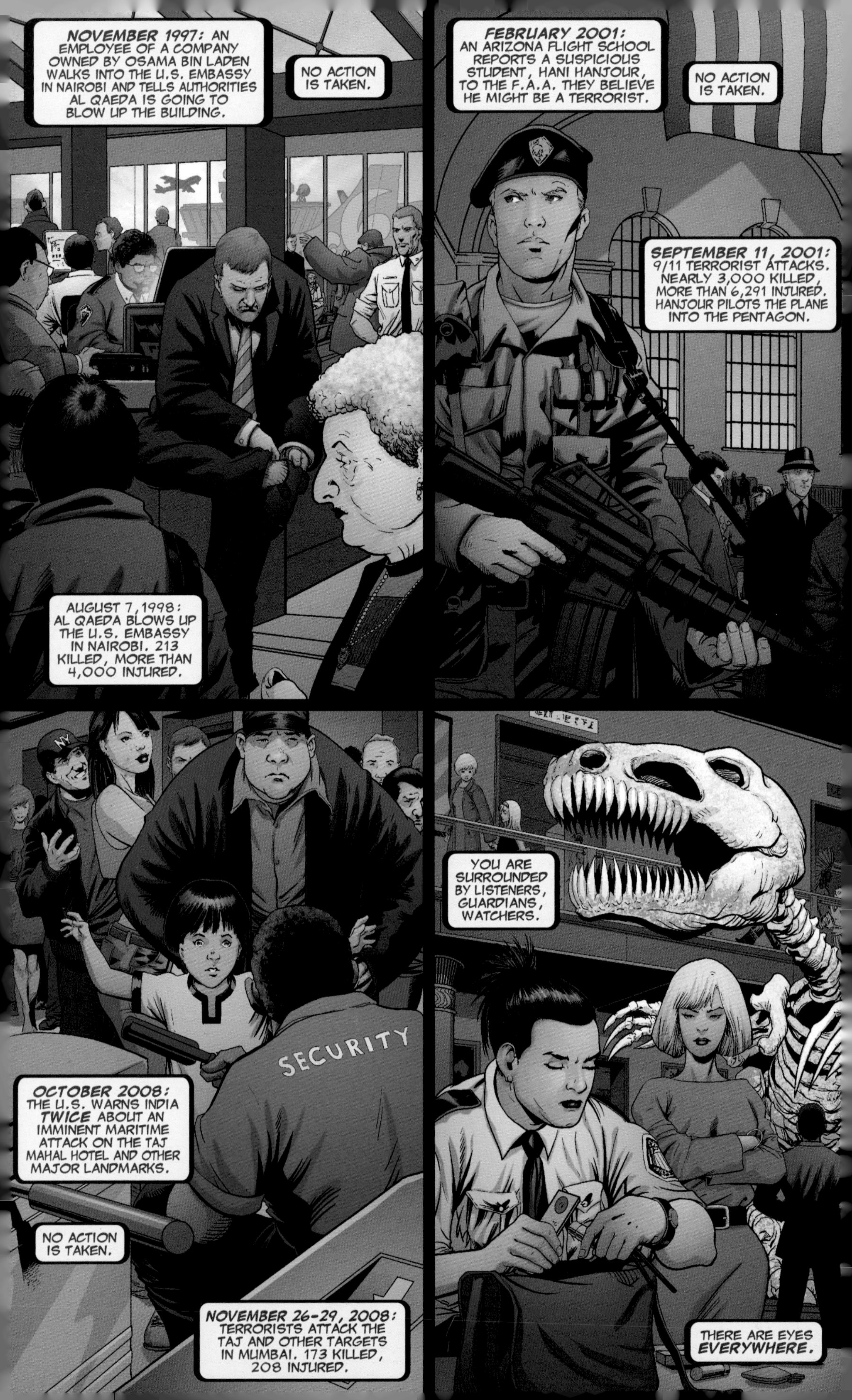
NOVEMBER 1997: AN EMPLOYEE OF A COMPANY OWNED BY OSAMA BIN LADEN WALKS INTO THE U.S. EMBASSY IN NAIROBI AND TELLS AUTHORITIES AL QAEDA IS GOING TO BLOW UP THE BUILDING.
NO ACTION IS TAKEN.
AUGUST 7, 1998: AL QAEDA BLOWS UP THE U.S. EMBASSY IN NAIROBI. 213 KILLED, MORE THAN 4,000 INJURED.
FEBRUARY 2001: AN ARIZONA FLIGHT SCHOOL REPORTS A SUSPICIOUS STUDENT, HANI HANJOUR, TO THE F.A.A. THEY BELIEVE HE MIGHT BE A TERRORIST.
NO ACTION IS TAKEN.
SEPTEMBER 11, 2001: 9/11 TERRORIST ATTACKS. NEARLY 3,000 KILLED, MORE THAN 6,291 INJURED. HANJOUR PILOTS THE PLANE INTO THE PENTAGON.
SECURITY
OCTOBER 2008: THE U.S. WARNS INDIA TWICE ABOUT AN IMMINENT MARITIME ATTACK ON THE TAJ MAHAL HOTEL AND OTHER MAJOR LANDMARKS.
NO ACTION IS TAKEN.
NOVEMBER 26-29, 2008: TERRORISTS ATTACK THE TAJ AND OTHER TARGETS IN MUMBAI. 173 KILLED, 208 INJURED.
YOU ARE SURROUNDED BY LISTENERS, GUARDIANS, WATCHERS.
THERE ARE EYES EVERYWHERE.

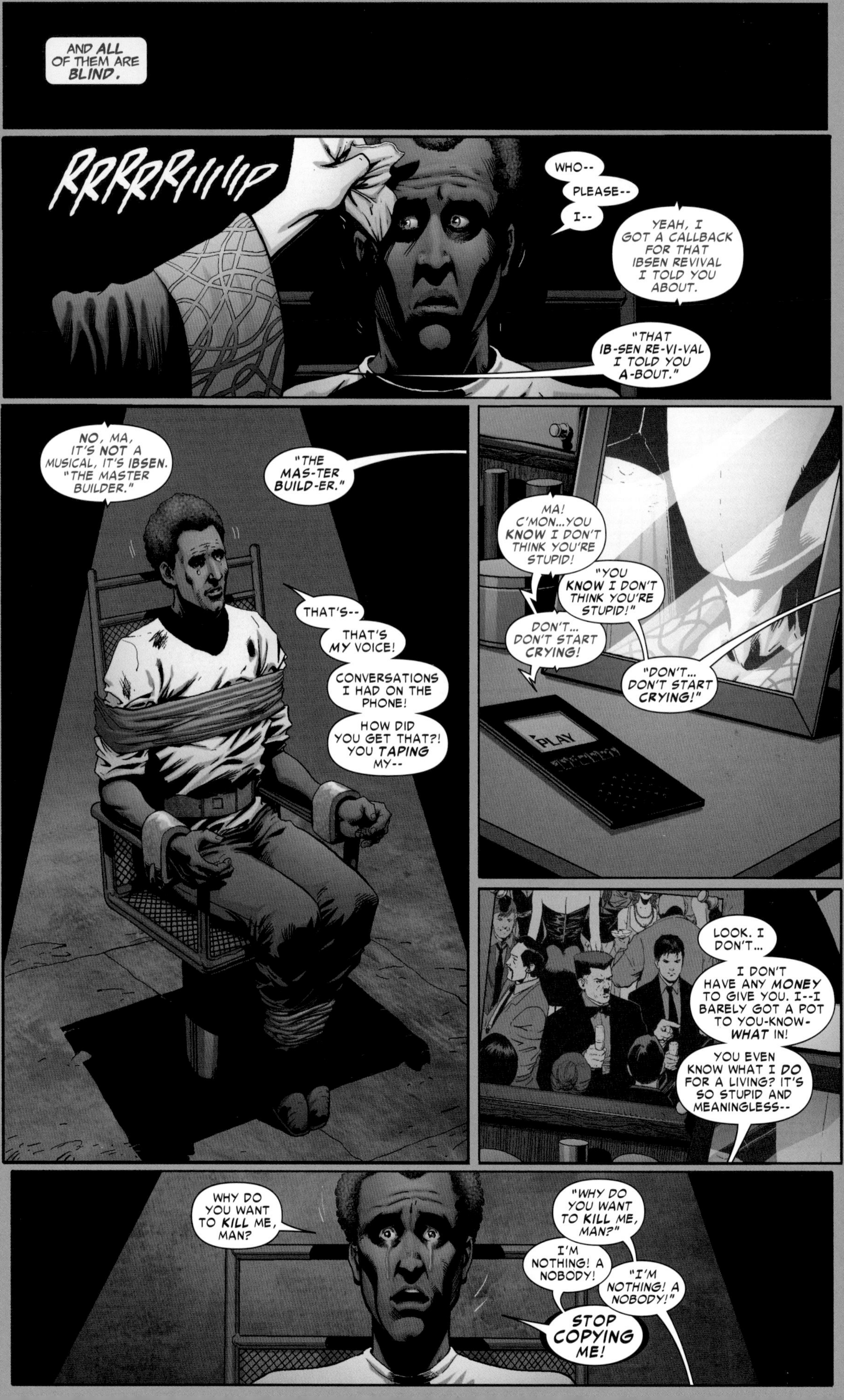
AND ALL OF THEM ARE BLIND.
RRRRRIIIIIP
WHO--
PLEASE--
I--
YEAH, I GOT A CALLBACK FOR THAT IBSEN REVIVAL I TOLD YOU ABOUT.
"THAT IB-SEN RE-VI-VAL I TOLD YOU A-BOUT."
NO, MA, IT'S NOT A MUSICAL, IT'S IBSEN. "THE MASTER BUILDER."
"THE MAS-TER BUILD-ER."
THAT'S--
THAT'S MY VOICE!
CONVERSATIONS I HAD ON THE PHONE!
HOW DID YOU GET THAT?! YOU TAPING MY--
MA! C'MON...YOU KNOW I DON'T THINK YOU'RE STUPID!
"YOU KNOW I DON'T THINK YOU'RE STUPID!"
DON'T... DON'T START CRYING!
"DON'T... DON'T START CRYING!"
PLAY
LOOK. I DON'T...
I DON'T HAVE ANY MONEY TO GIVE YOU. I--I BARELY GOT A POT TO YOU-KNOW-WHAT IN!
YOU EVEN KNOW WHAT I DO FOR A LIVING? IT'S SO STUPID AND MEANINGLESS--
WHY DO YOU WANT TO KILL ME, MAN?
"WHY DO YOU WANT TO KILL ME, MAN?"
I'M NOTHING! A NOBODY!
"I'M NOTHING! A NOBODY!"
STOP COPYING ME!

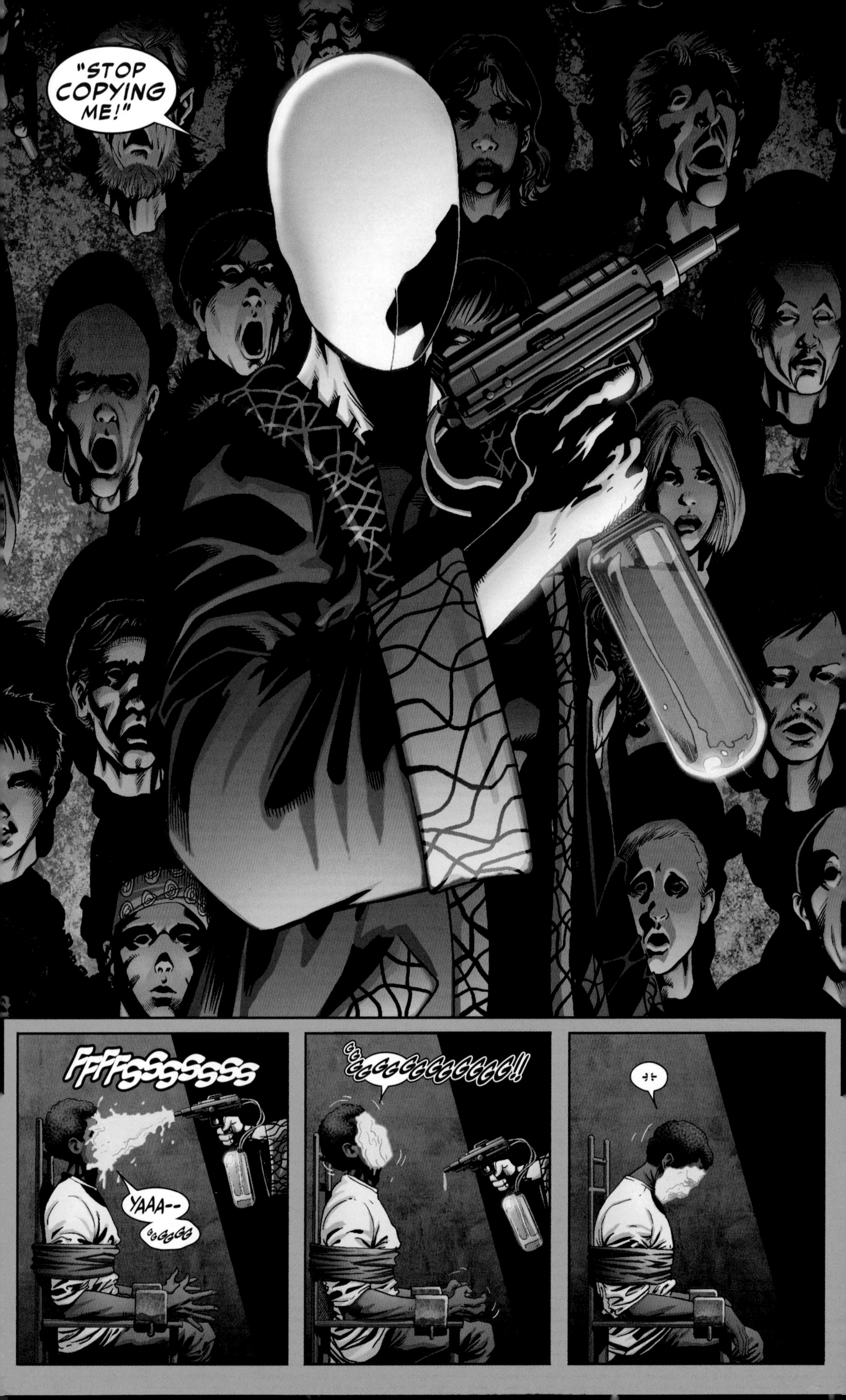
"STOP COPYING ME!"
FFFFSSSSSSSS
YAAA--
GGGGG
GGGGGGGGGGGGGGG!!

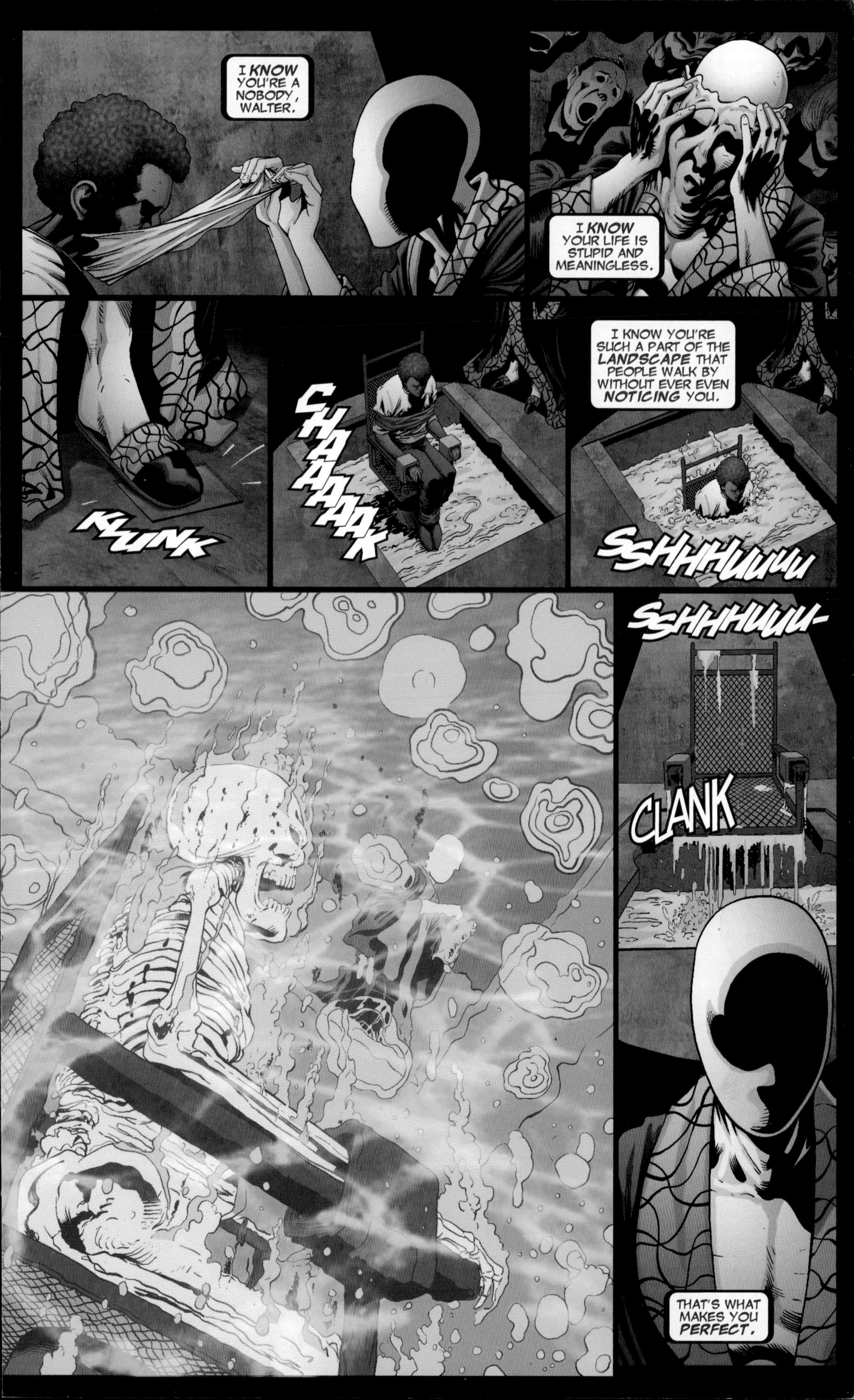
I KNOW YOU'RE A NOBODY, WALTER.
I KNOW YOUR LIFE IS STUPID AND MEANINGLESS.
KLUNK
CHAAAAAK
I KNOW YOU'RE SUCH A PART OF THE LANDSCAPE THAT PEOPLE WALK BY WITHOUT EVER EVEN NOTICING YOU.
SSHHHUUUU
SSHHHUUUU-
CLANK
THAT'S WHAT MAKES YOU PERFECT.

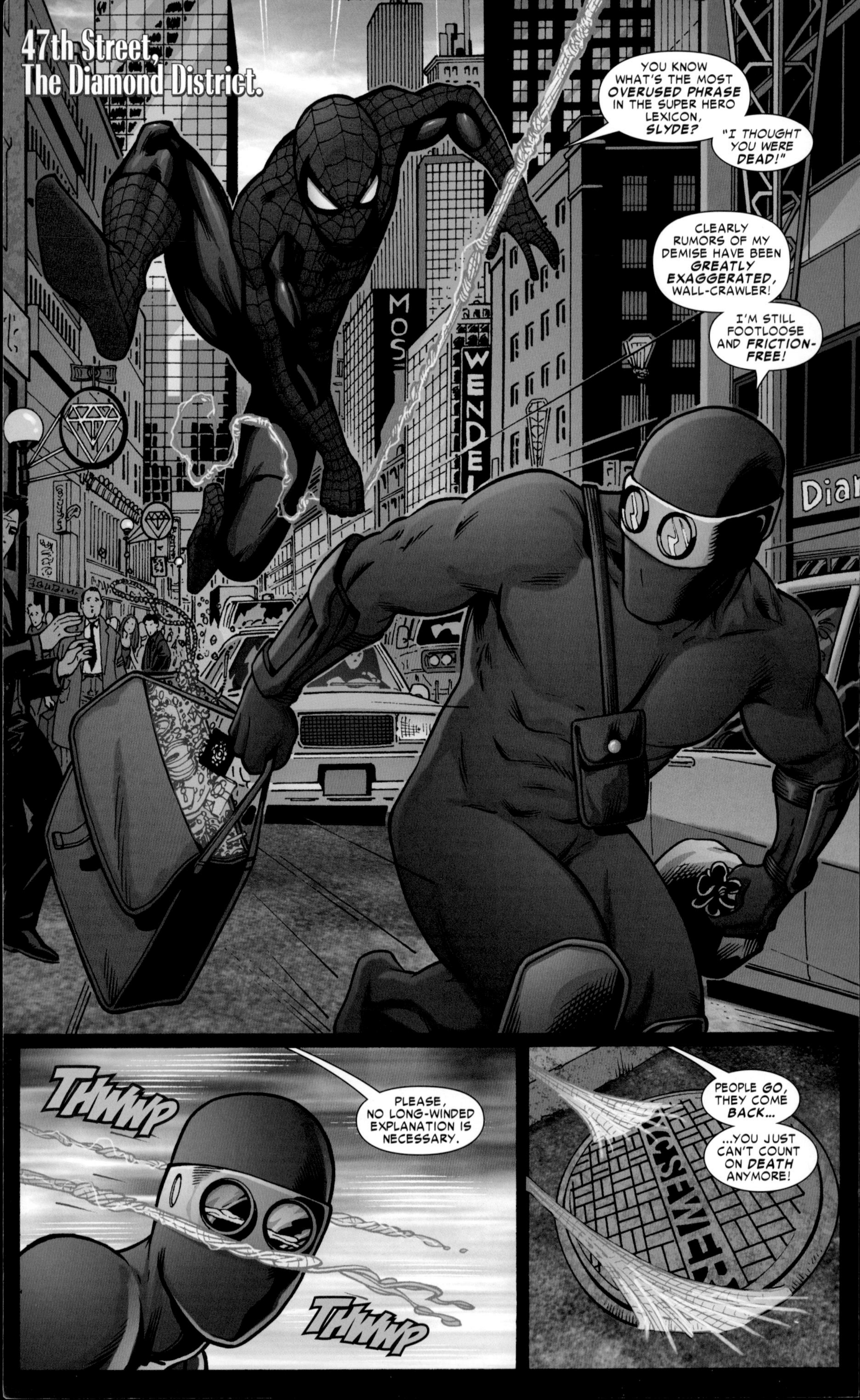
47th Street, The Diamond District.
YOU KNOW WHAT'S THE MOST OVERUSED PHRASE IN THE SUPER HERO LEXICON, SLYDE?
"I THOUGHT YOU WERE DEAD!"
CLEARLY RUMORS OF MY DEMISE HAVE BEEN GREATLY EXAGGERATED, WALL-CRAWLER!
I'M STILL FOOTLOOSE AND FRICTION-FREE!
THWWP
PLEASE, NO LONG-WINDED EXPLANATION IS NECESSARY.
THWWP
PEOPLE GO, THEY COME BACK...
...YOU JUST CAN'T COUNT ON DEATH ANYMORE!

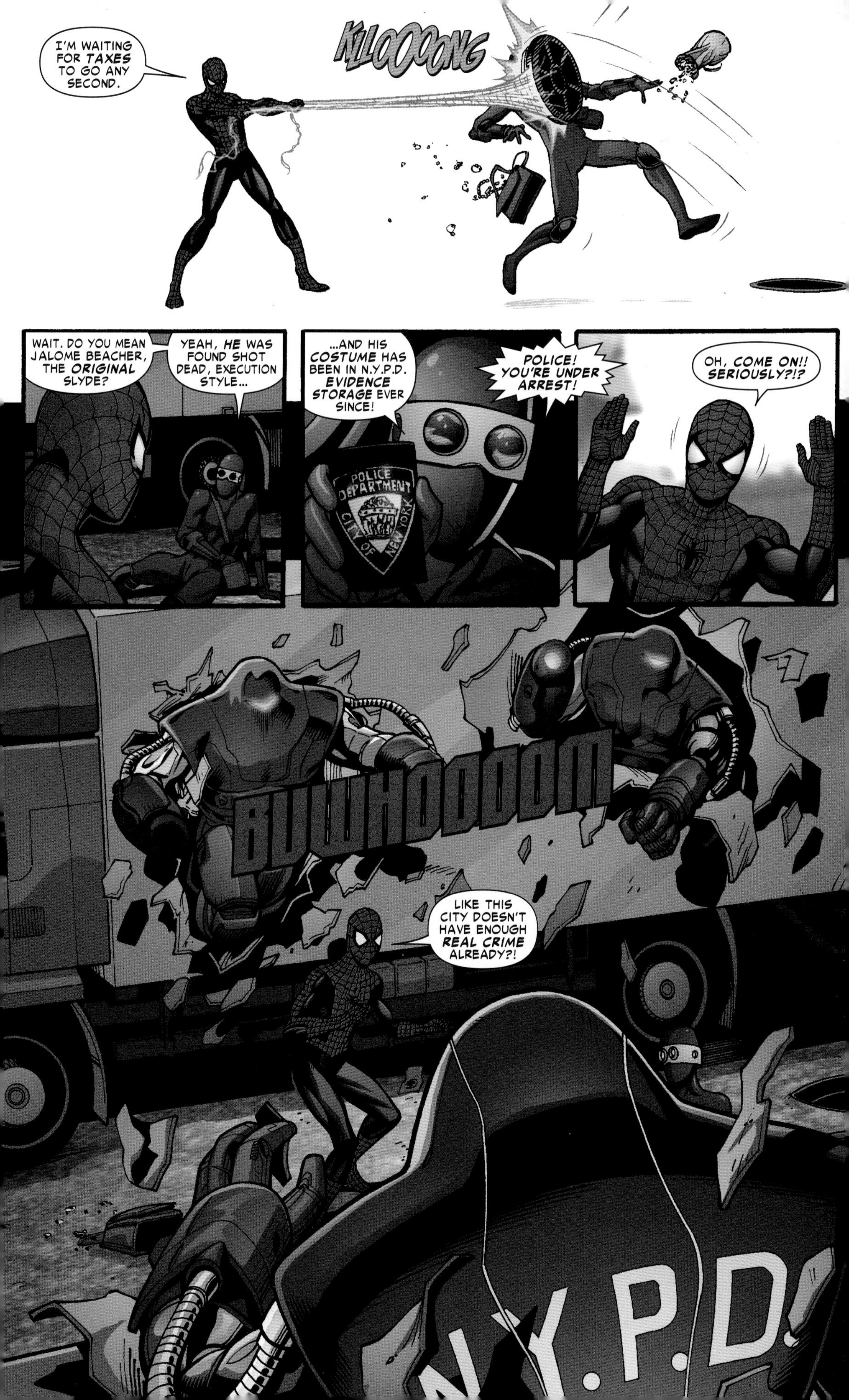
I'M WAITING FOR TAXES TO GO ANY SECOND.
KLLOOOOONG
WAIT. DO YOU MEAN JALOME BEACHER, THE ORIGINAL SLYDE?
YEAH, HE WAS FOUND SHOT DEAD, EXECUTION STYLE...
...AND HIS COSTUME HAS BEEN IN N.Y.P.D. EVIDENCE STORAGE EVER SINCE!
POLICE DEPARTMENT CITY OF NEW YORK
POLICE! YOU'RE UNDER ARREST!
OH, COME ON!! SERIOUSLY?!?
BWHOOOOM
LIKE THIS CITY DOESN'T HAVE ENOUGH REAL CRIME ALREADY?!
N.Y.P.D.

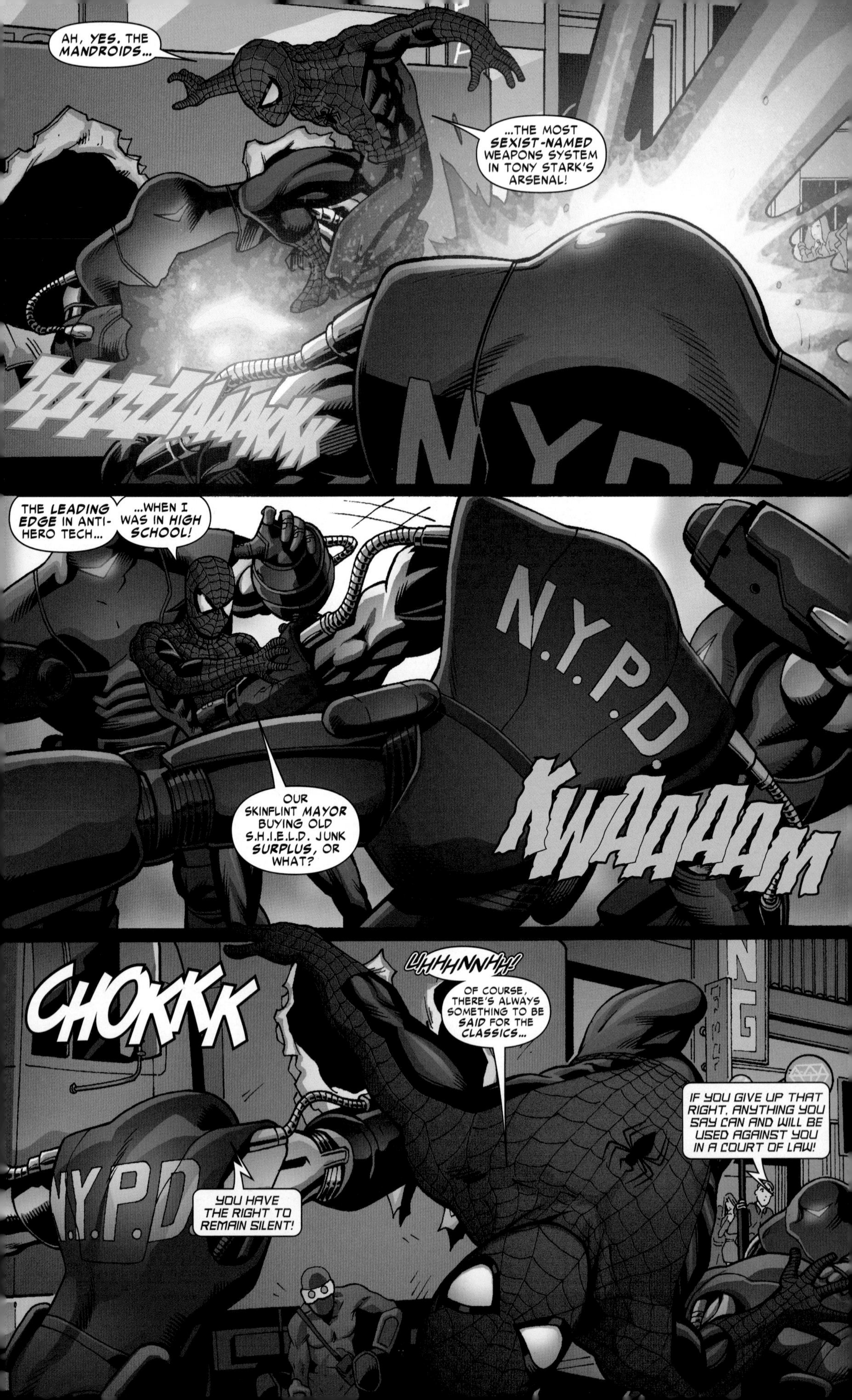
AH, YES. THE MANDROIDS...
...THE MOST SEXIST-NAMED WEAPONS SYSTEM IN TONY STARK'S ARSENAL!
THE LEADING EDGE IN ANTI-HERO TECH...
...WHEN I WAS IN HIGH SCHOOL!
N.Y.P.D.
OUR SKINFLINT MAYOR BUYING OLD S.H.I.E.L.D. JUNK SURPLUS, OR WHAT?
KWADAAM
CHOKKK
UHHHNNHH!
OF COURSE, THERE'S ALWAYS SOMETHING TO BE SAID FOR THE CLASSICS...
N.Y.P.D.
YOU HAVE THE RIGHT TO REMAIN SILENT!
IF YOU GIVE UP THAT RIGHT, ANYTHING YOU SAY CAN AND WILL BE USED AGAINST YOU IN A COURT OF LAW!

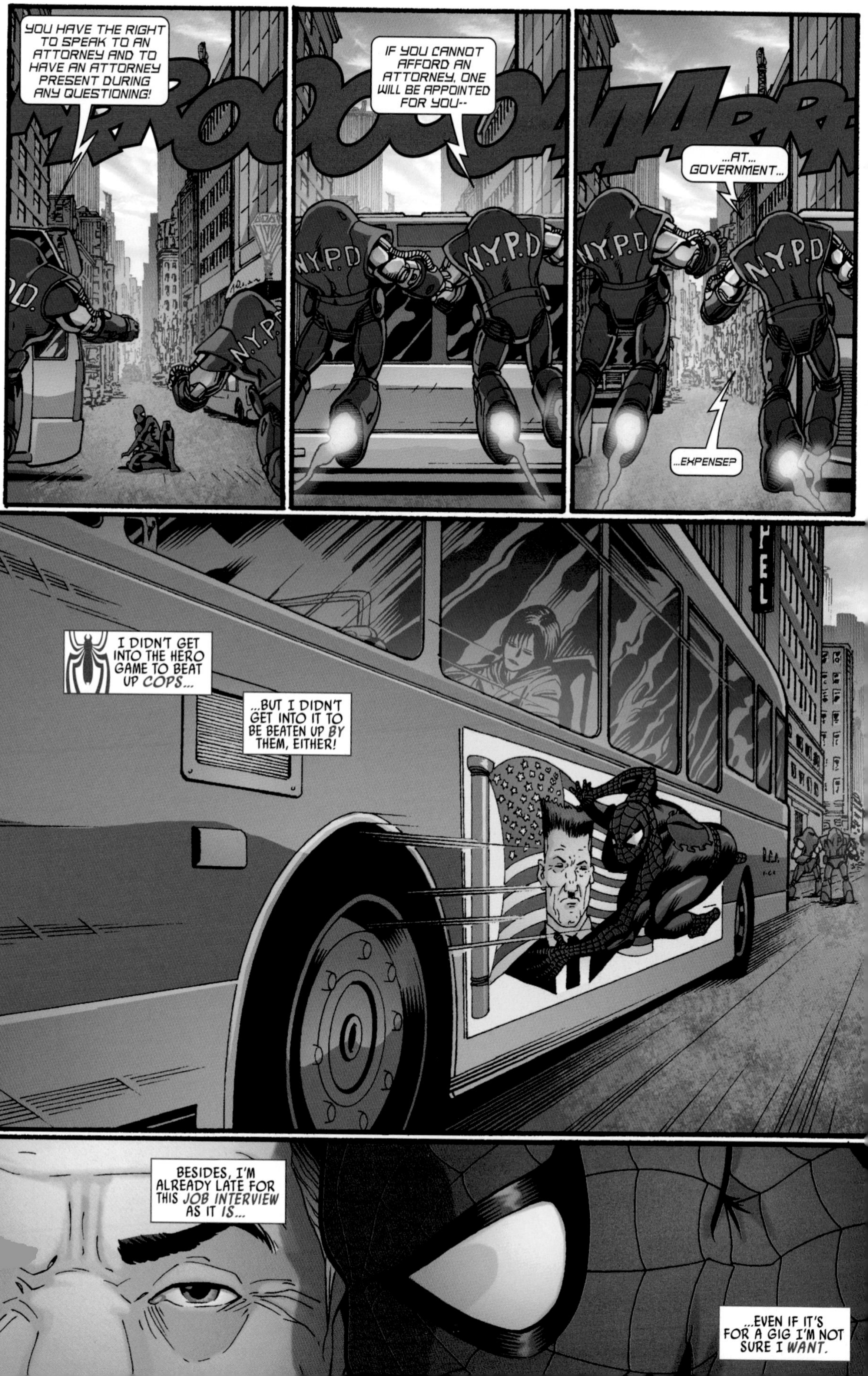
YOU HAVE THE RIGHT TO SPEAK TO AN ATTORNEY AND TO HAVE AN ATTORNEY PRESENT DURING ANY QUESTIONING!
IF YOU CANNOT AFFORD AN ATTORNEY, ONE WILL BE APPOINTED FOR YOU--
...AT... GOVERNMENT...
...EXPENSE?
I DIDN'T GET INTO THE HERO GAME TO BEAT UP COPS...
...BUT I DIDN'T GET INTO IT TO BE BEATEN UP BY THEM, EITHER!
BESIDES, I'M ALREADY LATE FOR THIS JOB INTERVIEW AS IT IS...
...EVEN IF IT'S FOR A GIG I'M NOT SURE I WANT.

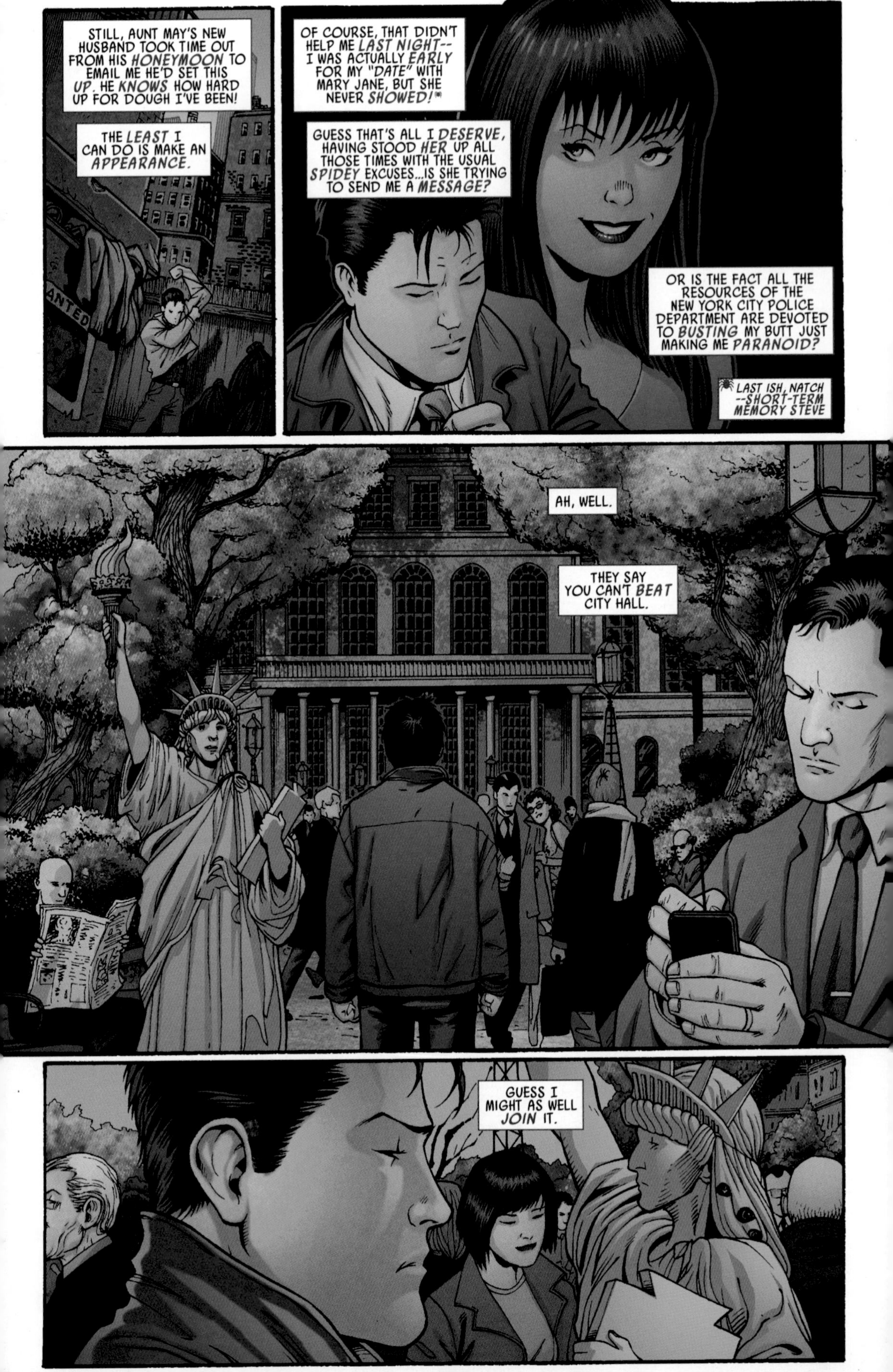
STILL, AUNT MAY'S NEW HUSBAND TOOK TIME OUT FROM HIS HONEYMOON TO EMAIL ME HE'D SET THIS UP. HE KNOWS HOW HARD UP FOR DOUGH I'VE BEEN!
THE LEAST I CAN DO IS MAKE AN APPEARANCE.
OF COURSE, THAT DIDN'T HELP ME LAST NIGHT-- I WAS ACTUALLY EARLY FOR MY "DATE" WITH MARY JANE, BUT SHE NEVER SHOWED!*
GUESS THAT'S ALL I DESERVE, HAVING STOOD HER UP ALL THOSE TIMES WITH THE USUAL SPIDEY EXCUSES...IS SHE TRYING TO SEND ME A MESSAGE?
OR IS THE FACT ALL THE RESOURCES OF THE NEW YORK CITY POLICE DEPARTMENT ARE DEVOTED TO BUSTING MY BUTT JUST MAKING ME PARANOID?
*LAST ISH, NATCH --SHORT-TERM MEMORY STEVE
AH, WELL.
THEY SAY YOU CAN'T BEAT CITY HALL.
GUESS I MIGHT AS WELL JOIN IT.

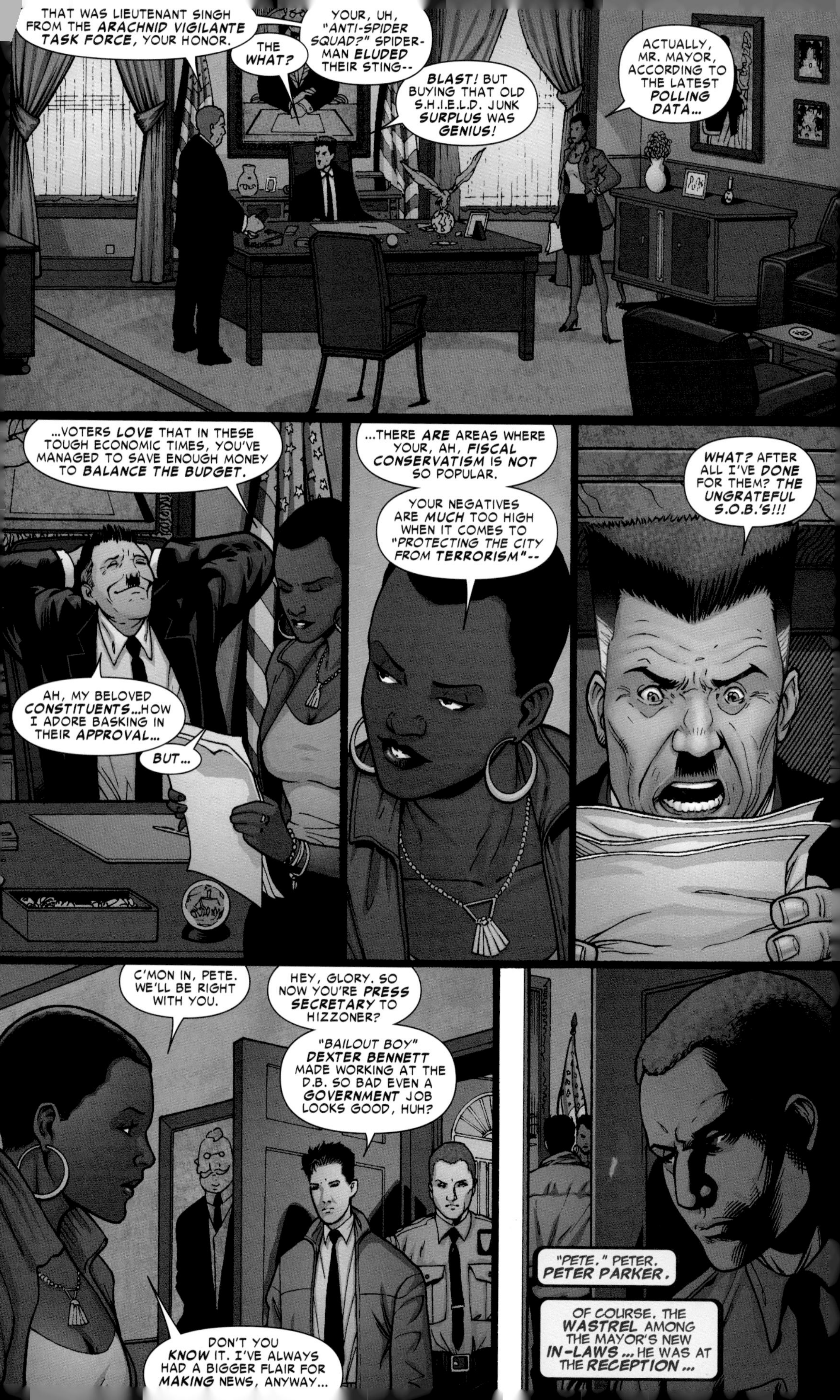
THAT WAS LIEUTENANT SINGH FROM THE ARACHNID VIGILANTE TASK FORCE, YOUR HONOR.
THE WHAT?
YOUR, UH, "ANTI-SPIDER SQUAD?" SPIDER-MAN ELUDED THEIR STING--
BLAST! BUT BUYING THAT OLD S.H.I.E.L.D. JUNK SURPLUS WAS GENIUS!
ACTUALLY, MR. MAYOR, ACCORDING TO THE LATEST POLLING DATA...
...VOTERS LOVE THAT IN THESE TOUGH ECONOMIC TIMES, YOU'VE MANAGED TO SAVE ENOUGH MONEY TO BALANCE THE BUDGET.
AH, MY BELOVED CONSTITUENTS...HOW I ADORE BASKING IN THEIR APPROVAL...
BUT...
...THERE ARE AREAS WHERE YOUR, AH, FISCAL CONSERVATISM IS NOT SO POPULAR.
YOUR NEGATIVES ARE MUCH TOO HIGH WHEN IT COMES TO "PROTECTING THE CITY FROM TERRORISM"--
WHAT? AFTER ALL I'VE DONE FOR THEM? THE UNGRATEFUL S.O.B.'S!!!
C'MON IN, PETE. WE'LL BE RIGHT WITH YOU.
HEY, GLORY. SO NOW YOU'RE PRESS SECRETARY TO HIZZONER?
"BAILOUT BOY" DEXTER BENNETT MADE WORKING AT THE D.B. SO BAD EVEN A GOVERNMENT JOB LOOKS GOOD, HUH?
DON'T YOU KNOW IT. I'VE ALWAYS HAD A BIGGER FLAIR FOR MAKING NEWS, ANYWAY...
"PETE." PETER. PETER PARKER.
OF COURSE. THE WASTREL AMONG THE MAYOR'S NEW IN-LAWS... HE WAS AT THE RECEPTION...

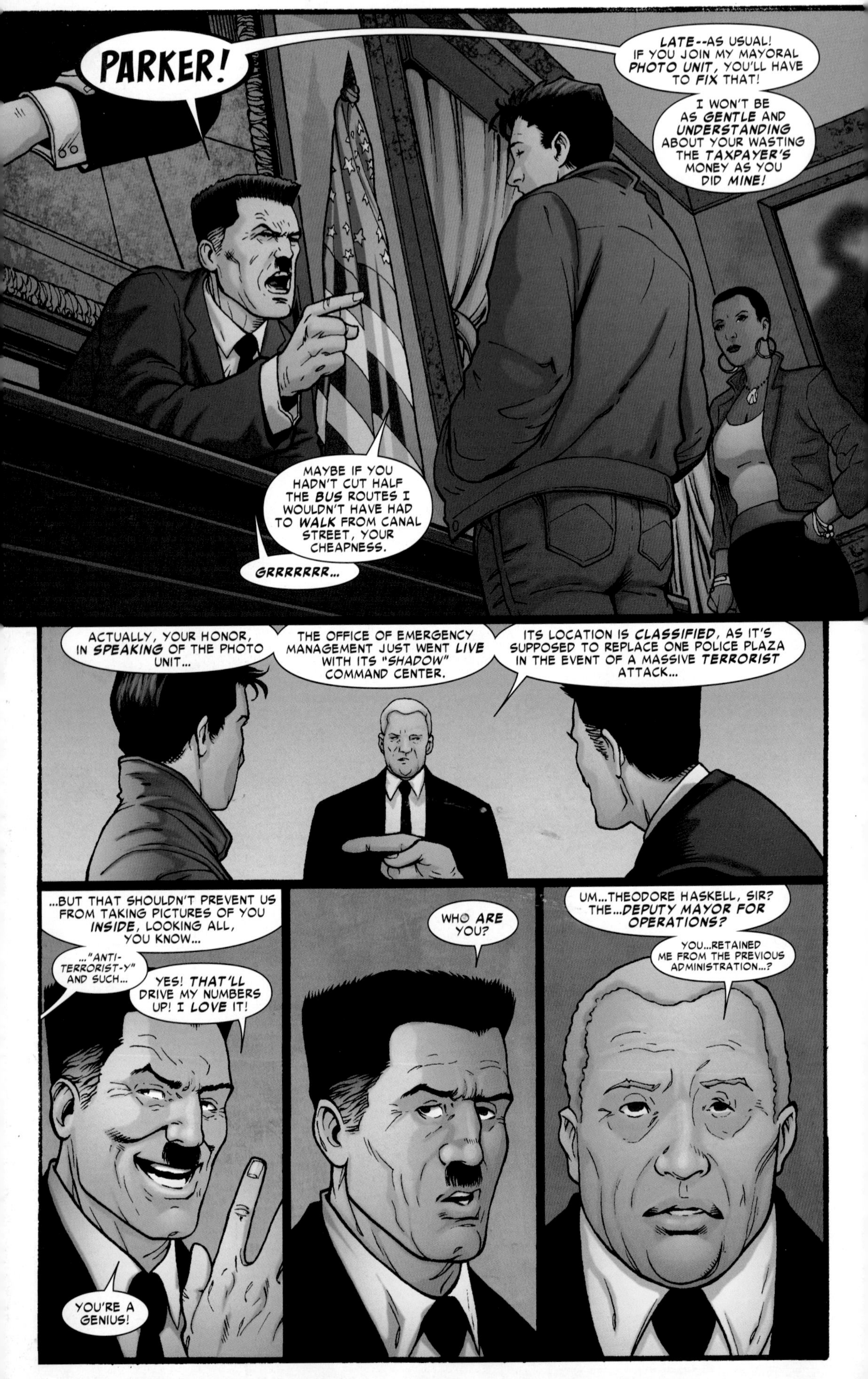
PARKER!
LATE--AS USUAL! IF YOU JOIN MY MAYORAL PHOTO UNIT, YOU'LL HAVE TO FIX THAT!
I WON'T BE AS GENTLE AND UNDERSTANDING ABOUT YOUR WASTING THE TAXPAYER'S MONEY AS YOU DID MINE!
MAYBE IF YOU HADN'T CUT HALF THE BUS ROUTES I WOULDN'T HAVE HAD TO WALK FROM CANAL STREET, YOUR CHEAPNESS.
GRRRRRRR...
ACTUALLY, YOUR HONOR, IN SPEAKING OF THE PHOTO UNIT...
THE OFFICE OF EMERGENCY MANAGEMENT JUST WENT LIVE WITH ITS "SHADOW" COMMAND CENTER.
ITS LOCATION IS CLASSIFIED, AS IT'S SUPPOSED TO REPLACE ONE POLICE PLAZA IN THE EVENT OF A MASSIVE TERRORIST ATTACK...
...BUT THAT SHOULDN'T PREVENT US FROM TAKING PICTURES OF YOU INSIDE, LOOKING ALL, YOU KNOW...
..."ANTI-TERRORIST-Y" AND SUCH...
YES! THAT'LL DRIVE MY NUMBERS UP! I LOVE IT!
YOU'RE A GENIUS!
WHO ARE YOU?
UM...THEODORE HASKELL, SIR? THE...DEPUTY MAYOR FOR OPERATIONS?
YOU...RETAINED ME FROM THE PREVIOUS ADMINISTRATION...?

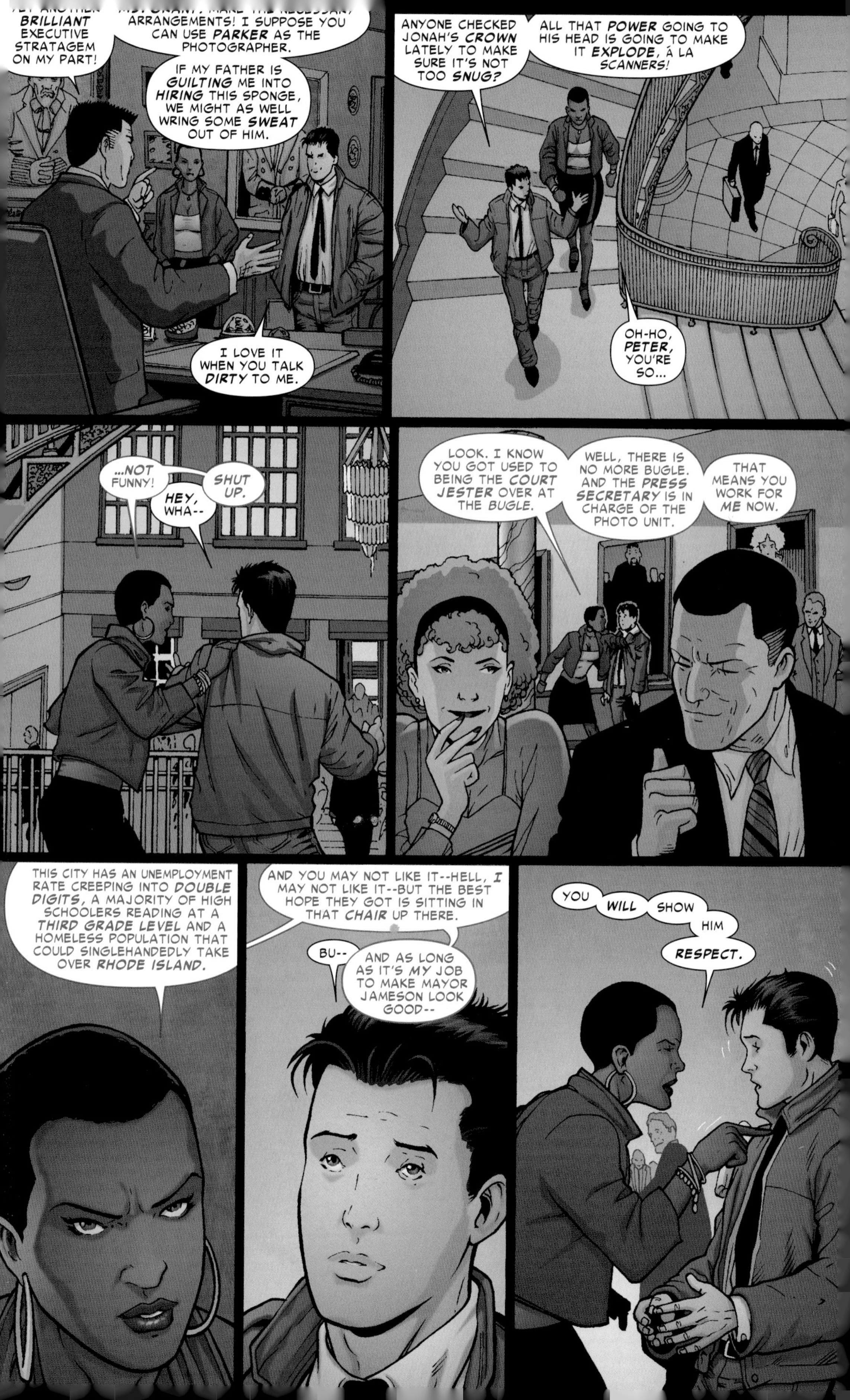
BRILLIANT EXECUTIVE STRATAGEM ON MY PART!
ARRANGEMENTS! I SUPPOSE YOU CAN USE PARKER AS THE PHOTOGRAPHER.
IF MY FATHER IS GUILTING ME INTO HIRING THIS SPONGE, WE MIGHT AS WELL WRING SOME SWEAT OUT OF HIM.
I LOVE IT WHEN YOU TALK DIRTY TO ME.
ANYONE CHECKED JONAH'S CROWN LATELY TO MAKE SURE IT'S NOT TOO SNUG?
ALL THAT POWER GOING TO HIS HEAD IS GOING TO MAKE IT EXPLODE, Á LA SCANNERS!
OH-HO, PETER, YOU'RE SO...
...NOT FUNNY!
HEY, WHA--
SHUT UP.
LOOK. I KNOW YOU GOT USED TO BEING THE COURT JESTER OVER AT THE BUGLE.
WELL, THERE IS NO MORE BUGLE. AND THE PRESS SECRETARY IS IN CHARGE OF THE PHOTO UNIT.
THAT MEANS YOU WORK FOR ME NOW.
THIS CITY HAS AN UNEMPLOYMENT RATE CREEPING INTO DOUBLE DIGITS, A MAJORITY OF HIGH SCHOOLERS READING AT A THIRD GRADE LEVEL AND A HOMELESS POPULATION THAT COULD SINGLEHANDEDLY TAKE OVER RHODE ISLAND.
AND YOU MAY NOT LIKE IT--HELL, I MAY NOT LIKE IT--BUT THE BEST HOPE THEY GOT IS SITTING IN THAT CHAIR UP THERE.
BU--
AND AS LONG AS IT'S MY JOB TO MAKE MAYOR JAMESON LOOK GOOD--
YOU WILL SHOW HIM RESPECT.

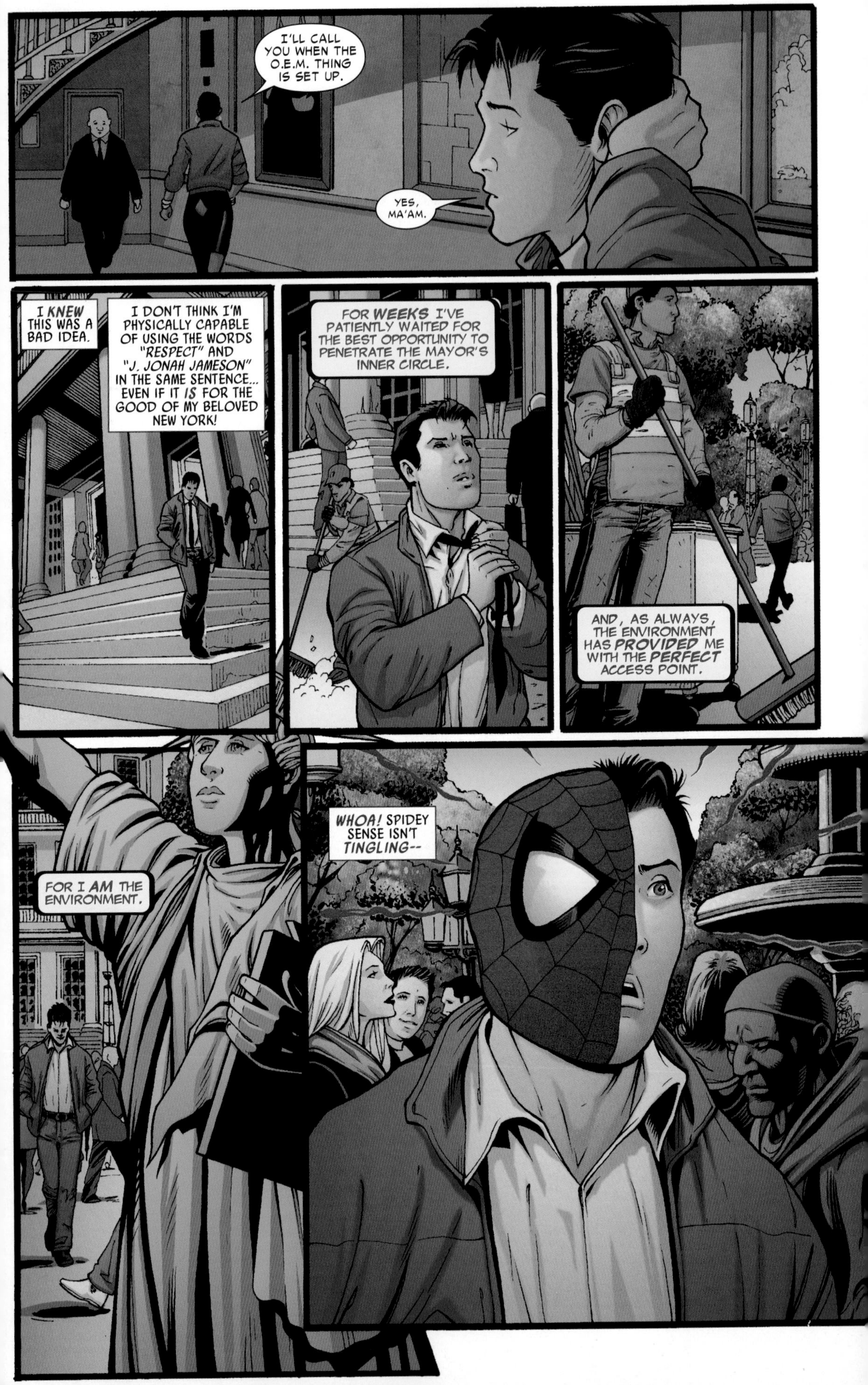
I'LL CALL YOU WHEN THE O.E.M. THING IS SET UP.
YES, MA'AM.
I KNEW THIS WAS A BAD IDEA.
I DON'T THINK I'M PHYSICALLY CAPABLE OF USING THE WORDS "RESPECT" AND "J. JONAH JAMESON" IN THE SAME SENTENCE... EVEN IF IT IS FOR THE GOOD OF MY BELOVED NEW YORK!
FOR WEEKS I'VE PATIENTLY WAITED FOR THE BEST OPPORTUNITY TO PENETRATE THE MAYOR'S INNER CIRCLE.
AND, AS ALWAYS, THE ENVIRONMENT HAS PROVIDED ME WITH THE PERFECT ACCESS POINT.
FOR I AM THE ENVIRONMENT.
WHOA! SPIDEY SENSE ISN'T TINGLING--

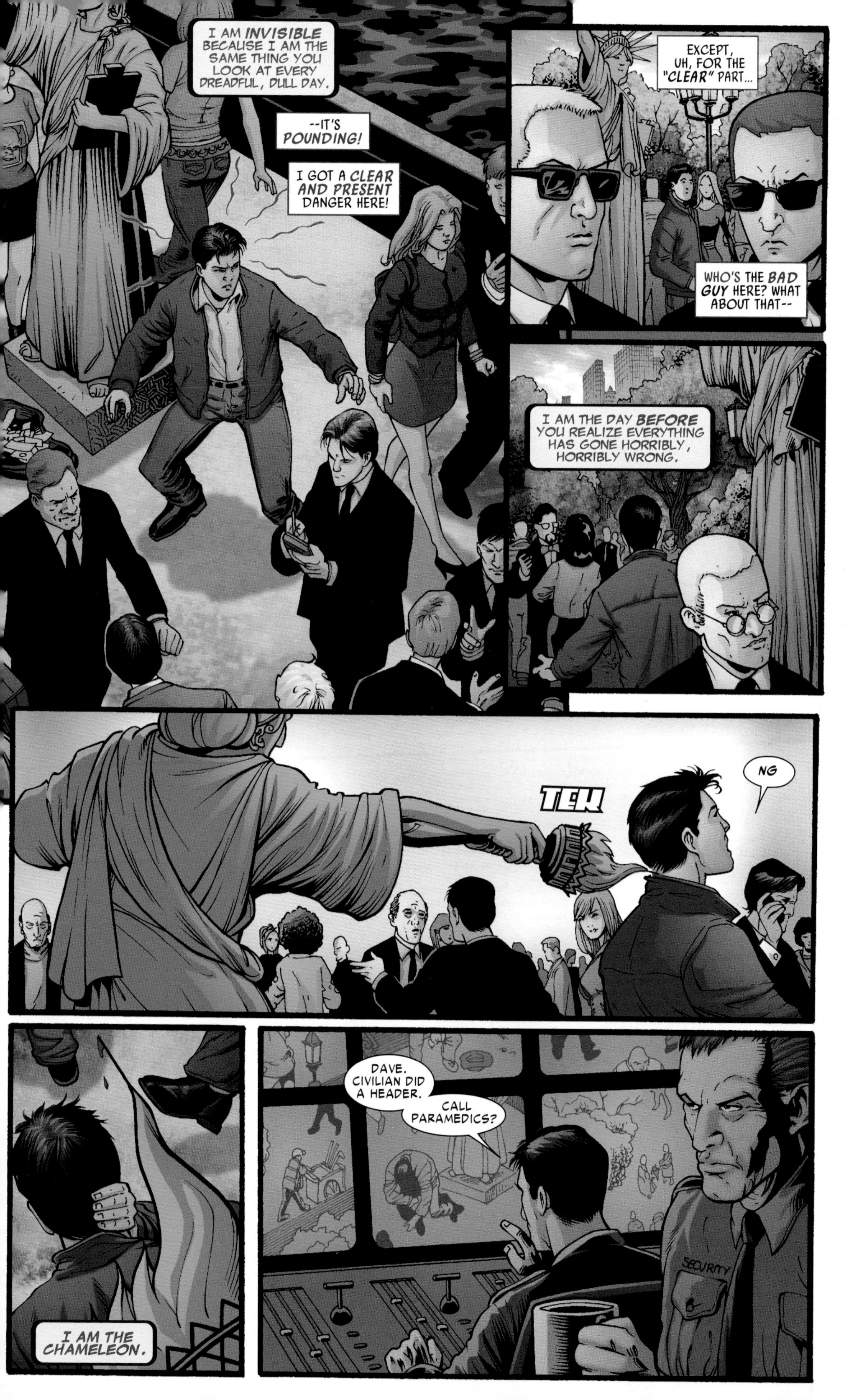
I AM INVISIBLE BECAUSE I AM THE SAME THING YOU LOOK AT EVERY DREADFUL, DULL DAY.
--IT'S POUNDING!
I GOT A CLEAR AND PRESENT DANGER HERE!
EXCEPT, UH, FOR THE "CLEAR" PART...
WHO'S THE BAD GUY HERE? WHAT ABOUT THAT--
I AM THE DAY BEFORE YOU REALIZE EVERYTHING HAS GONE HORRIBLY, HORRIBLY WRONG.
TEK
NG
I AM THE CHAMELEON.
DAVE. CIVILIAN DID A HEADER.
CALL PARAMEDICS?
SECURITY

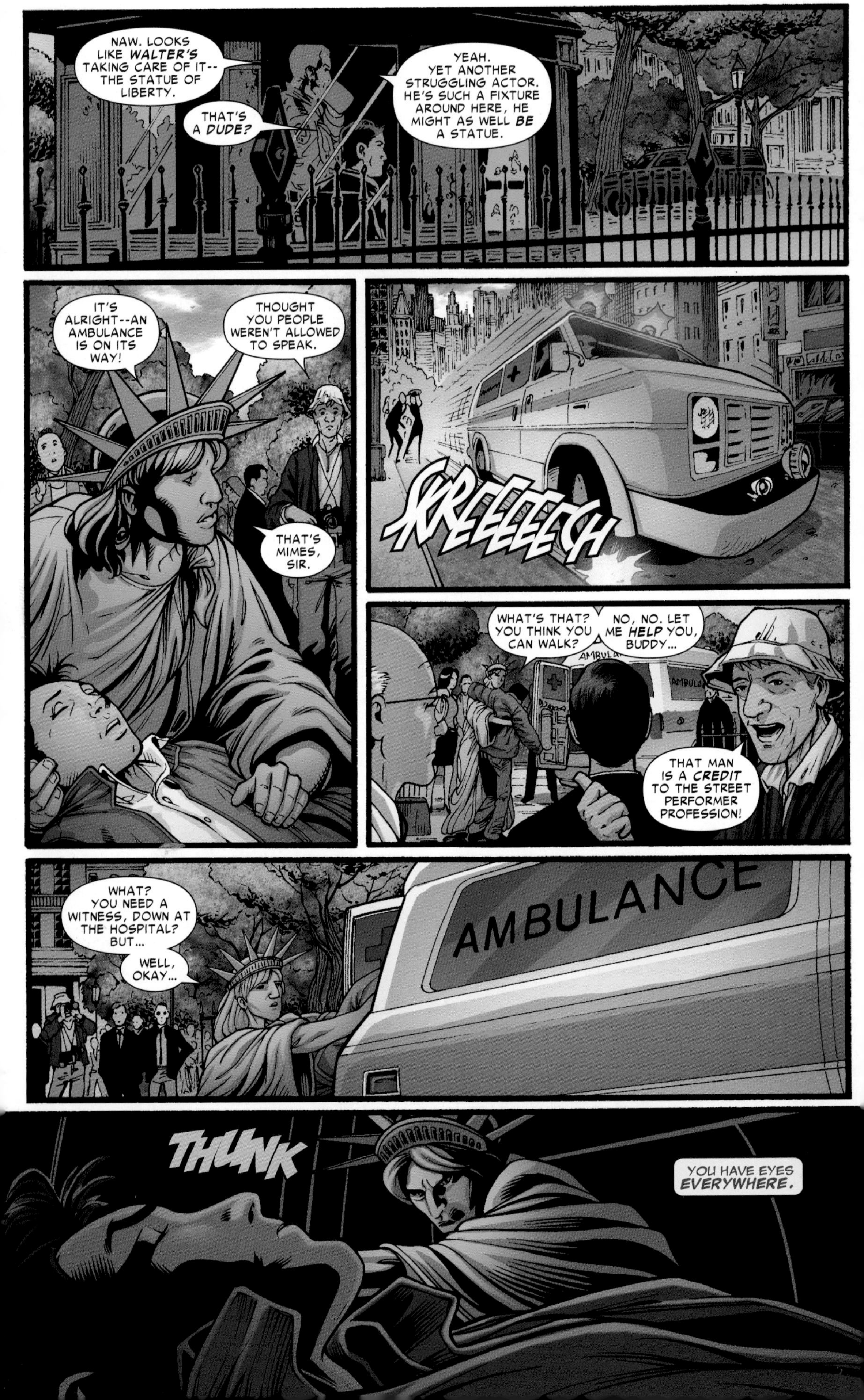
NAW. LOOKS LIKE WALTER'S TAKING CARE OF IT-- THE STATUE OF LIBERTY.
THAT'S A DUDE?
YEAH. YET ANOTHER STRUGGLING ACTOR. HE'S SUCH A FIXTURE AROUND HERE, HE MIGHT AS WELL BE A STATUE.
IT'S ALRIGHT--AN AMBULANCE IS ON ITS WAY!
THOUGHT YOU PEOPLE WEREN'T ALLOWED TO SPEAK.
THAT'S MIMES, SIR.
SKREEEEEECH
WHAT'S THAT? YOU THINK YOU CAN WALK?
NO, NO. LET ME HELP YOU, BUDDY...
THAT MAN IS A CREDIT TO THE STREET PERFORMER PROFESSION!
WHAT? YOU NEED A WITNESS, DOWN AT THE HOSPITAL? BUT...
WELL, OKAY...
AMBULANCE
THUNK
YOU HAVE EYES EVERYWHERE.

LAIR SIX.

SKREEE

AND ALL OF THEM ARE BLIND.

CITY HALL IS LOCKED DOWN FAIRLY TIGHT THESE DAYS.

AUER, WALTER

PERMIT FOR STREET PERFORMANCE NEW YORK CITY

VITATIS NOVI EBORACI

NOT THE EASIEST INTEL-GATHERING LOCATION.

JULY IV MDCCLXXI

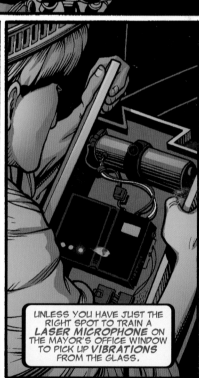

UNLESS YOU HAVE JUST THE RIGHT SPOT TO TRAIN A LASER MICROPHONE ON THE MAYOR'S OFFICE WINDOW TO PICK UP VIBRATIONS FROM THE GLASS.

NOW I HAVE EVERYTHING I NEED TO COMPLETE MY MISSION.

AND TEACH NEW YORK IT WILL NEVER FORGET...

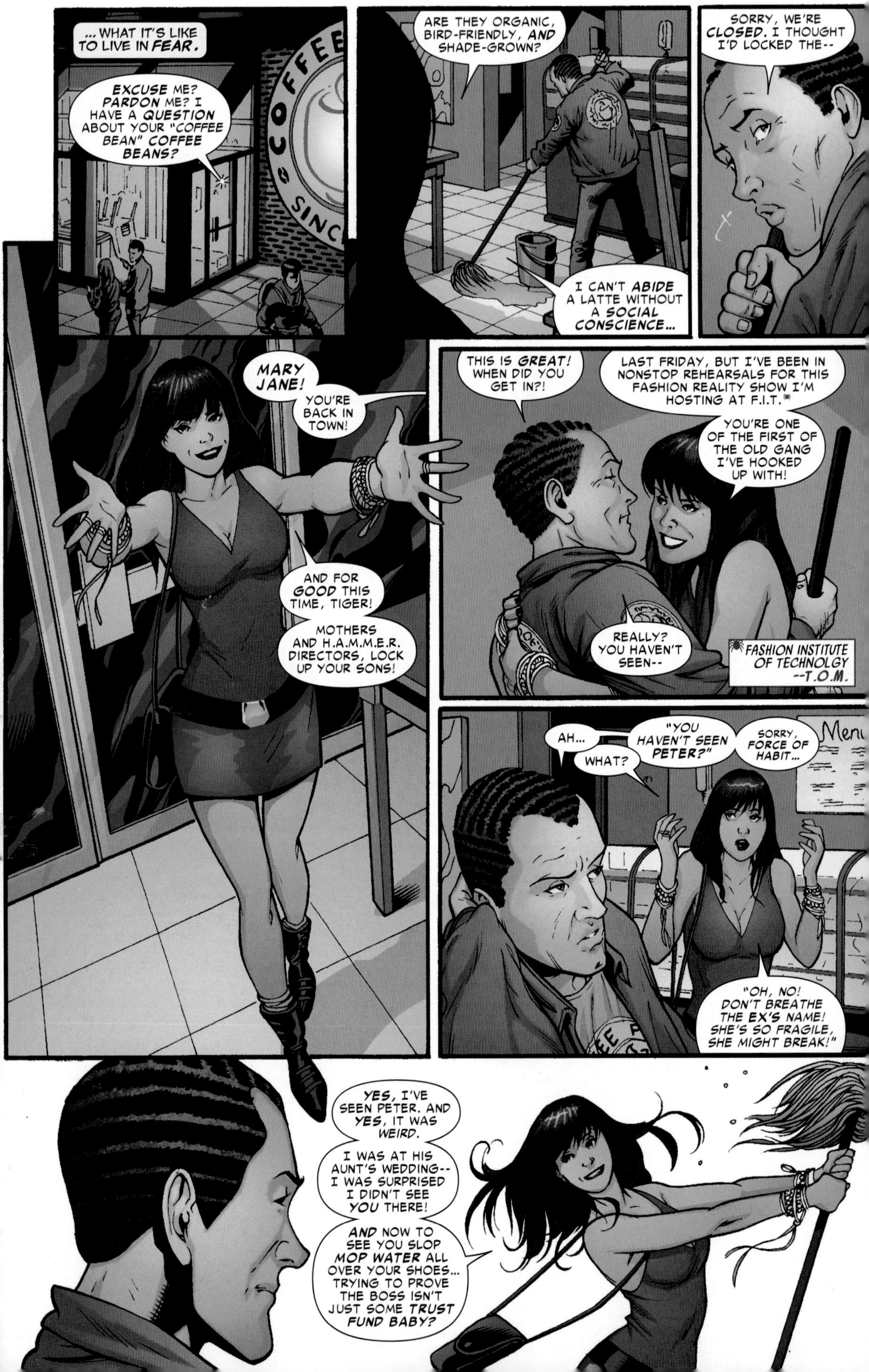

...WHAT IT'S LIKE TO LIVE IN FEAR.
EXCUSE ME? PARDON ME? I HAVE A QUESTION ABOUT YOUR "COFFEE BEAN" COFFEE BEANS?
COFFEE
SINC
ARE THEY ORGANIC, BIRD-FRIENDLY, AND SHADE-GROWN?
I CAN'T ABIDE A LATTE WITHOUT A SOCIAL CONSCIENCE...
SORRY, WE'RE CLOSED. I THOUGHT I'D LOCKED THE--
MARY JANE!
YOU'RE BACK IN TOWN!
AND FOR GOOD THIS TIME, TIGER!
MOTHERS AND H.A.M.M.E.R. DIRECTORS, LOCK UP YOUR SONS!
THIS IS GREAT! WHEN DID YOU GET IN?!
LAST FRIDAY, BUT I'VE BEEN IN NONSTOP REHEARSALS FOR THIS FASHION REALITY SHOW I'M HOSTING AT F.I.T.*
YOU'RE ONE OF THE FIRST OF THE OLD GANG I'VE HOOKED UP WITH!
REALLY? YOU HAVEN'T SEEN--
*FASHION INSTITUTE OF TECHNOLGY --T.O.M.
AH...
WHAT?
"YOU HAVEN'T SEEN PETER?"
SORRY, FORCE OF HABIT...
Menu
"OH, NO! DON'T BREATHE THE EX'S NAME! SHE'S SO FRAGILE, SHE MIGHT BREAK!"
YES, I'VE SEEN PETER. AND YES, IT WAS WEIRD.
I WAS AT HIS AUNT'S WEDDING-- I WAS SURPRISED I DIDN'T SEE YOU THERE!
AND NOW TO SEE YOU SLOP MOP WATER ALL OVER YOUR SHOES... TRYING TO PROVE THE BOSS ISN'T JUST SOME TRUST FUND BABY?

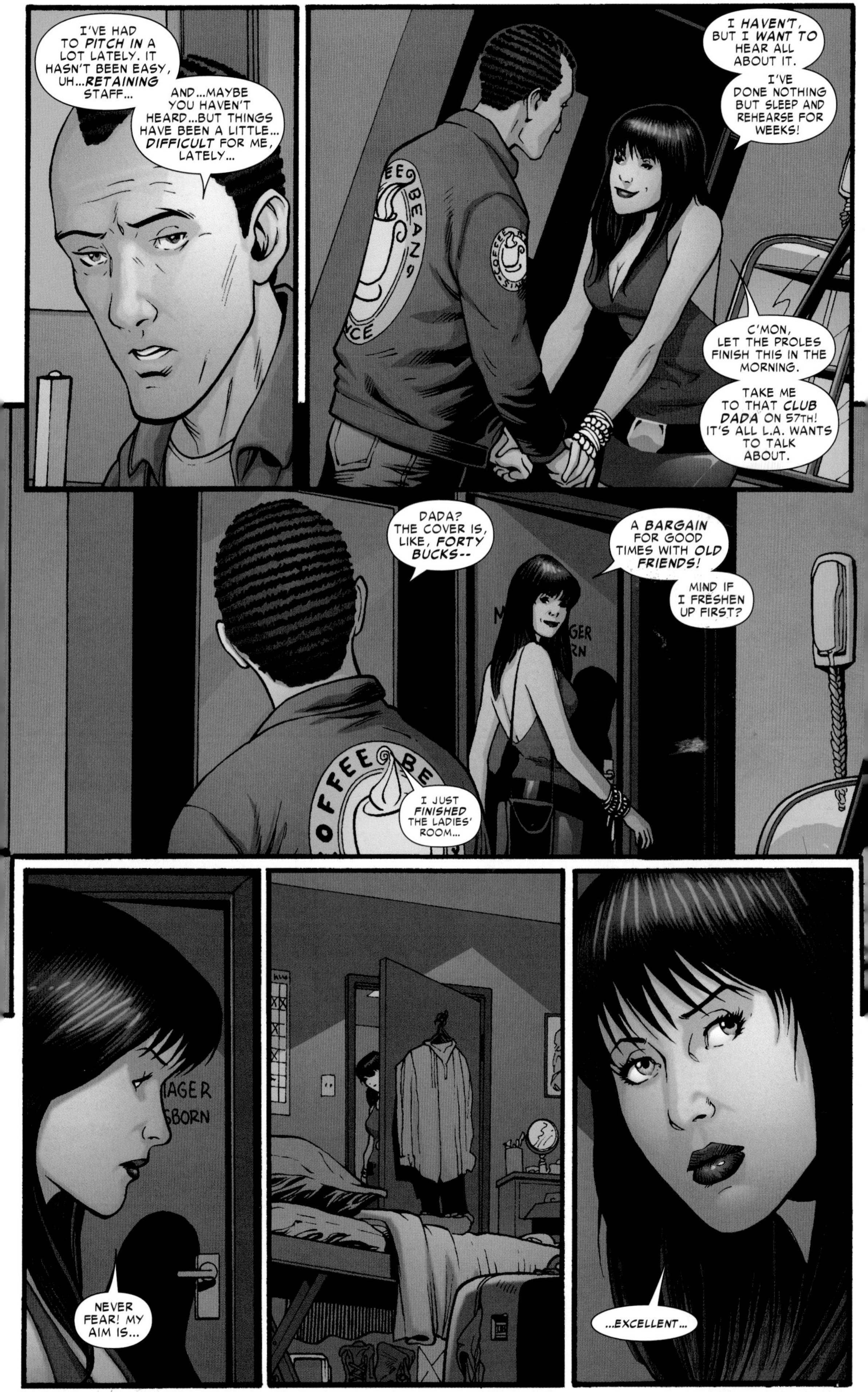

I'VE HAD TO *PITCH IN* A LOT LATELY. IT HASN'T BEEN EASY, UH...*RETAINING* STAFF...
AND...MAYBE YOU HAVEN'T HEARD...BUT THINGS HAVE BEEN A LITTLE... *DIFFICULT* FOR ME, LATELY...
I *HAVEN'T*, BUT I *WANT TO* HEAR ALL ABOUT IT.
I'VE DONE NOTHING BUT SLEEP AND REHEARSE FOR WEEKS!
C'MON, LET THE PROLES FINISH THIS IN THE MORNING.
TAKE ME TO THAT *CLUB DADA* ON 57TH! IT'S ALL L.A. WANTS TO TALK ABOUT.
DADA? THE COVER IS, LIKE, *FORTY BUCKS*--
A *BARGAIN* FOR GOOD TIMES WITH *OLD FRIENDS!*
MIND IF I FRESHEN UP FIRST?
I JUST *FINISHED* THE LADIES' ROOM...
NEVER FEAR! MY AIM IS...
...EXCELLENT...

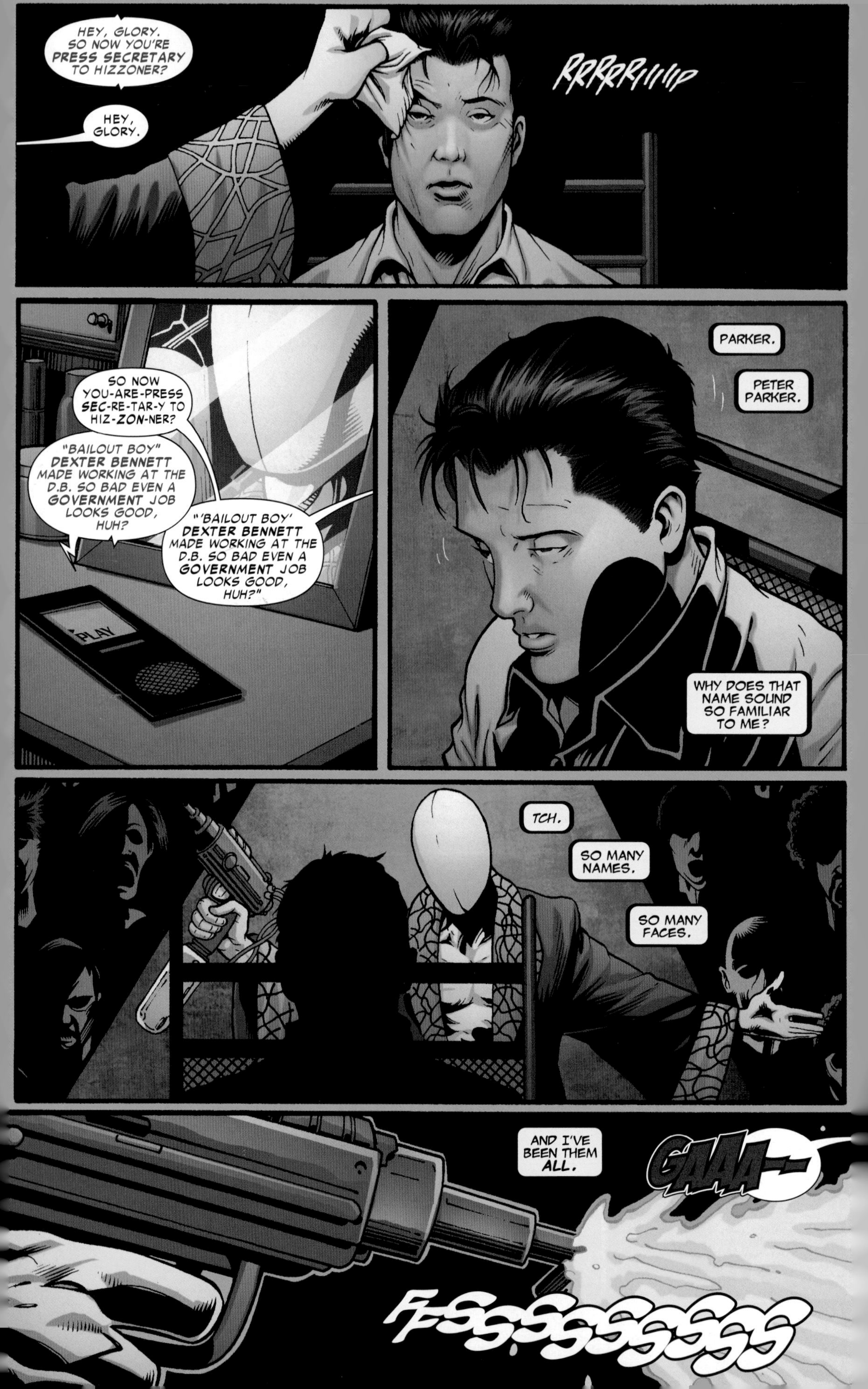

HEY, GLORY. SO NOW YOU'RE PRESS SECRETARY TO HIZZONER?
HEY, GLORY.
RRRRRIIIIP
SO NOW YOU-ARE-PRESS SEC-RE-TAR-Y TO HIZ-ZON-NER?
"BAILOUT BOY" DEXTER BENNETT MADE WORKING AT THE D.B. SO BAD EVEN A GOVERNMENT JOB LOOKS GOOD, HUH?
"'BAILOUT BOY' DEXTER BENNETT MADE WORKING AT THE D.B. SO BAD EVEN A GOVERNMENT JOB LOOKS GOOD, HUH?"
PLAY
PARKER.
PETER PARKER.
WHY DOES THAT NAME SOUND SO FAMILIAR TO ME?
TCH.
SO MANY NAMES.
SO MANY FACES.
AND I'VE BEEN THEM ALL.
GAAA--
FFSSSSSSSSSS

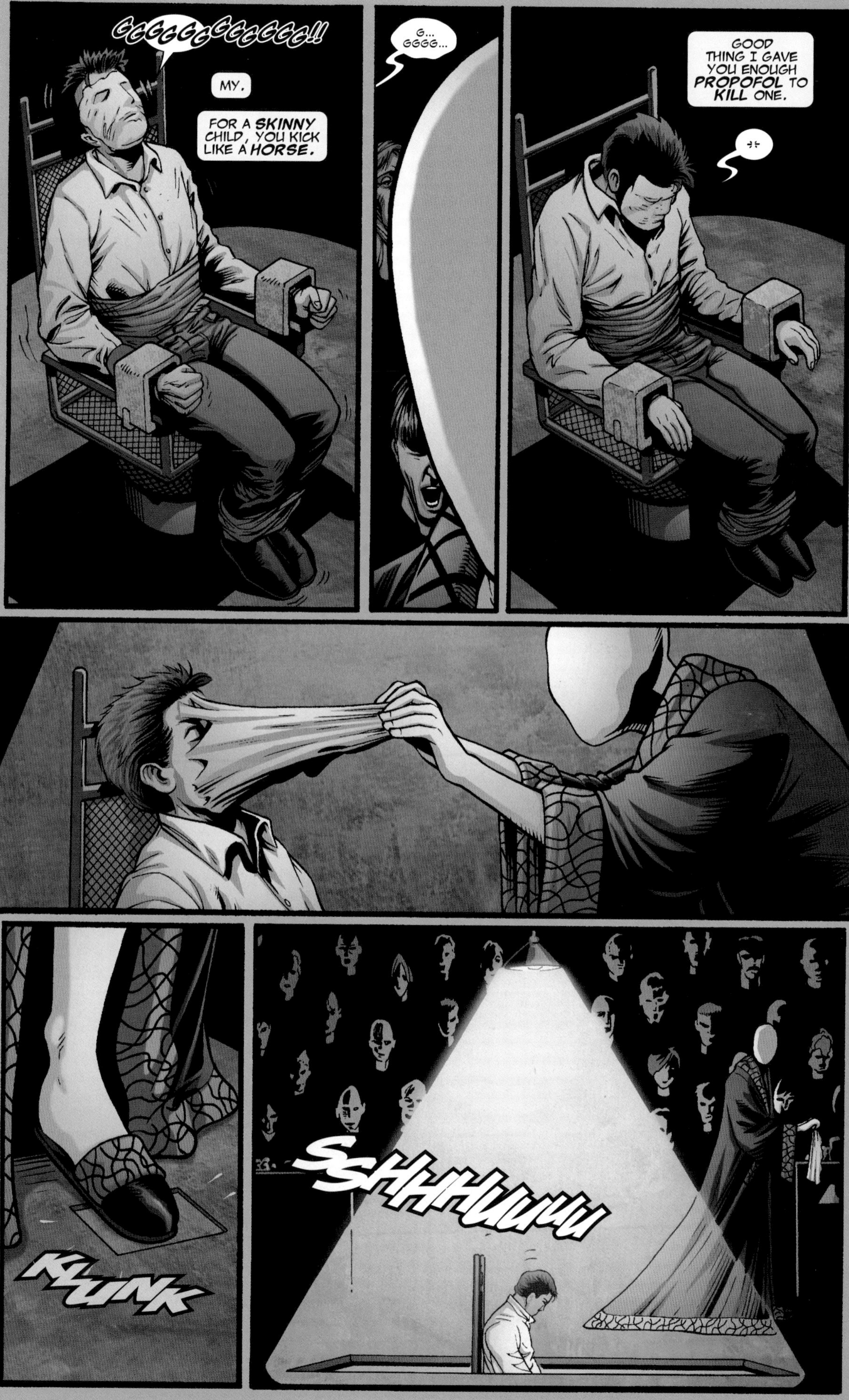
GGGGGGGGGGGGG!!
MY.
FOR A SKINNY CHILD, YOU KICK LIKE A HORSE.
G... GGGG...
GOOD THING I GAVE YOU ENOUGH PROPOFOL TO KILL ONE.
KLUNK
SSHHHUUUU

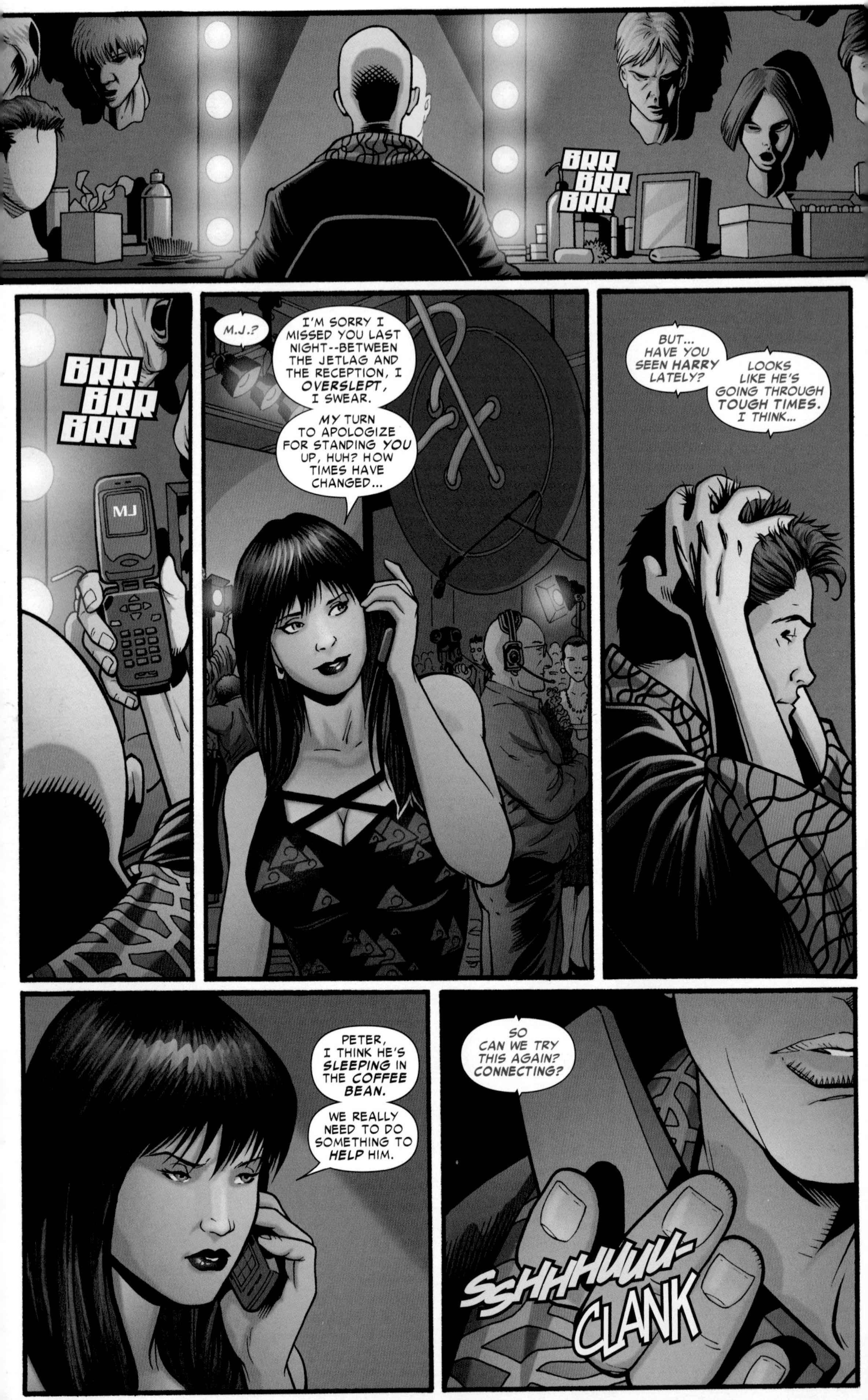
BRR BRR BRR
BRR BRR BRR
MJ
M.J.?
I'M SORRY I MISSED YOU LAST NIGHT--BETWEEN THE JETLAG AND THE RECEPTION, I OVERSLEPT, I SWEAR.
MY TURN TO APOLOGIZE FOR STANDING YOU UP, HUH? HOW TIMES HAVE CHANGED...
BUT... HAVE YOU SEEN HARRY LATELY?
LOOKS LIKE HE'S GOING THROUGH TOUGH TIMES. I THINK...
PETER, I THINK HE'S SLEEPING IN THE COFFEE BEAN.
WE REALLY NEED TO DO SOMETHING TO HELP HIM.
SO CAN WE TRY THIS AGAIN? CONNECTING?
SSHHHUUU-CLANK

SURE, MARY JANE.

NAME THE TIME AND THE PLACE... ...AND I'LL BE THERE.

RED-HEADED STRANGER:
TENTH OF SEPTEMBER

FRED VAN LENTE WRITER | BARRY KITSON PENCILER | RICK KETCHAM & BARRY KITSON INKERS | JEROMY COX COLORIST | VC'S JOE CARAMAGNA LETTERER | TOM BRENNAN ASST. EDITOR | STEPHEN WACKER EDITOR | TOM BREVOORT EXEC. EDITOR | JOE QUESADA EDITOR IN CHIEF | DAN BUCKLEY PUBLISHER | ALAN FINE EXEC. PRODUCER

GALE, GUGGENHEIM, KELLY, SLOTT, VAN LENTE, WAID & WELLS WEB-HEADS

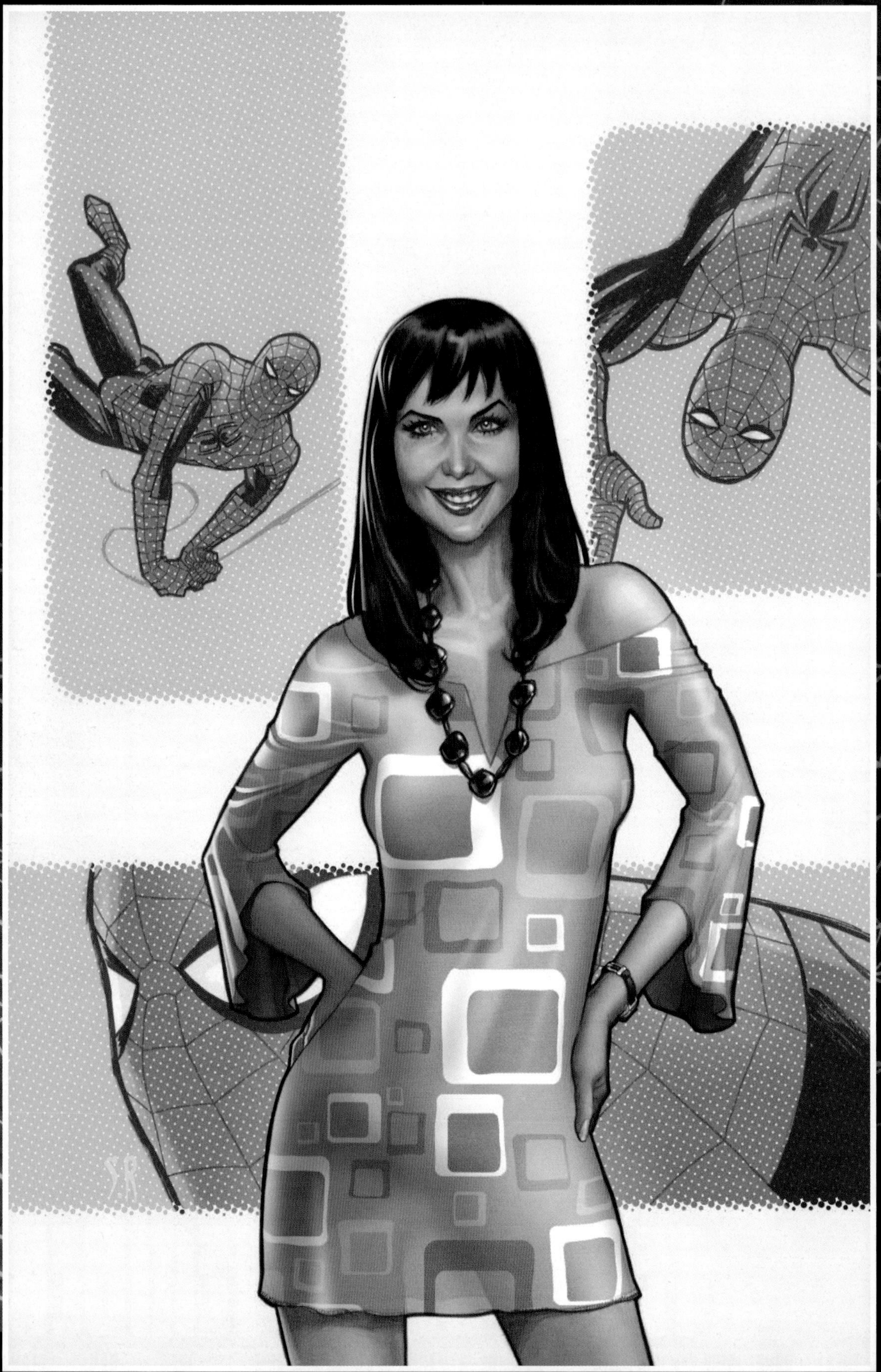

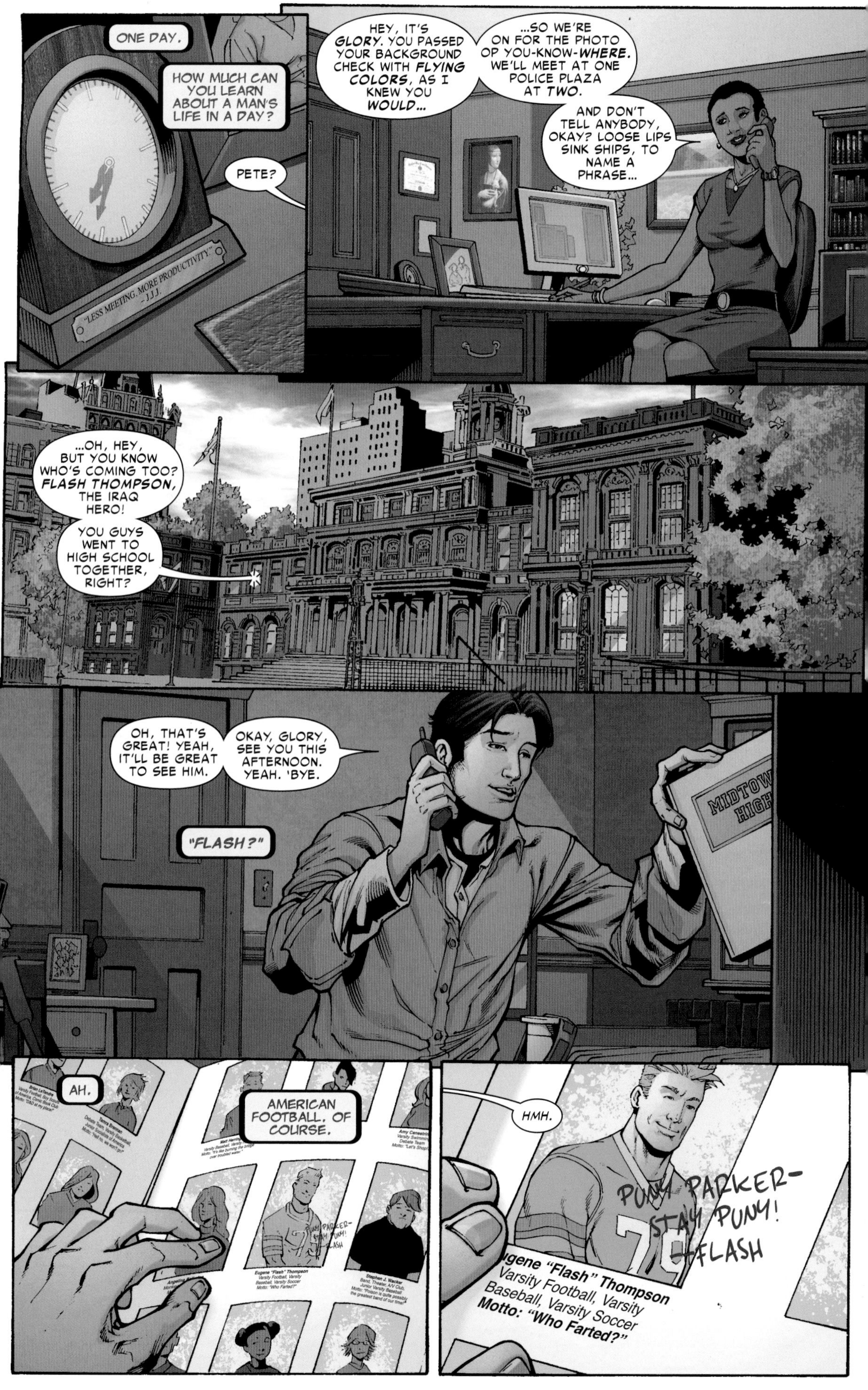
ONE DAY.
HOW MUCH CAN YOU LEARN ABOUT A MAN'S LIFE IN A DAY?
"LESS MEETING, MORE PRODUCTIVITY." -J.J.J.
PETE?
HEY, IT'S GLORY. YOU PASSED YOUR BACKGROUND CHECK WITH FLYING COLORS, AS I KNEW YOU WOULD...
...SO WE'RE ON FOR THE PHOTO OP YOU-KNOW-WHERE. WE'LL MEET AT ONE POLICE PLAZA AT TWO.
AND DON'T TELL ANYBODY, OKAY? LOOSE LIPS SINK SHIPS, TO NAME A PHRASE...
...OH, HEY, BUT YOU KNOW WHO'S COMING TOO? FLASH THOMPSON, THE IRAQ HERO!
YOU GUYS WENT TO HIGH SCHOOL TOGETHER, RIGHT?
OH, THAT'S GREAT! YEAH, IT'LL BE GREAT TO SEE HIM.
OKAY, GLORY, SEE YOU THIS AFTERNOON. YEAH. 'BYE.
"FLASH?"
AH.
AMERICAN FOOTBALL, OF COURSE.
HMH.
PUNY PARKER- STAY PUNY! -FLASH
Eugene "Flash" Thompson
Varsity Football, Varsity Baseball, Varsity Soccer
Motto: "Who Farted?"

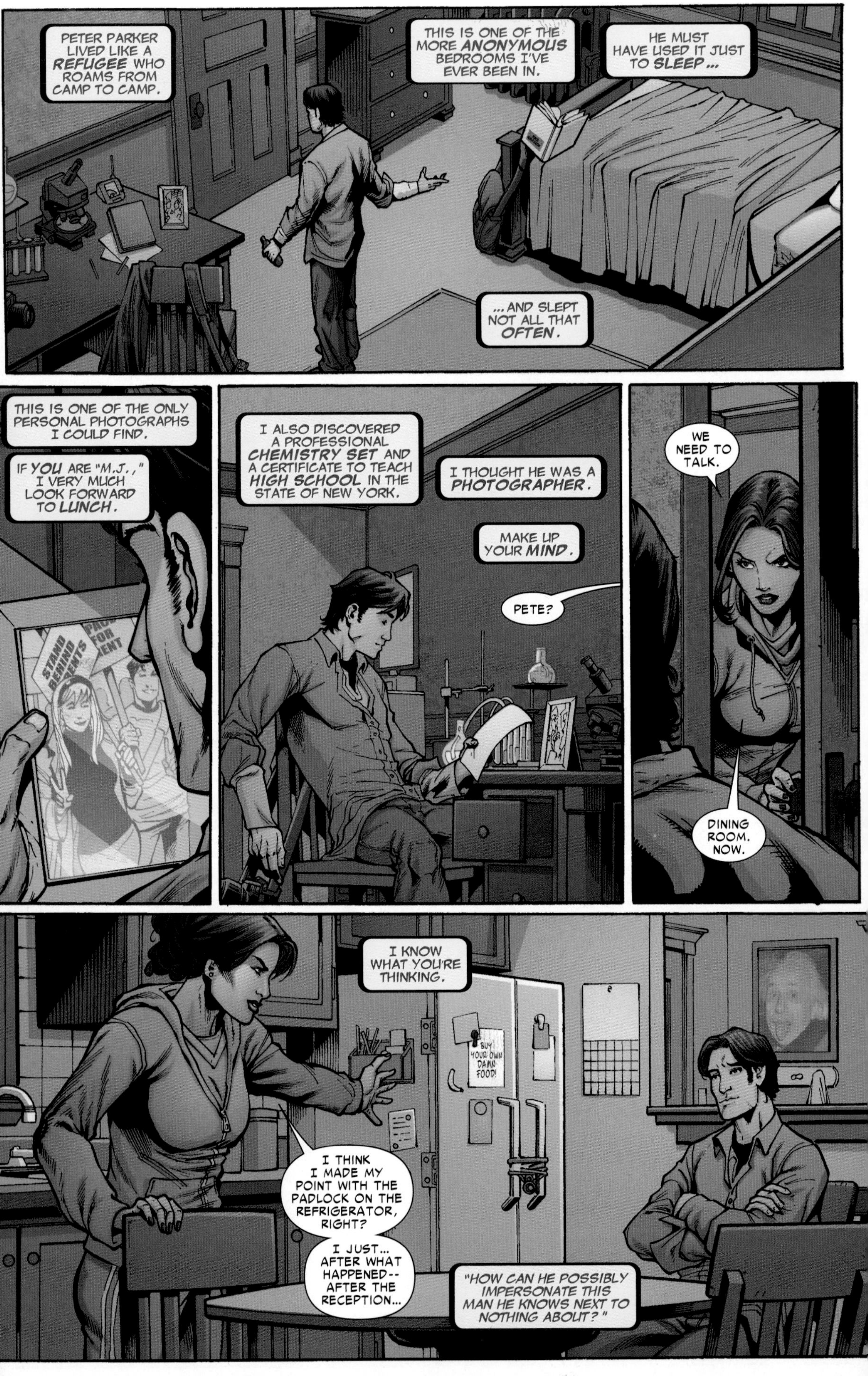

PETER PARKER LIVED LIKE A REFUGEE WHO ROAMS FROM CAMP TO CAMP.
THIS IS ONE OF THE MORE ANONYMOUS BEDROOMS I'VE EVER BEEN IN.
HE MUST HAVE USED IT JUST TO SLEEP...
...AND SLEPT NOT ALL THAT OFTEN.
THIS IS ONE OF THE ONLY PERSONAL PHOTOGRAPHS I COULD FIND.
IF YOU ARE "M.J.," I VERY MUCH LOOK FORWARD TO LUNCH.
I ALSO DISCOVERED A PROFESSIONAL CHEMISTRY SET AND A CERTIFICATE TO TEACH HIGH SCHOOL IN THE STATE OF NEW YORK.
I THOUGHT HE WAS A PHOTOGRAPHER.
MAKE UP YOUR MIND.
PETE?
WE NEED TO TALK.
DINING ROOM. NOW.
I KNOW WHAT YOU'RE THINKING.
BUY YOUR OWN DAMN FOOD!
I THINK I MADE MY POINT WITH THE PADLOCK ON THE REFRIGERATOR, RIGHT?
I JUST... AFTER WHAT HAPPENED-- AFTER THE RECEPTION...
"HOW CAN HE POSSIBLY IMPERSONATE THIS MAN HE KNOWS NEXT TO NOTHING ABOUT?"

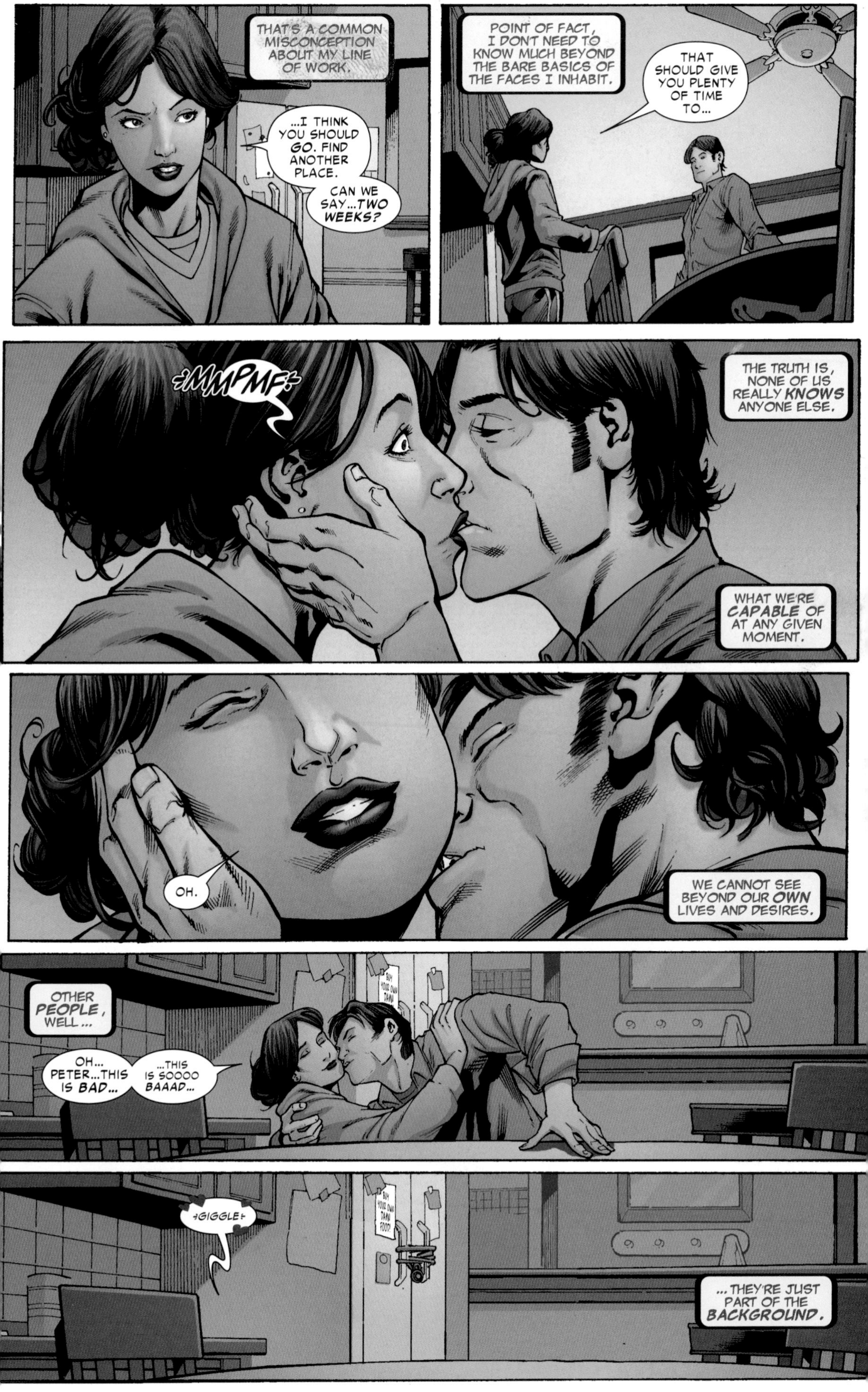
THAT'S A COMMON MISCONCEPTION ABOUT MY LINE OF WORK.
...I THINK YOU SHOULD GO. FIND ANOTHER PLACE.
CAN WE SAY...TWO WEEKS?
POINT OF FACT, I DON'T NEED TO KNOW MUCH BEYOND THE BARE BASICS OF THE FACES I INHABIT.
THAT SHOULD GIVE YOU PLENTY OF TIME TO...
MMPMF
THE TRUTH IS, NONE OF US REALLY KNOWS ANYONE ELSE.
WHAT WE'RE CAPABLE OF AT ANY GIVEN MOMENT.
OH.
WE CANNOT SEE BEYOND OUR OWN LIVES AND DESIRES.
OTHER PEOPLE, WELL...
OH... PETER...THIS IS BAD...
...THIS IS SOOOO BAAAD...
GIGGLE
...THEY'RE JUST PART OF THE BACKGROUND.

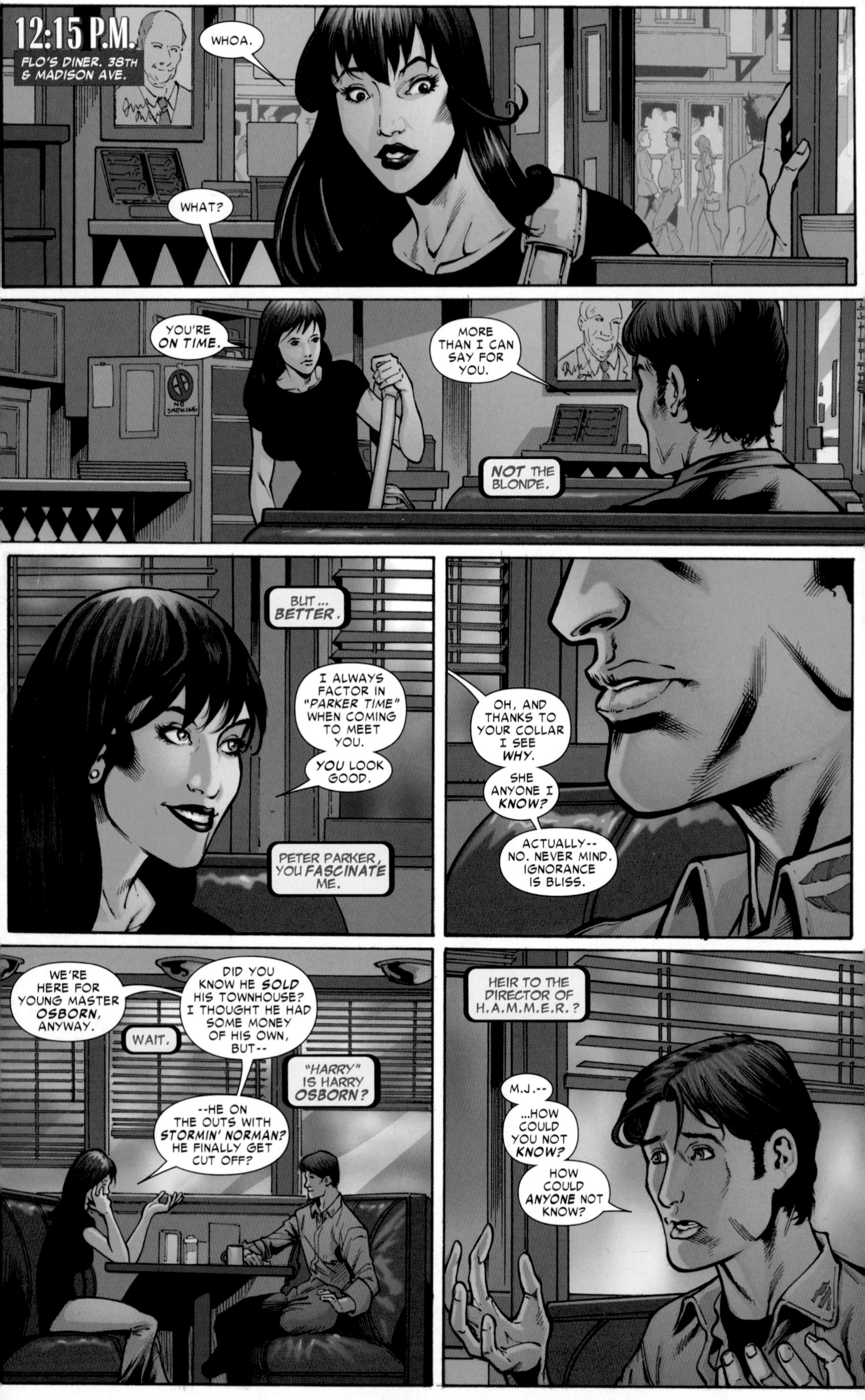
12:15 P.M.
FLO'S DINER. 38TH & MADISON AVE.
WHOA.
WHAT?
YOU'RE ON TIME.
MORE THAN I CAN SAY FOR YOU.
NOT THE BLONDE.
BUT... BETTER.
I ALWAYS FACTOR IN "PARKER TIME" WHEN COMING TO MEET YOU.
YOU LOOK GOOD.
PETER PARKER, YOU FASCINATE ME.
OH, AND THANKS TO YOUR COLLAR I SEE WHY.
SHE ANYONE I KNOW?
ACTUALLY-- NO. NEVER MIND. IGNORANCE IS BLISS.
WE'RE HERE FOR YOUNG MASTER OSBORN, ANYWAY.
DID YOU KNOW HE SOLD HIS TOWNHOUSE? I THOUGHT HE HAD SOME MONEY OF HIS OWN, BUT--
WAIT.
"HARRY" IS HARRY OSBORN?
--HE ON THE OUTS WITH STORMIN' NORMAN? HE FINALLY GET CUT OFF?
HEIR TO THE DIRECTOR OF H.A.M.M.E.R.?
M.J.--
...HOW COULD YOU NOT KNOW?
HOW COULD ANYONE NOT KNOW?

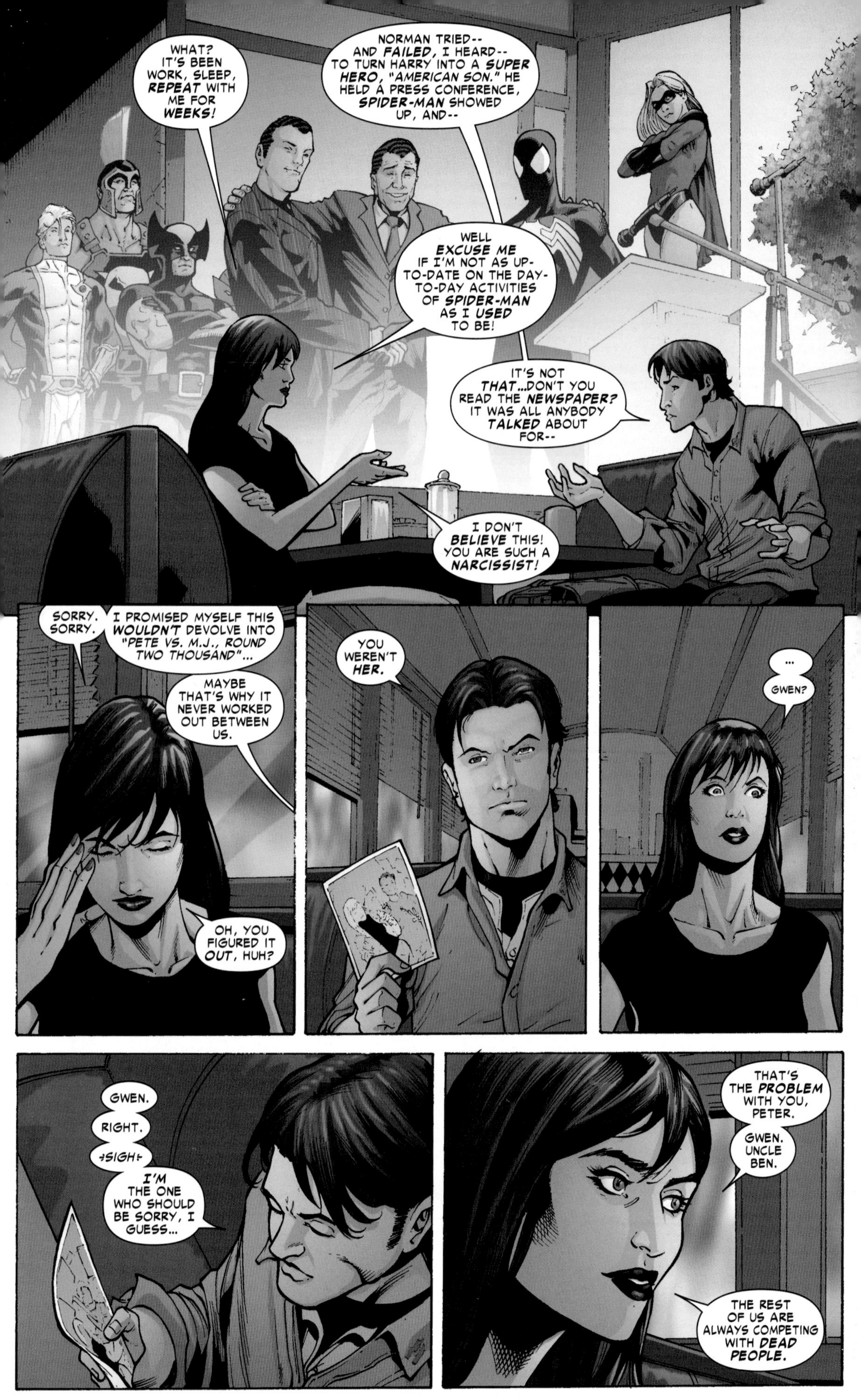
WHAT? IT'S BEEN WORK, SLEEP, REPEAT WITH ME FOR WEEKS!
NORMAN TRIED-- AND FAILED, I HEARD-- TO TURN HARRY INTO A SUPER HERO, "AMERICAN SON." HE HELD A PRESS CONFERENCE, SPIDER-MAN SHOWED UP, AND--
WELL EXCUSE ME IF I'M NOT AS UP-TO-DATE ON THE DAY-TO-DAY ACTIVITIES OF SPIDER-MAN AS I USED TO BE!
IT'S NOT THAT...DON'T YOU READ THE NEWSPAPER? IT WAS ALL ANYBODY TALKED ABOUT FOR--
I DON'T BELIEVE THIS! YOU ARE SUCH A NARCISSIST!
SORRY. SORRY.
I PROMISED MYSELF THIS WOULDN'T DEVOLVE INTO "PETE VS. M.J., ROUND TWO THOUSAND"...
MAYBE THAT'S WHY IT NEVER WORKED OUT BETWEEN US.
OH, YOU FIGURED IT OUT, HUH?
YOU WEREN'T HER.
...
GWEN?
GWEN.
RIGHT.
-SIGH-
I'M THE ONE WHO SHOULD BE SORRY, I GUESS...
THAT'S THE PROBLEM WITH YOU, PETER.
GWEN. UNCLE BEN.
THE REST OF US ARE ALWAYS COMPETING WITH DEAD PEOPLE.

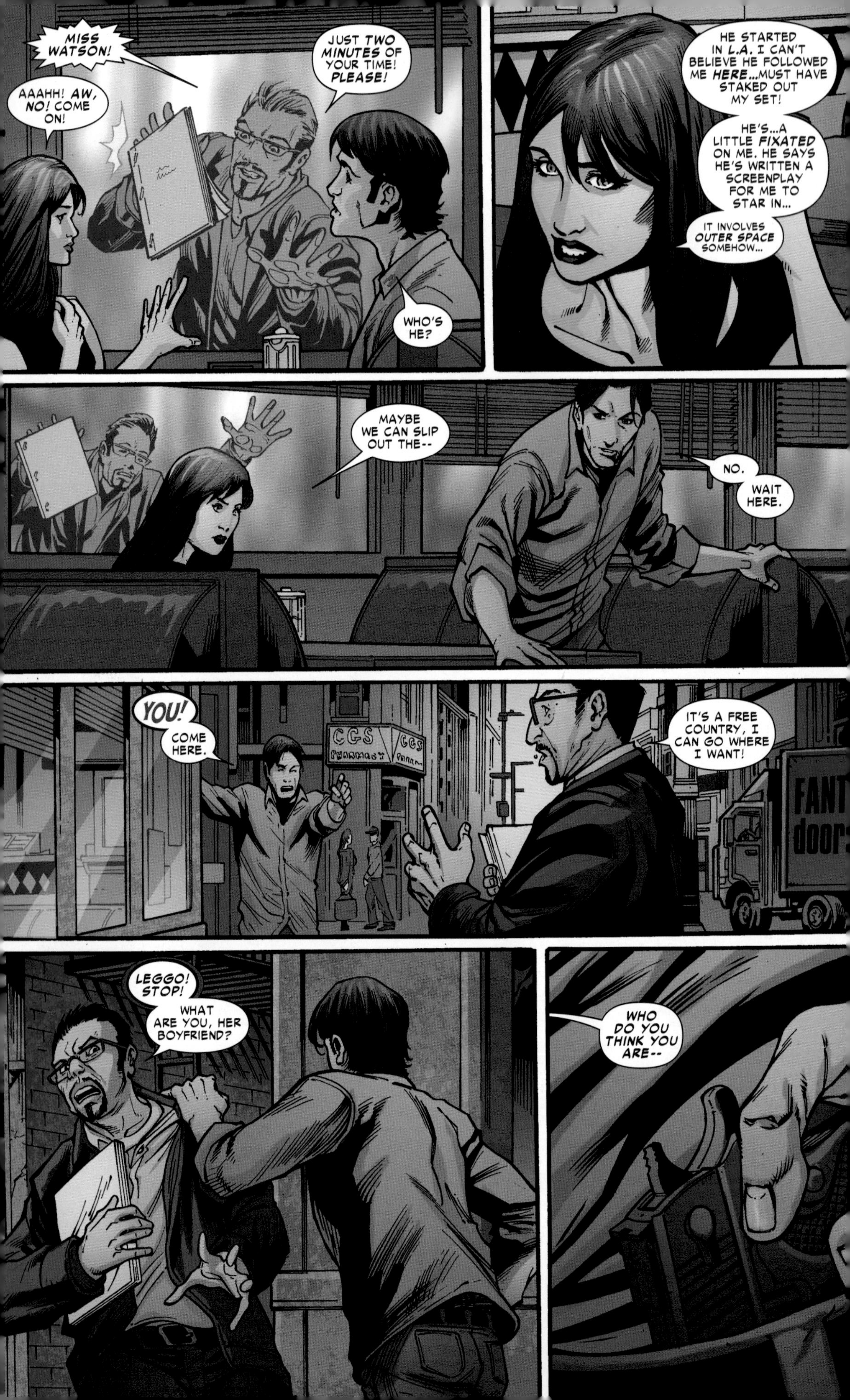
MISS WATSON!
AAAHH! AW, NO! COME ON!
JUST TWO MINUTES OF YOUR TIME! PLEASE!
WHO'S HE?
HE STARTED IN L.A. I CAN'T BELIEVE HE FOLLOWED ME HERE...MUST HAVE STAKED OUT MY SET!
HE'S...A LITTLE FIXATED ON ME. HE SAYS HE'S WRITTEN A SCREENPLAY FOR ME TO STAR IN...
IT INVOLVES OUTER SPACE SOMEHOW...
MAYBE WE CAN SLIP OUT THE--
NO.
WAIT HERE.
YOU! COME HERE.
CGS PHARMACY
IT'S A FREE COUNTRY, I CAN GO WHERE I WANT!
FANT doors
LEGGO! STOP!
WHAT ARE YOU, HER BOYFRIEND?
WHO DO YOU THINK YOU ARE--

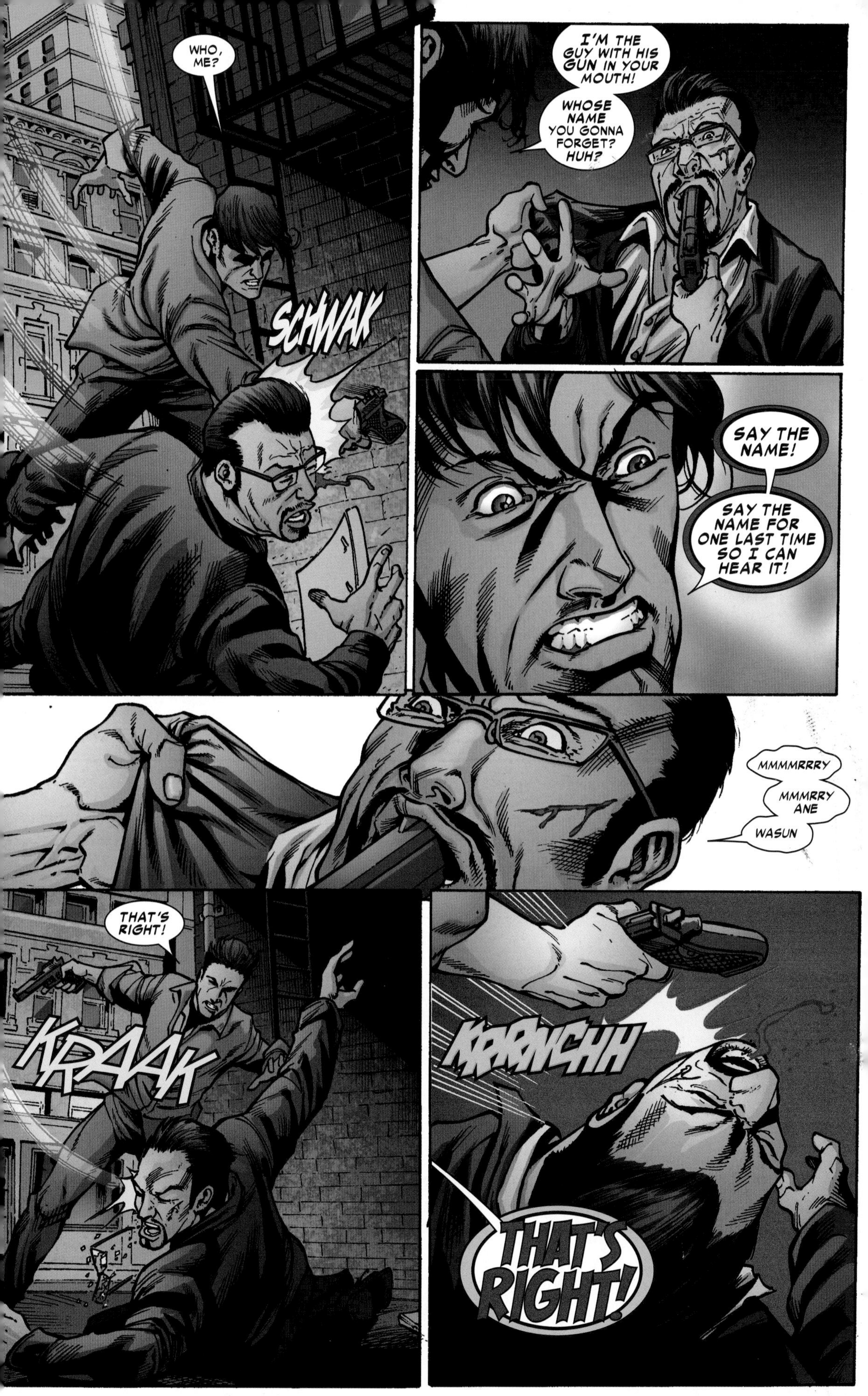
WHO, ME?
SCHWAK
I'M THE GUY WITH HIS GUN IN YOUR MOUTH!
WHOSE NAME YOU GONNA FORGET? HUH?
SAY THE NAME!
SAY THE NAME FOR ONE LAST TIME SO I CAN HEAR IT!
MMMMRRRY
MMMRRY ANE
WASUN
THAT'S RIGHT!
KRAAK
KRRRNCHH
THAT'S RIGHT!

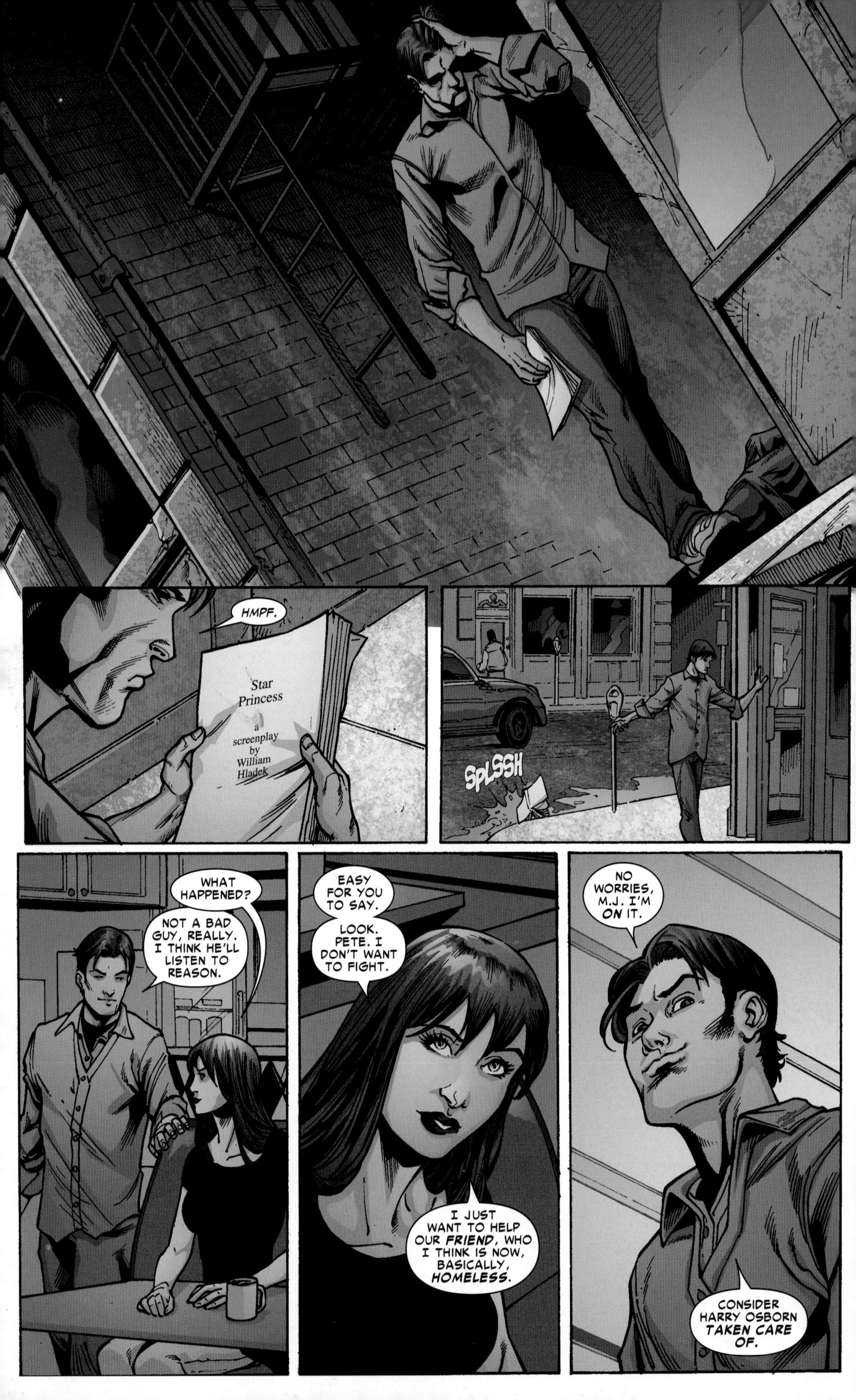
HMPF.
Star Princess a screenplay by William Hladek
SPLSSH
WHAT HAPPENED?
NOT A BAD GUY, REALLY. I THINK HE'LL LISTEN TO REASON.
EASY FOR YOU TO SAY.
LOOK. PETE. I DON'T WANT TO FIGHT.
I JUST WANT TO HELP OUR FRIEND, WHO I THINK IS NOW, BASICALLY, HOMELESS.
NO WORRIES, M.J. I'M ON IT.
CONSIDER HARRY OSBORN TAKEN CARE OF.

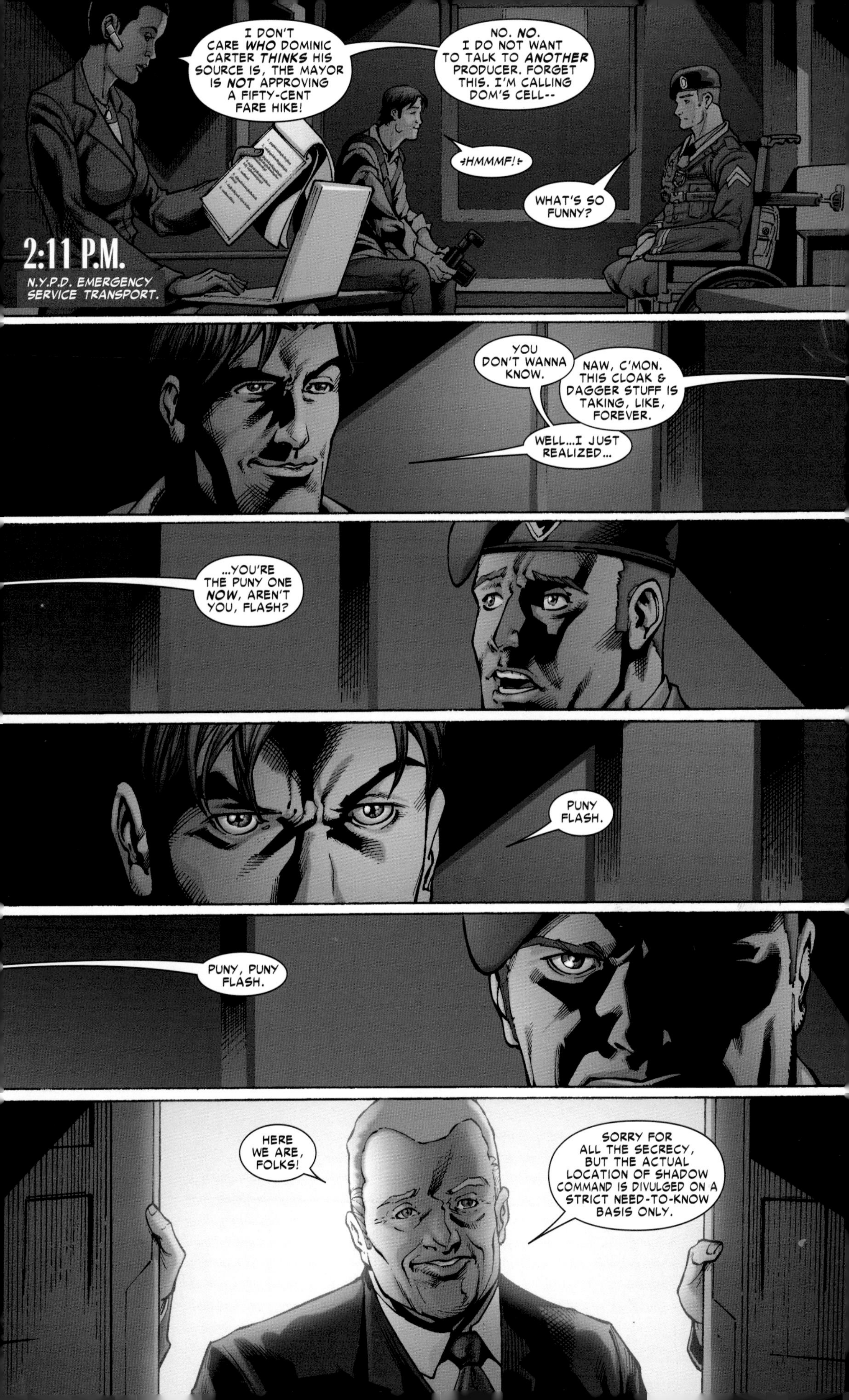
2:11 P.M.
N.Y.P.D. EMERGENCY SERVICE TRANSPORT.
I DON'T CARE WHO DOMINIC CARTER THINKS HIS SOURCE IS, THE MAYOR IS NOT APPROVING A FIFTY-CENT FARE HIKE!
NO. NO. I DO NOT WANT TO TALK TO ANOTHER PRODUCER. FORGET THIS. I'M CALLING DOM'S CELL--
HMMMF!
WHAT'S SO FUNNY?
YOU DON'T WANNA KNOW.
NAW, C'MON. THIS CLOAK & DAGGER STUFF IS TAKING, LIKE, FOREVER.
WELL...I JUST REALIZED...
...YOU'RE THE PUNY ONE NOW, AREN'T YOU, FLASH?
PUNY FLASH.
PUNY, PUNY FLASH.
HERE WE ARE, FOLKS!
SORRY FOR ALL THE SECRECY, BUT THE ACTUAL LOCATION OF SHADOW COMMAND IS DIVULGED ON A STRICT NEED-TO-KNOW BASIS ONLY.

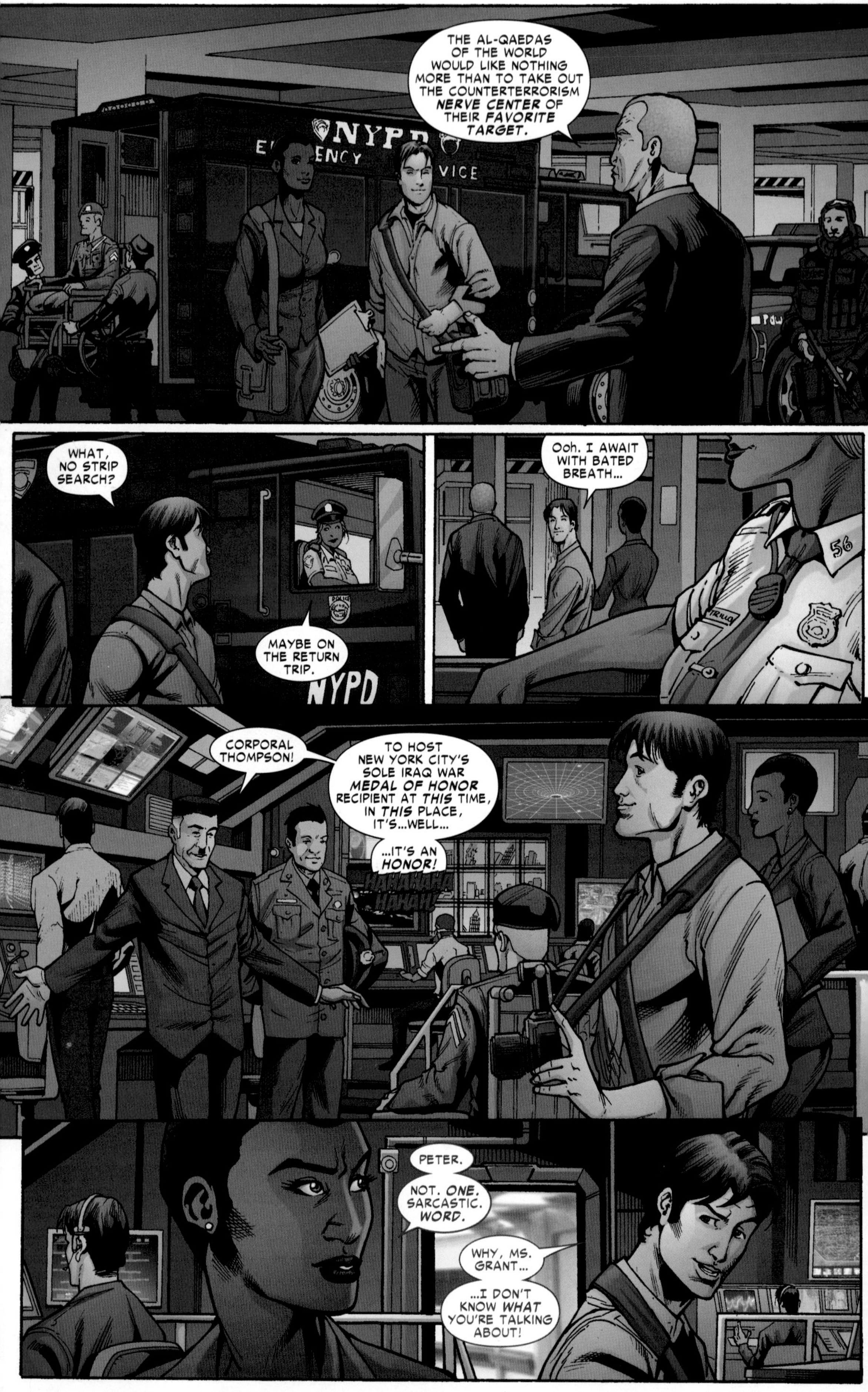
THE AL-QAEDAS OF THE WORLD WOULD LIKE NOTHING MORE THAN TO TAKE OUT THE COUNTERTERRORISM NERVE CENTER OF THEIR FAVORITE TARGET.
NYPD
WHAT, NO STRIP SEARCH?
MAYBE ON THE RETURN TRIP.
NYPD
Ooh. I AWAIT WITH BATED BREATH...
56
CORPORAL THOMPSON!
TO HOST NEW YORK CITY'S SOLE IRAQ WAR MEDAL OF HONOR RECIPIENT AT THIS TIME, IN THIS PLACE, IT'S...WELL...
...IT'S AN HONOR!
PETER.
NOT. ONE. SARCASTIC. WORD.
WHY, MS. GRANT...
...I DON'T KNOW WHAT YOU'RE TALKING ABOUT!

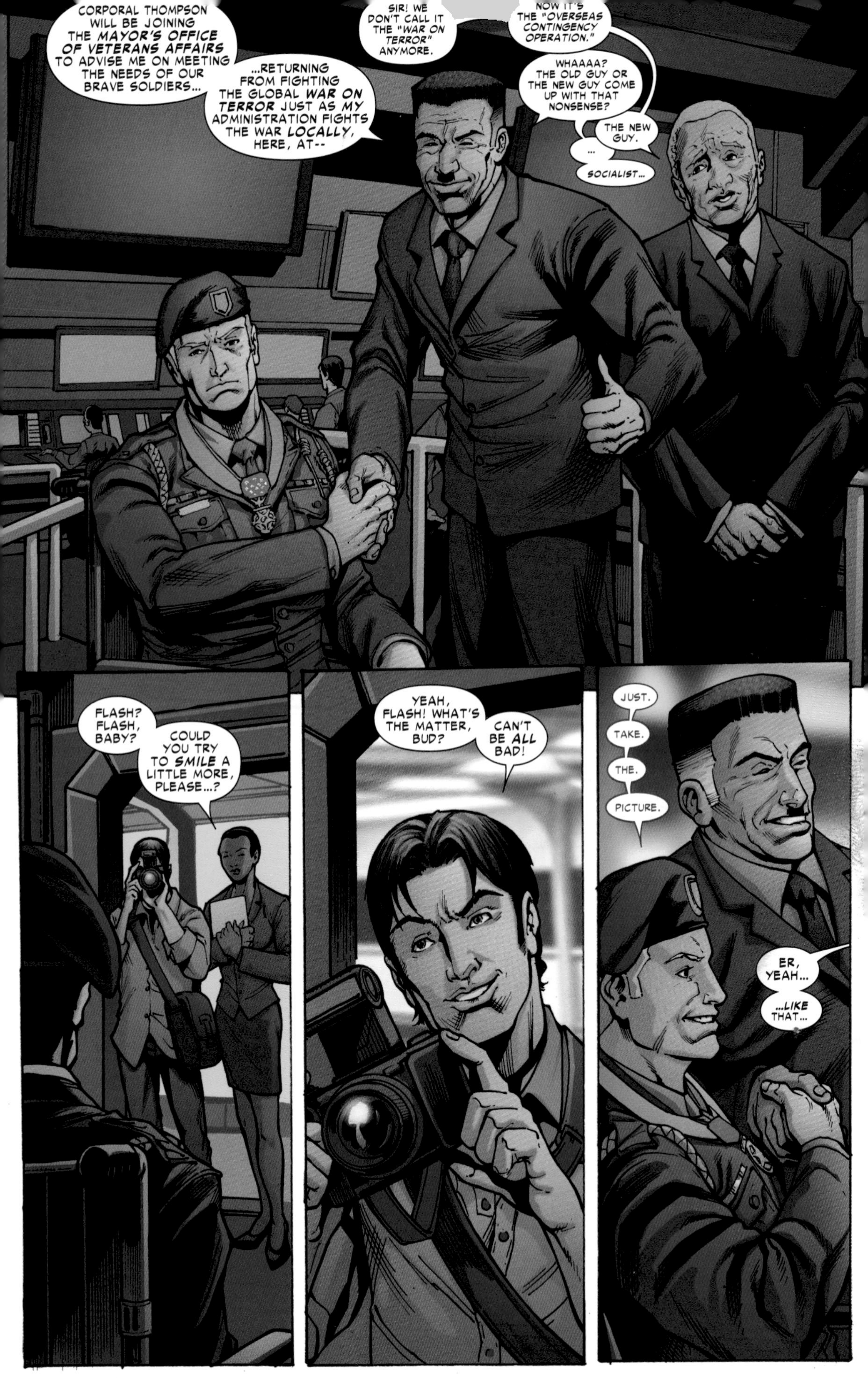

CORPORAL THOMPSON WILL BE JOINING THE MAYOR'S OFFICE OF VETERANS AFFAIRS TO ADVISE ME ON MEETING THE NEEDS OF OUR BRAVE SOLDIERS...
...RETURNING FROM FIGHTING THE GLOBAL WAR ON TERROR JUST AS MY ADMINISTRATION FIGHTS THE WAR LOCALLY, HERE, AT--
SIR! WE DON'T CALL IT THE "WAR ON TERROR" ANYMORE.
NOW IT'S THE "OVERSEAS CONTINGENCY OPERATION."
WHAAAA? THE OLD GUY OR THE NEW GUY COME UP WITH THAT NONSENSE?
THE NEW GUY.
...
SOCIALIST...
FLASH? FLASH, BABY?
COULD YOU TRY TO SMILE A LITTLE MORE, PLEASE...?
YEAH, FLASH! WHAT'S THE MATTER, BUD?
CAN'T BE ALL BAD!
JUST.
TAKE.
THE.
PICTURE.
ER, YEAH...
...LIKE THAT...

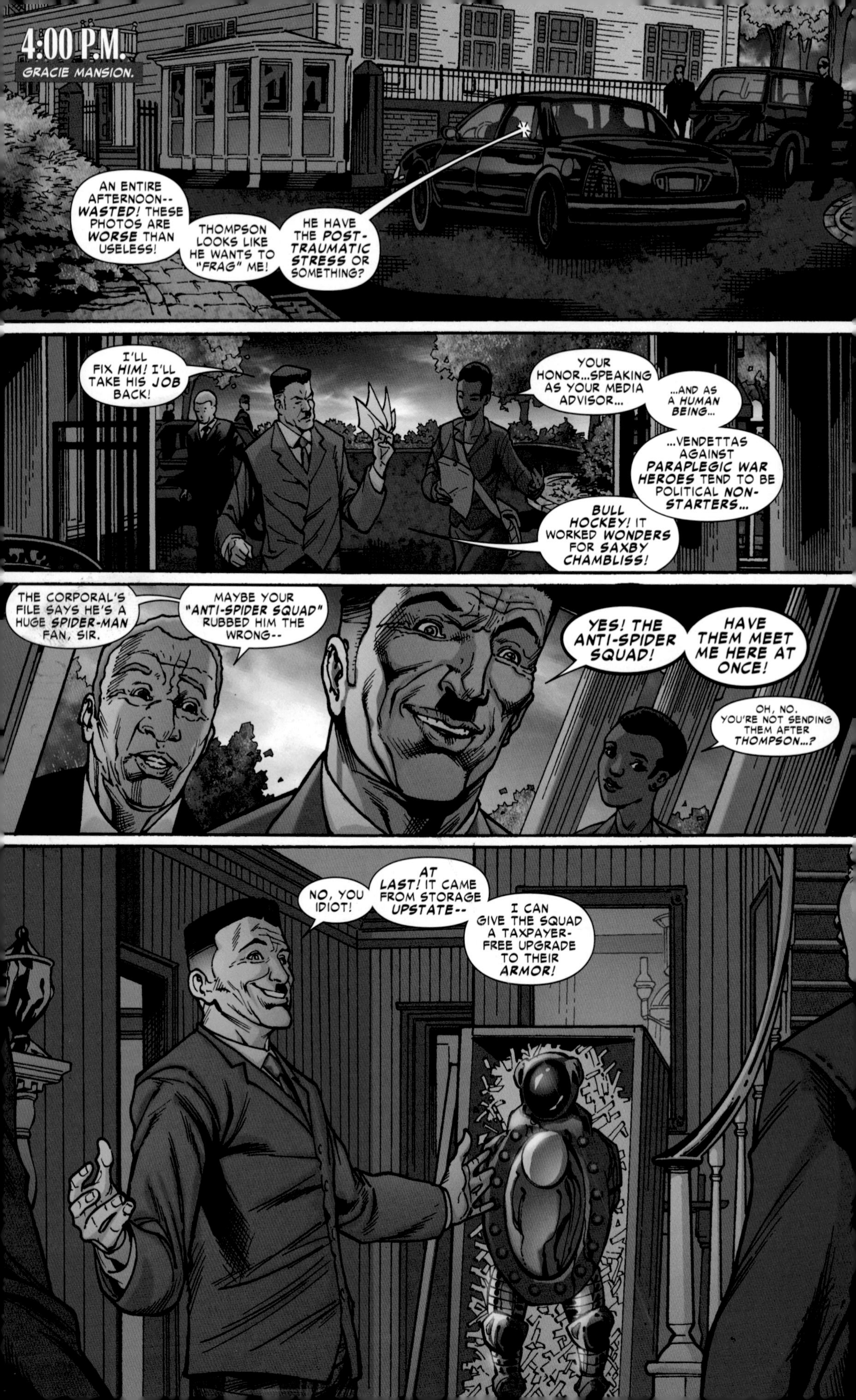
4:00 P.M.
GRACIE MANSION.
AN ENTIRE AFTERNOON-- WASTED! THESE PHOTOS ARE WORSE THAN USELESS!
THOMPSON LOOKS LIKE HE WANTS TO "FRAG" ME!
HE HAVE THE POST-TRAUMATIC STRESS OR SOMETHING?
I'LL FIX HIM! I'LL TAKE HIS JOB BACK!
YOUR HONOR...SPEAKING AS YOUR MEDIA ADVISOR...
...AND AS A HUMAN BEING...
...VENDETTAS AGAINST PARAPLEGIC WAR HEROES TEND TO BE POLITICAL NON-STARTERS...
BULL HOCKEY! IT WORKED WONDERS FOR SAXBY CHAMBLISS!
THE CORPORAL'S FILE SAYS HE'S A HUGE SPIDER-MAN FAN, SIR.
MAYBE YOUR "ANTI-SPIDER SQUAD" RUBBED HIM THE WRONG--
YES! THE ANTI-SPIDER SQUAD!
HAVE THEM MEET ME HERE AT ONCE!
OH, NO. YOU'RE NOT SENDING THEM AFTER THOMPSON...?
NO, YOU IDIOT!
AT LAST! IT CAME FROM STORAGE UPSTATE--
I CAN GIVE THE SQUAD A TAXPAYER-FREE UPGRADE TO THEIR ARMOR!

4:45 P.M.

THERE IT IS.

SHADOW COMMAND-- FROM THE OUTSIDE.

JUST ANOTHER UNASSUMING WAREHOUSE IN LONG ISLAND CITY.

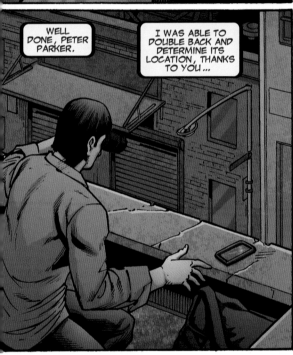

WELL DONE, PETER PARKER.

I WAS ABLE TO DOUBLE BACK AND DETERMINE ITS LOCATION, THANKS TO YOU...

...AS WELL AS THE HOMING DEVICE I LEFT IN THE MEN'S ROOM.

I'LL TAKE ONE OF THOSE CELL PHONES TOO.

5:03 P.M.

I FOUND THE RIGHT ADDRESS. DELIVERY WILL BE MADE AT NOON TOMORROW.

FINALLY.

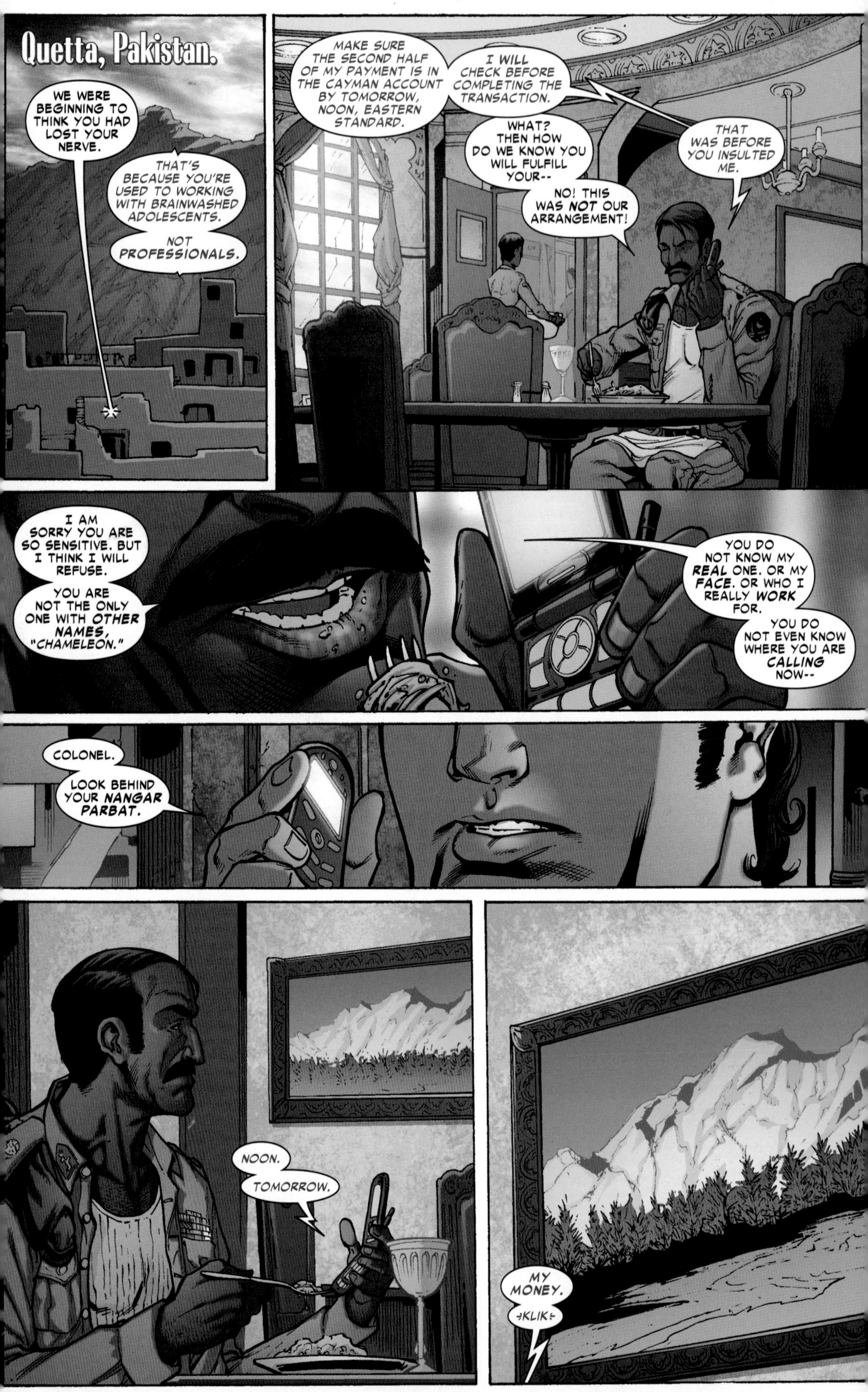
Quetta, Pakistan.
WE WERE BEGINNING TO THINK YOU HAD LOST YOUR NERVE.
THAT'S BECAUSE YOU'RE USED TO WORKING WITH BRAINWASHED ADOLESCENTS.
NOT PROFESSIONALS.
MAKE SURE THE SECOND HALF OF MY PAYMENT IS IN THE CAYMAN ACCOUNT BY TOMORROW, NOON, EASTERN STANDARD.
I WILL CHECK BEFORE COMPLETING THE TRANSACTION.
WHAT? THEN HOW DO WE KNOW YOU WILL FULFILL YOUR--
NO! THIS WAS NOT OUR ARRANGEMENT!
THAT WAS BEFORE YOU INSULTED ME.
I AM SORRY YOU ARE SO SENSITIVE. BUT I THINK I WILL REFUSE.
YOU ARE NOT THE ONLY ONE WITH OTHER NAMES, "CHAMELEON."
YOU DO NOT KNOW MY REAL ONE. OR MY FACE. OR WHO I REALLY WORK FOR.
YOU DO NOT EVEN KNOW WHERE YOU ARE CALLING NOW--
COLONEL.
LOOK BEHIND YOUR NANGAR PARBAT.
NOON.
TOMORROW.
MY MONEY.
KLIK

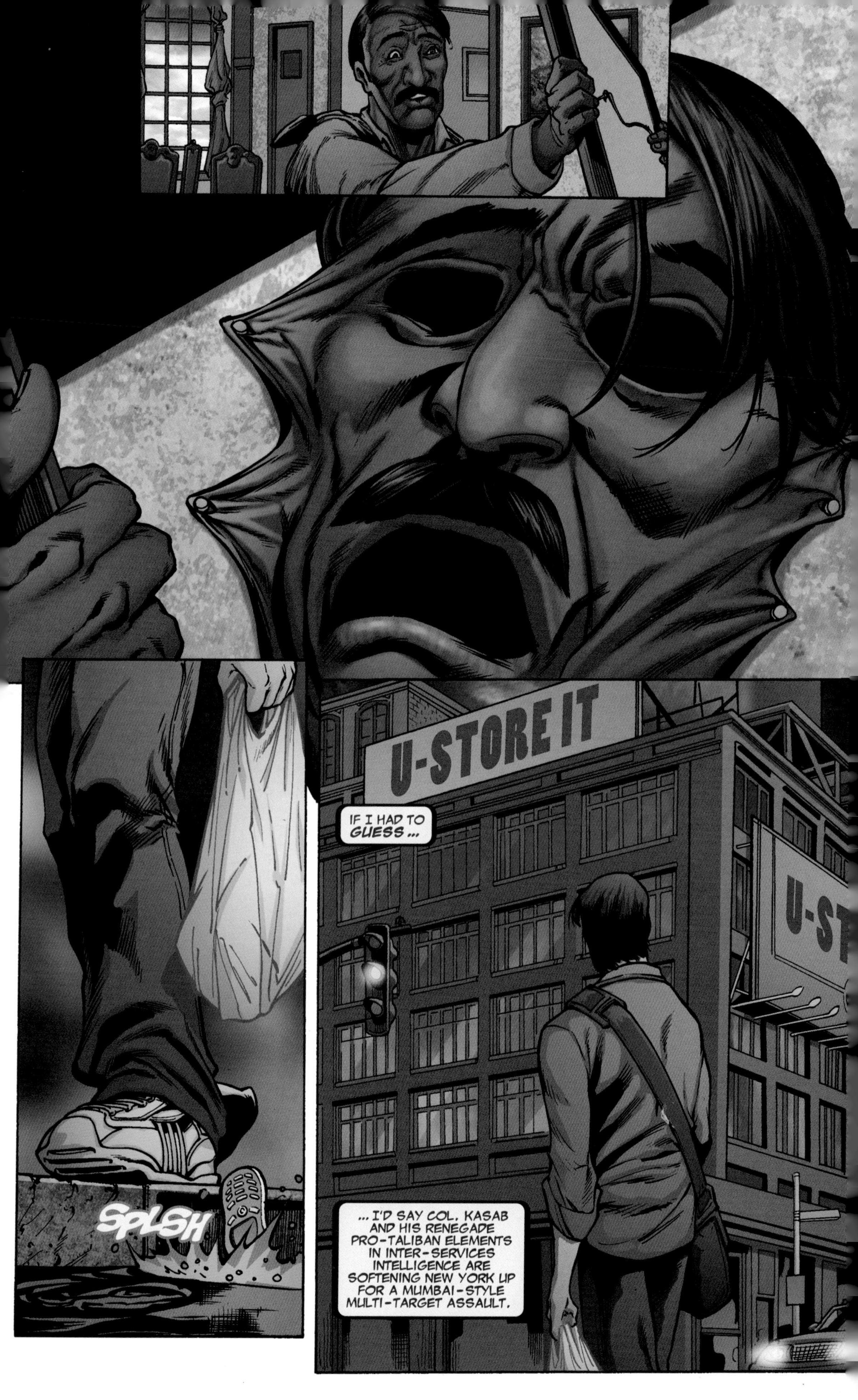

SPLSH
U-STORE IT
IF I HAD TO GUESS...
U-S
...I'D SAY COL. KASAB AND HIS RENEGADE PRO-TALIBAN ELEMENTS IN INTER-SERVICES INTELLIGENCE ARE SOFTENING NEW YORK UP FOR A MUMBAI-STYLE MULTI-TARGET ASSAULT.

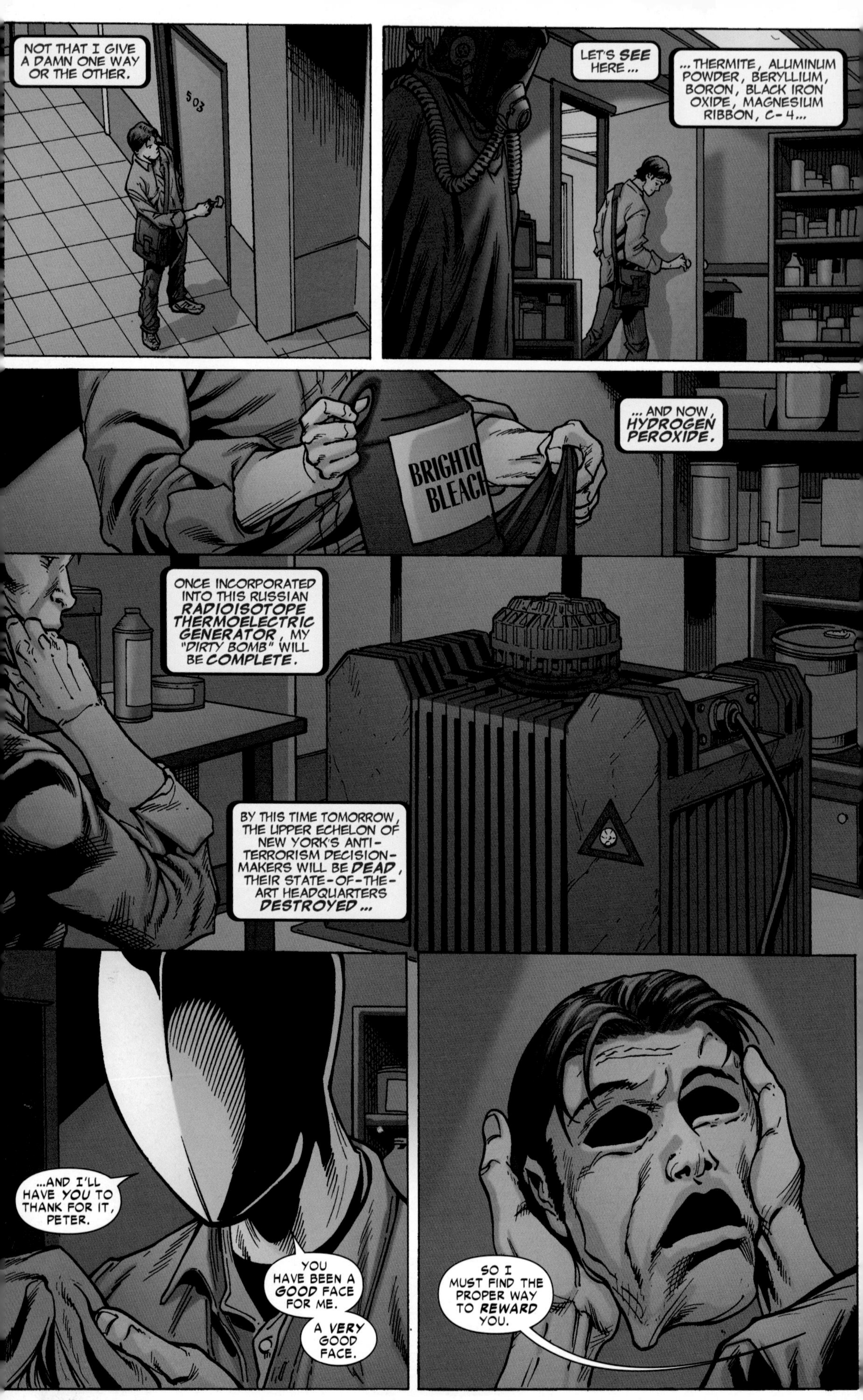
NOT THAT I GIVE A DAMN ONE WAY OR THE OTHER.
503
LET'S SEE HERE...
...THERMITE, ALUMINUM POWDER, BERYLLIUM, BORON, BLACK IRON OXIDE, MAGNESIUM RIBBON, C-4...
BRIGHTO BLEACH
...AND NOW, HYDROGEN PEROXIDE.
ONCE INCORPORATED INTO THIS RUSSIAN RADIOISOTOPE THERMOELECTRIC GENERATOR, MY "DIRTY BOMB" WILL BE COMPLETE.
BY THIS TIME TOMORROW, THE UPPER ECHELON OF NEW YORK'S ANTI-TERRORISM DECISION-MAKERS WILL BE DEAD, THEIR STATE-OF-THE-ART HEADQUARTERS DESTROYED...
...AND I'LL HAVE YOU TO THANK FOR IT, PETER.
YOU HAVE BEEN A GOOD FACE FOR ME.
A VERY GOOD FACE.
SO I MUST FIND THE PROPER WAY TO REWARD YOU.

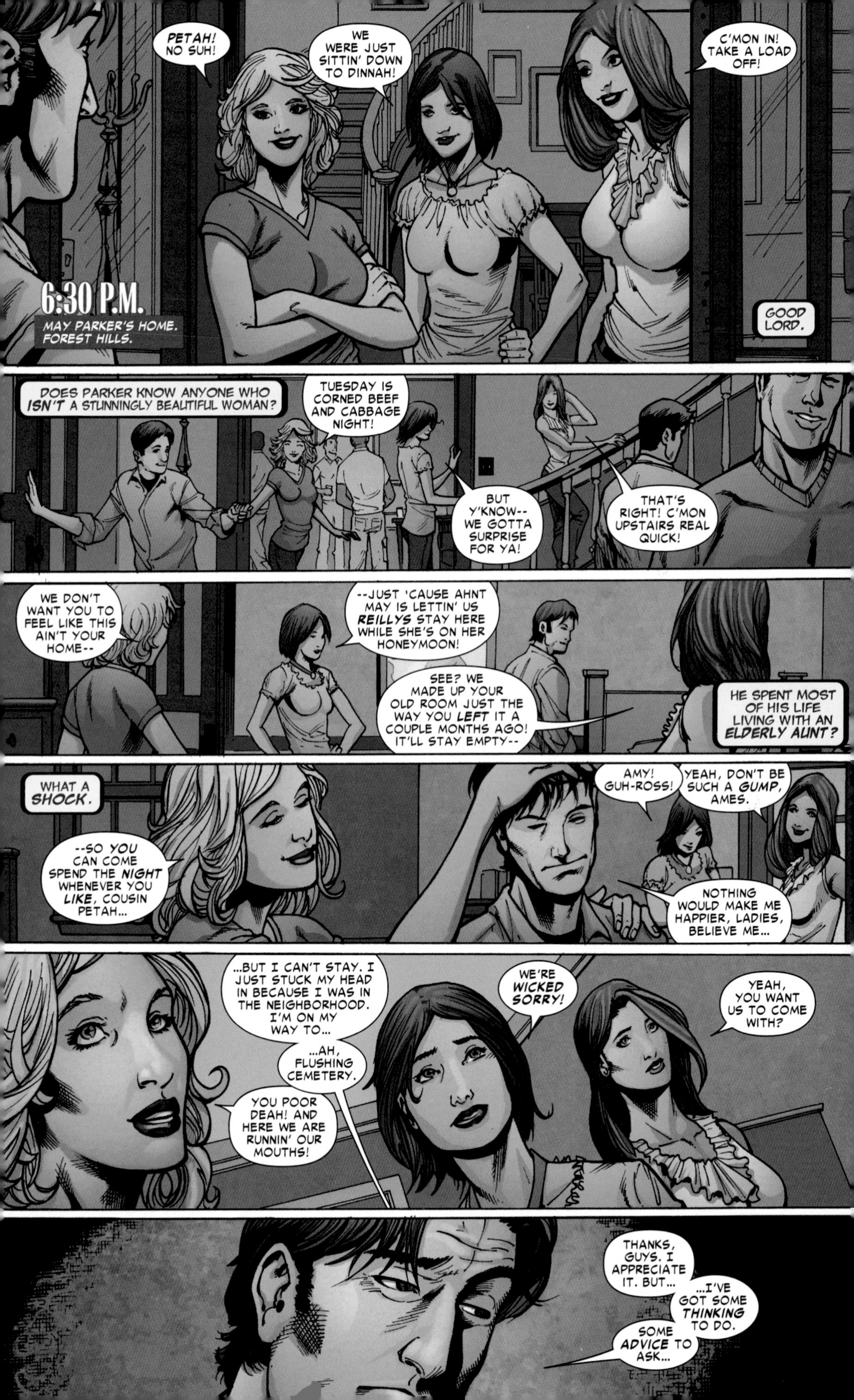
PETAH! NO SUH!
WE WERE JUST SITTIN' DOWN TO DINNAH!
C'MON IN! TAKE A LOAD OFF!
6:30 P.M.
MAY PARKER'S HOME. FOREST HILLS.
GOOD LORD.
DOES PARKER KNOW ANYONE WHO ISN'T A STUNNINGLY BEAUTIFUL WOMAN?
TUESDAY IS CORNED BEEF AND CABBAGE NIGHT!
BUT Y'KNOW-- WE GOTTA SURPRISE FOR YA!
THAT'S RIGHT! C'MON UPSTAIRS REAL QUICK!
WE DON'T WANT YOU TO FEEL LIKE THIS AIN'T YOUR HOME--
--JUST 'CAUSE AHNT MAY IS LETTIN' US REILLYS STAY HERE WHILE SHE'S ON HER HONEYMOON!
SEE? WE MADE UP YOUR OLD ROOM JUST THE WAY YOU LEFT IT A COUPLE MONTHS AGO! IT'LL STAY EMPTY--
HE SPENT MOST OF HIS LIFE LIVING WITH AN ELDERLY AUNT?
WHAT A SHOCK.
--SO YOU CAN COME SPEND THE NIGHT WHENEVER YOU LIKE, COUSIN PETAH...
AMY! GUH-ROSS!
YEAH, DON'T BE SUCH A GUMP, AMES.
NOTHING WOULD MAKE ME HAPPIER, LADIES, BELIEVE ME...
...BUT I CAN'T STAY. I JUST STUCK MY HEAD IN BECAUSE I WAS IN THE NEIGHBORHOOD. I'M ON MY WAY TO...
...AH, FLUSHING CEMETERY.
WE'RE WICKED SORRY!
YEAH, YOU WANT US TO COME WITH?
YOU POOR DEAH! AND HERE WE ARE RUNNIN' OUR MOUTHS!
THANKS, GUYS. I APPRECIATE IT. BUT...
...I'VE GOT SOME THINKING TO DO.
SOME ADVICE TO ASK...

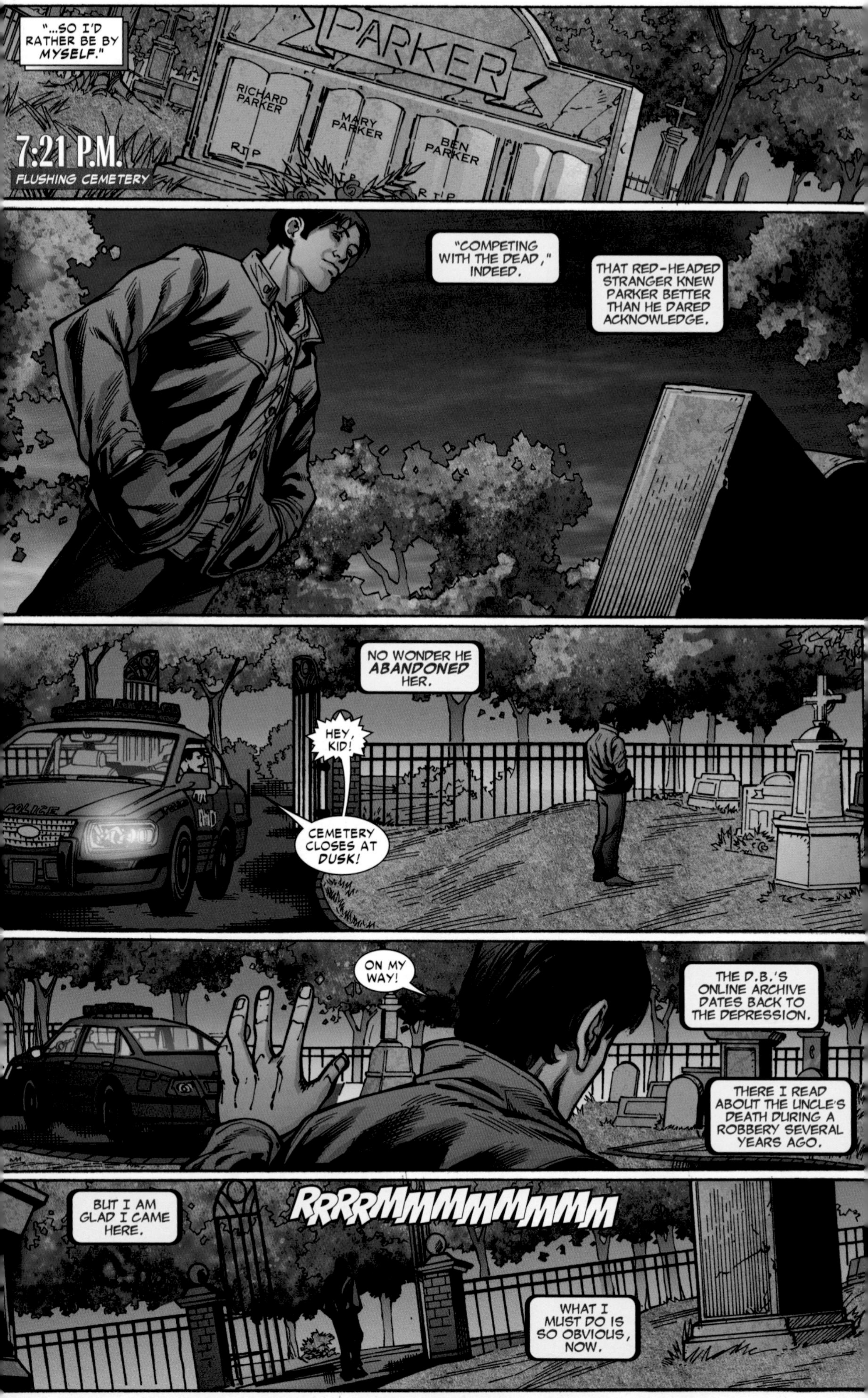

"...SO I'D RATHER BE BY *MYSELF*."
PARKER
RICHARD PARKER
MARY PARKER
BEN PARKER
7:21 P.M.
FLUSHING CEMETERY
"COMPETING WITH THE DEAD," INDEED.
THAT RED-HEADED STRANGER KNEW PARKER BETTER THAN HE DARED ACKNOWLEDGE.
NO WONDER HE *ABANDONED* HER.
HEY, KID!
CEMETERY CLOSES AT *DUSK*!
POLICE
ON MY WAY!
THE D.B.'S ONLINE ARCHIVE DATES BACK TO THE DEPRESSION.
THERE I READ ABOUT THE UNCLE'S DEATH DURING A ROBBERY SEVERAL YEARS AGO.
BUT I AM GLAD I CAME HERE.
RRRRMMMMMMMMMM
WHAT I MUST DO IS SO OBVIOUS, NOW.

AND THOMPSON MAKES A PERFECT TOUCHDOWN PASS...

THE FAMOUS BASEBALLER, JACKIE ROBINSON, HE ONCE SAID:

LEADING MIDTOWN HIGH TO ANOTHER THRILLING VICTORY OVER LONGTIME RIVALS--

"A LIFE IS NOT IMPORTANT EXCEPT IN THE IMPACT IT HAS ON OTHER LIVES."

I COULD NOT AGREE MORE.

MARY JANE, WE NEED YOU IN FIFTEEN!

FRONT LINE

SPIDER-MAN E... MORE... N.Y.P.D. STING...

THAT IS WHY I TRY TO MAKE AS MUCH IMPACT ON MY FACES' LIVES AS POSSIBLE.

AFTER ALL, THEY HAVE DONE SO MUCH FOR ME. IT IS THE LEAST I CAN DO.

UNLIKE THEM, I NEED NOT FEAR WHAT PEOPLE THINK OF ME...

SO I CAN BE BRAVE WHERE THEY ARE WEAK.

...FLIGHT TO LOS ANGELES WILL TAKE ABOUT FIVE-AND-A-HALF HOURS...

FOR I WILL JUST BE SOMEONE ELSE TOMORROW.

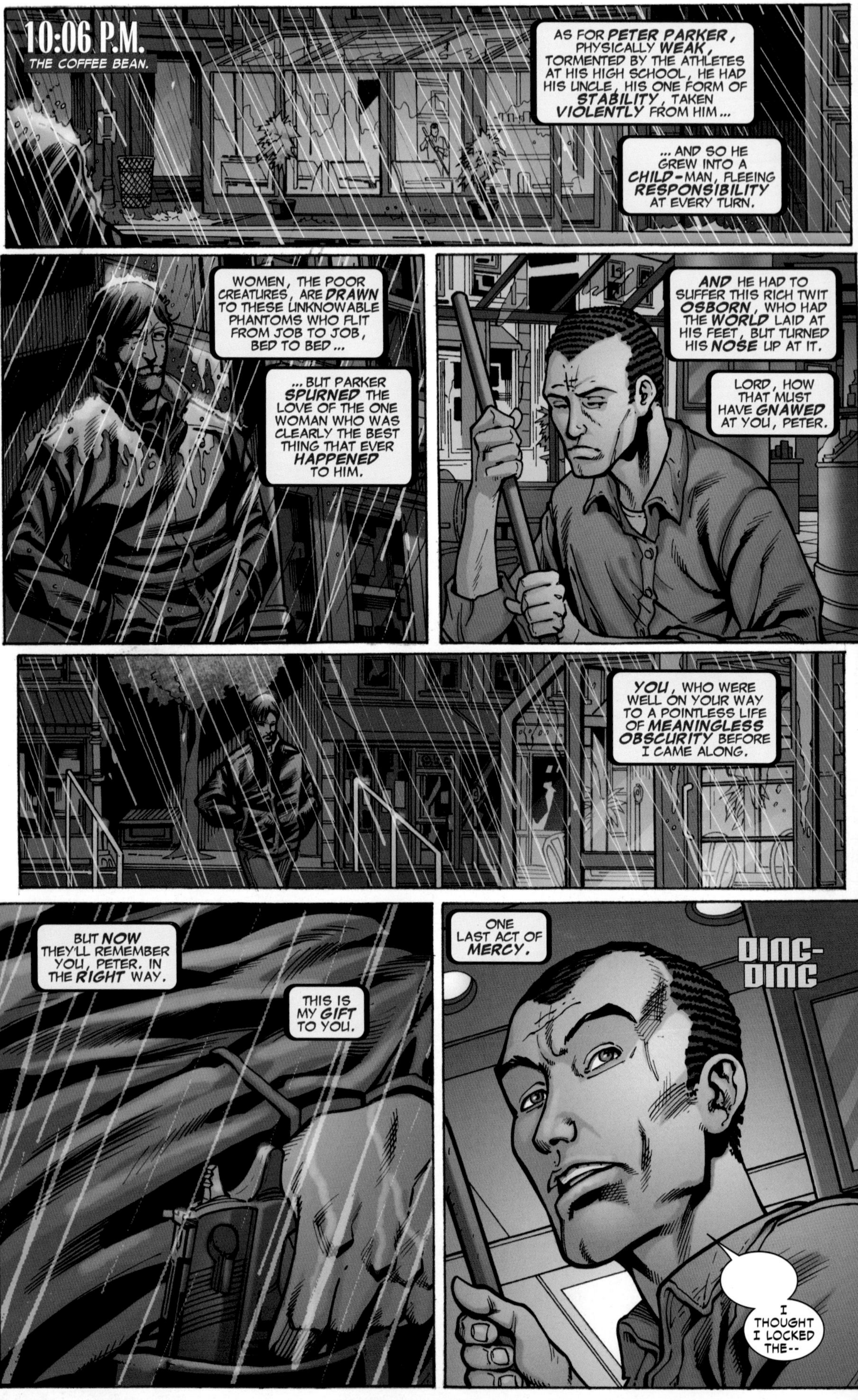
10:06 P.M.
THE COFFEE BEAN.
AS FOR PETER PARKER, PHYSICALLY WEAK, TORMENTED BY THE ATHLETES AT HIS HIGH SCHOOL, HE HAD HIS UNCLE, HIS ONE FORM OF STABILITY, TAKEN VIOLENTLY FROM HIM...
...AND SO HE GREW INTO A CHILD-MAN, FLEEING RESPONSIBILITY AT EVERY TURN.
WOMEN, THE POOR CREATURES, ARE DRAWN TO THESE UNKNOWABLE PHANTOMS WHO FLIT FROM JOB TO JOB, BED TO BED...
...BUT PARKER SPURNED THE LOVE OF THE ONE WOMAN WHO WAS CLEARLY THE BEST THING THAT EVER HAPPENED TO HIM.
AND HE HAD TO SUFFER THIS RICH TWIT OSBORN, WHO HAD THE WORLD LAID AT HIS FEET, BUT TURNED HIS NOSE UP AT IT.
LORD, HOW THAT MUST HAVE GNAWED AT YOU, PETER.
YOU, WHO WERE WELL ON YOUR WAY TO A POINTLESS LIFE OF MEANINGLESS OBSCURITY BEFORE I CAME ALONG.
BUT NOW THEY'LL REMEMBER YOU, PETER. IN THE RIGHT WAY.
THIS IS MY GIFT TO YOU.
ONE LAST ACT OF MERCY.
DING-DING
I THOUGHT I LOCKED THE--

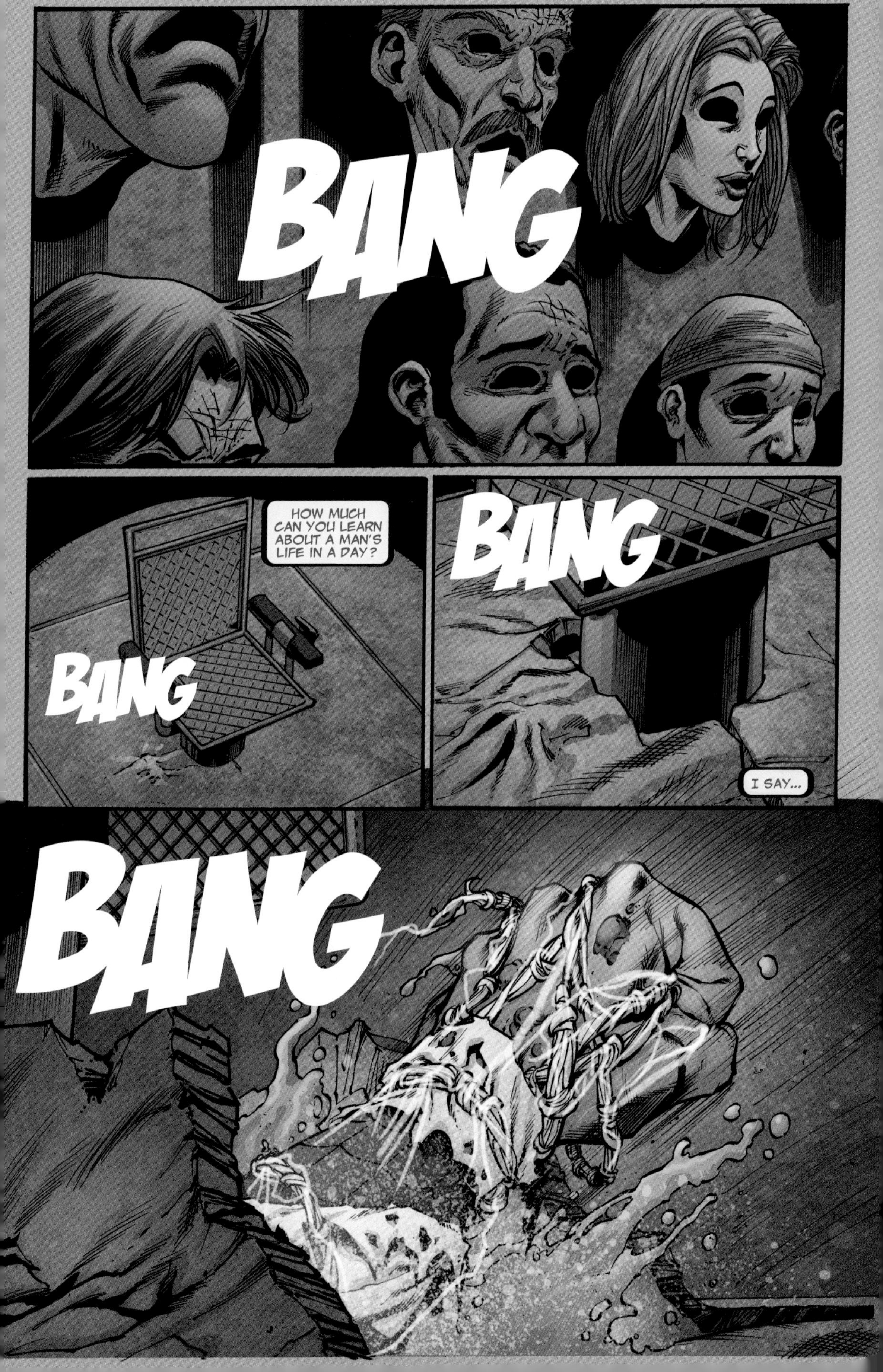
BANG
HOW MUCH CAN YOU LEARN ABOUT A MAN'S LIFE IN A DAY?
BANG
BANG
I SAY...
BANG

RED-HEADED STRANGER:
DECONSTRUCTING PETER

...EVERYTHING.

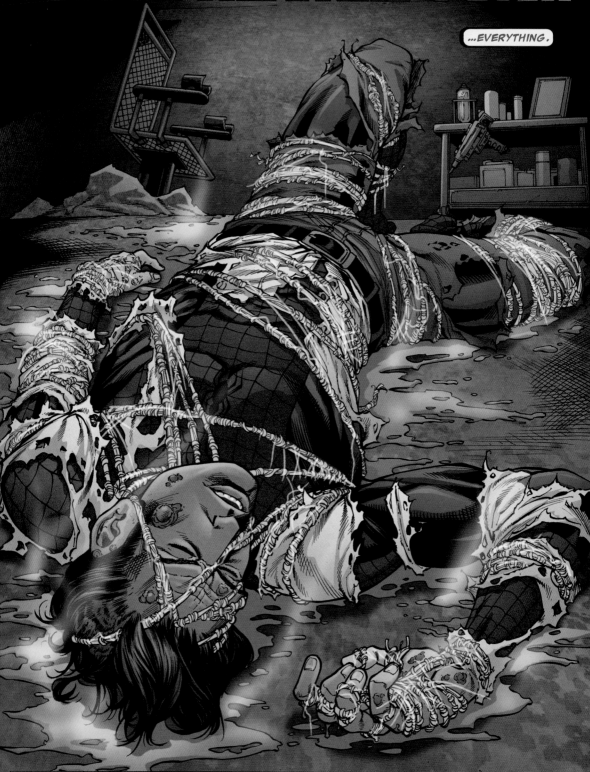

FRED VAN LENTE	ROBERT ATKINS	VICTOR OLAZABA	JEROMY COX	VC'S JOE CARAMAGNA	TOM BRENNAN	STEPHEN WACKER	TOM BREVOORT	JOE QUESADA	DAN BUCKLEY	ALAN FINE
WRITER	PENCILER	INKER	COLORIST	LETTERER	ASST. EDITOR	R.I.P.	EXEC. EDITOR	EDITOR IN CHIEF	PUBLISHER	EXEC. PRODUCER

GALE, GUGGENHEIM, KELLY, SLOTT, VAN LENTE, WAID & WELLS WEB-HEADS

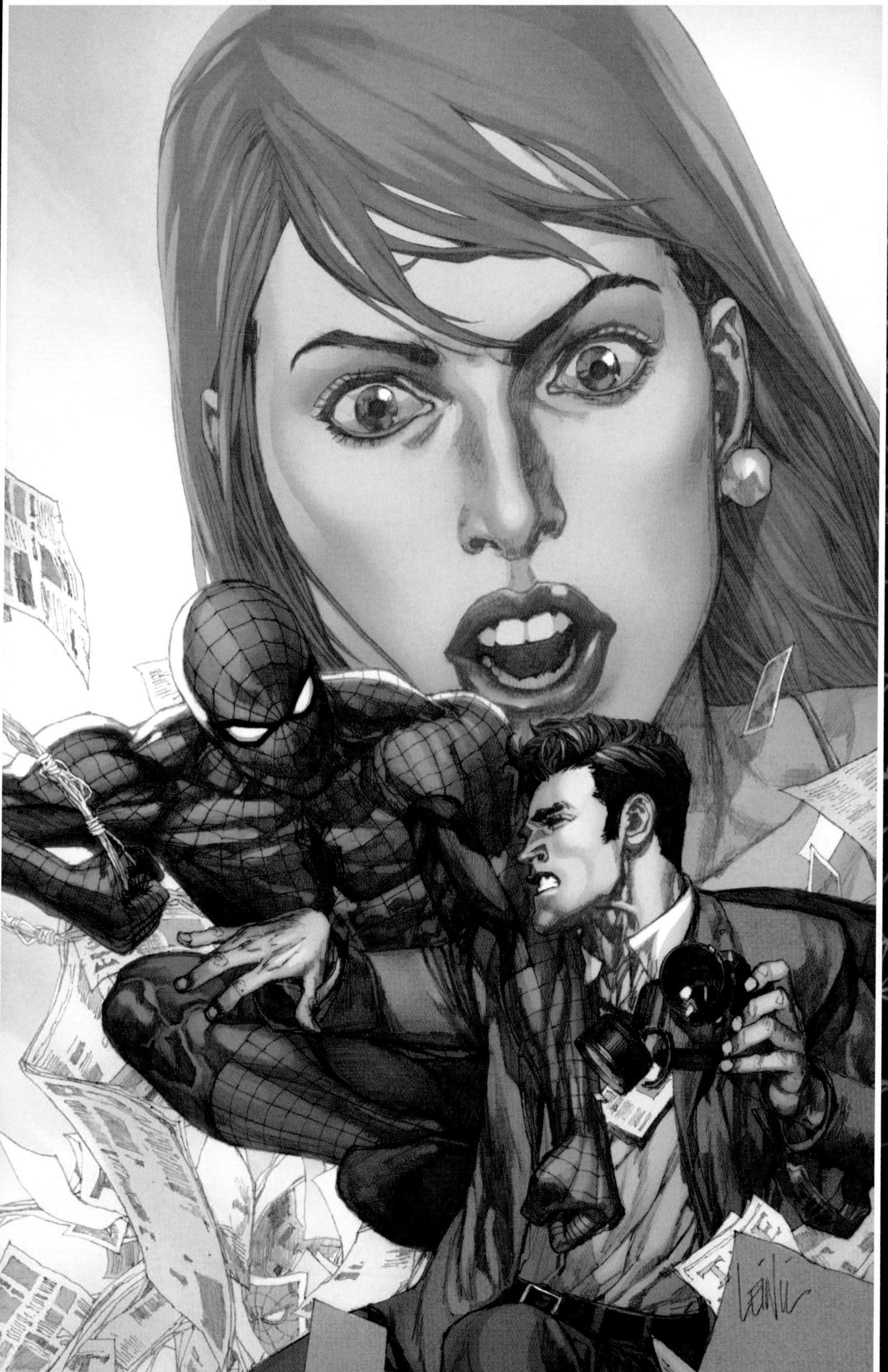

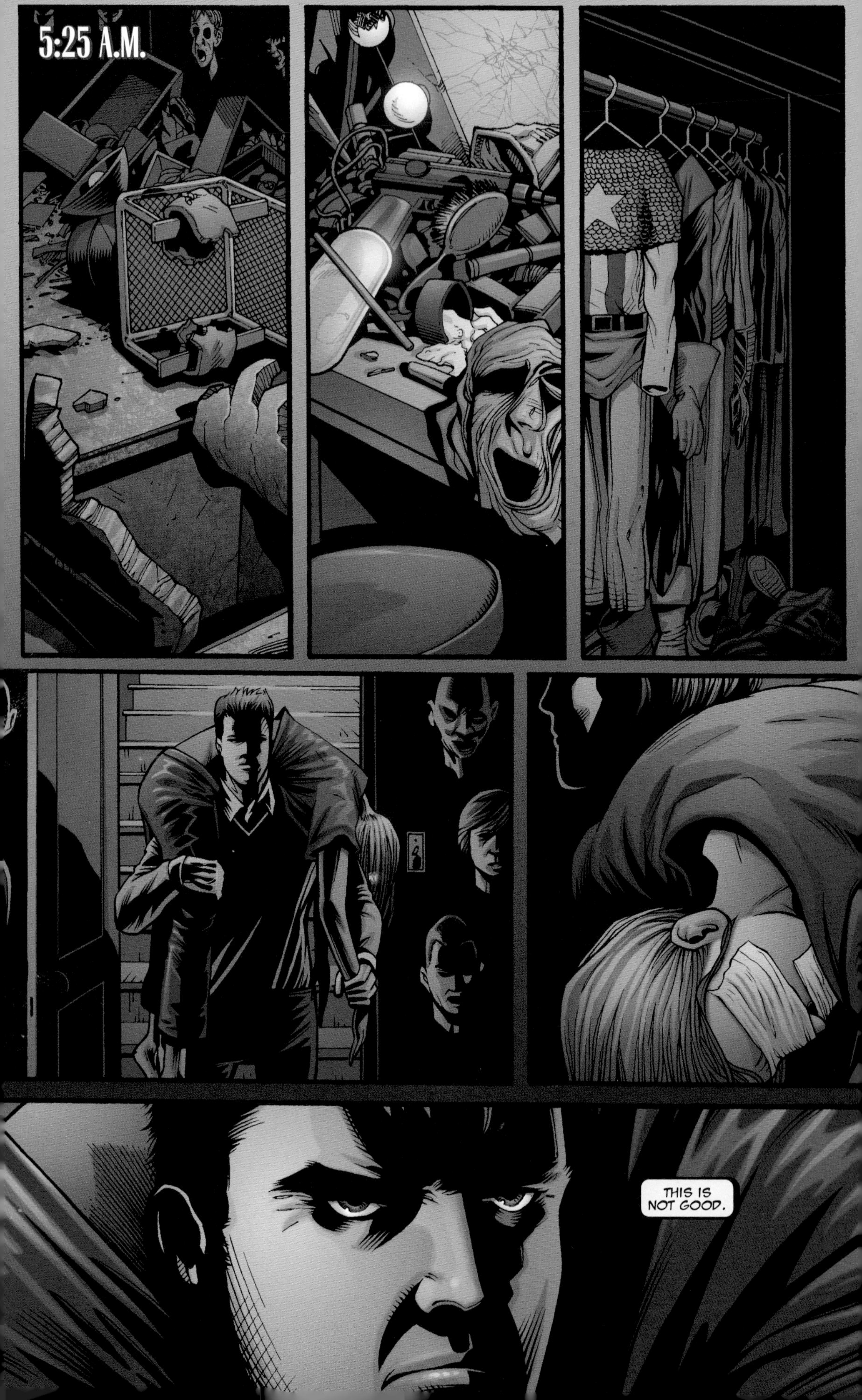
5:25 A.M.
THIS IS NOT GOOD.

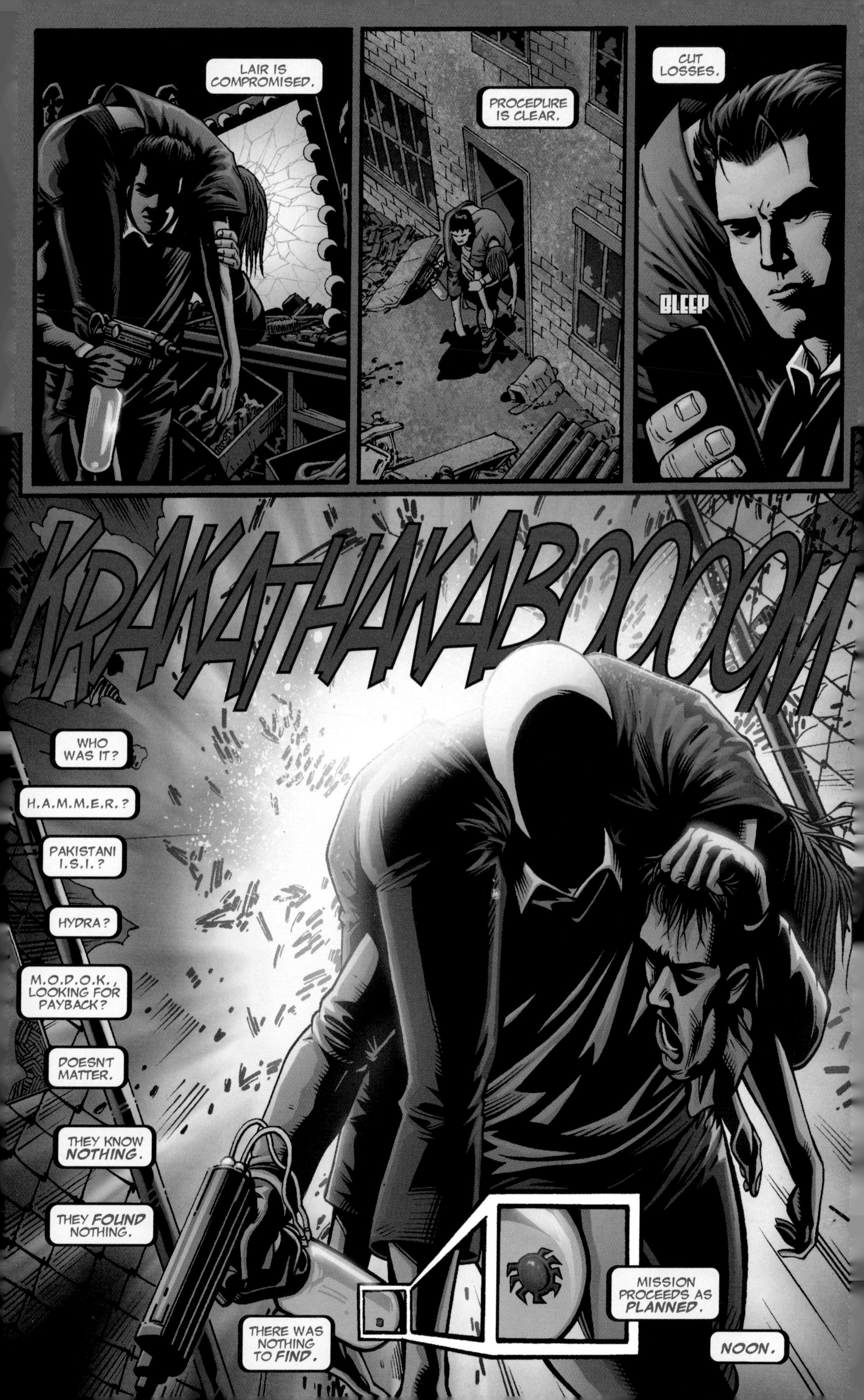
LAIR IS COMPROMISED.
PROCEDURE IS CLEAR.
CUT LOSSES.
BLEEP
KRAKATHAKABOOOOOM
WHO WAS IT?
H.A.M.M.E.R.?
PAKISTANI I.S.I.?
HYDRA?
M.O.D.O.K., LOOKING FOR PAYBACK?
DOESN'T MATTER.
THEY KNOW NOTHING.
THEY FOUND NOTHING.
THERE WAS NOTHING TO FIND.
MISSION PROCEEDS AS PLANNED.
NOON.

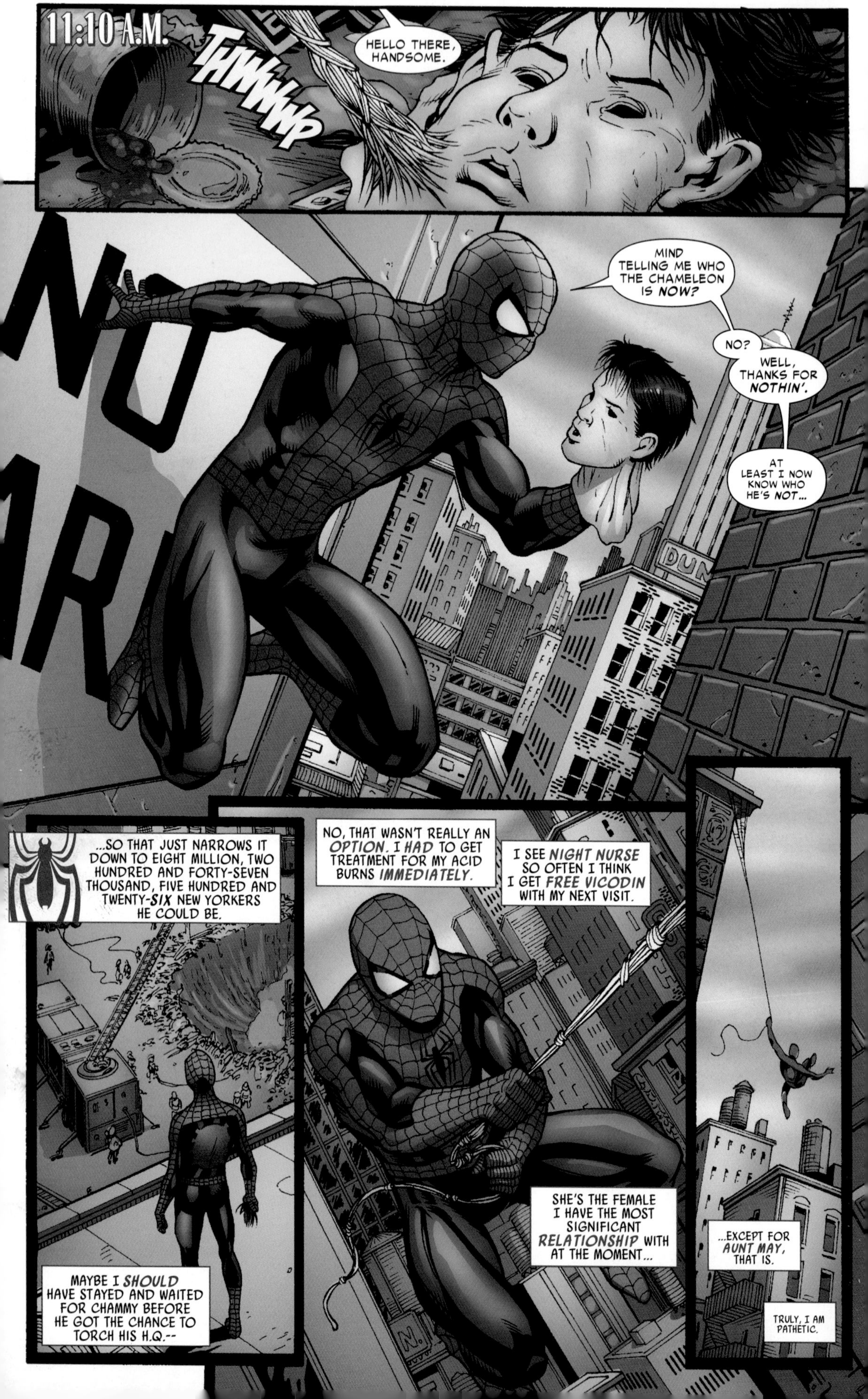
11:10 A.M.
THWWWP
HELLO THERE, HANDSOME.
MIND TELLING ME WHO THE CHAMELEON IS NOW?
NO?
WELL, THANKS FOR NOTHIN'.
AT LEAST I NOW KNOW WHO HE'S NOT...
...SO THAT JUST NARROWS IT DOWN TO EIGHT MILLION, TWO HUNDRED AND FORTY-SEVEN THOUSAND, FIVE HUNDRED AND TWENTY-SIX NEW YORKERS HE COULD BE.
MAYBE I SHOULD HAVE STAYED AND WAITED FOR CHAMMY BEFORE HE GOT THE CHANCE TO TORCH HIS H.Q.--
NO, THAT WASN'T REALLY AN OPTION. I HAD TO GET TREATMENT FOR MY ACID BURNS IMMEDIATELY.
I SEE NIGHT NURSE SO OFTEN I THINK I GET FREE VICODIN WITH MY NEXT VISIT.
SHE'S THE FEMALE I HAVE THE MOST SIGNIFICANT RELATIONSHIP WITH AT THE MOMENT...
...EXCEPT FOR AUNT MAY, THAT IS.
TRULY, I AM PATHETIC.

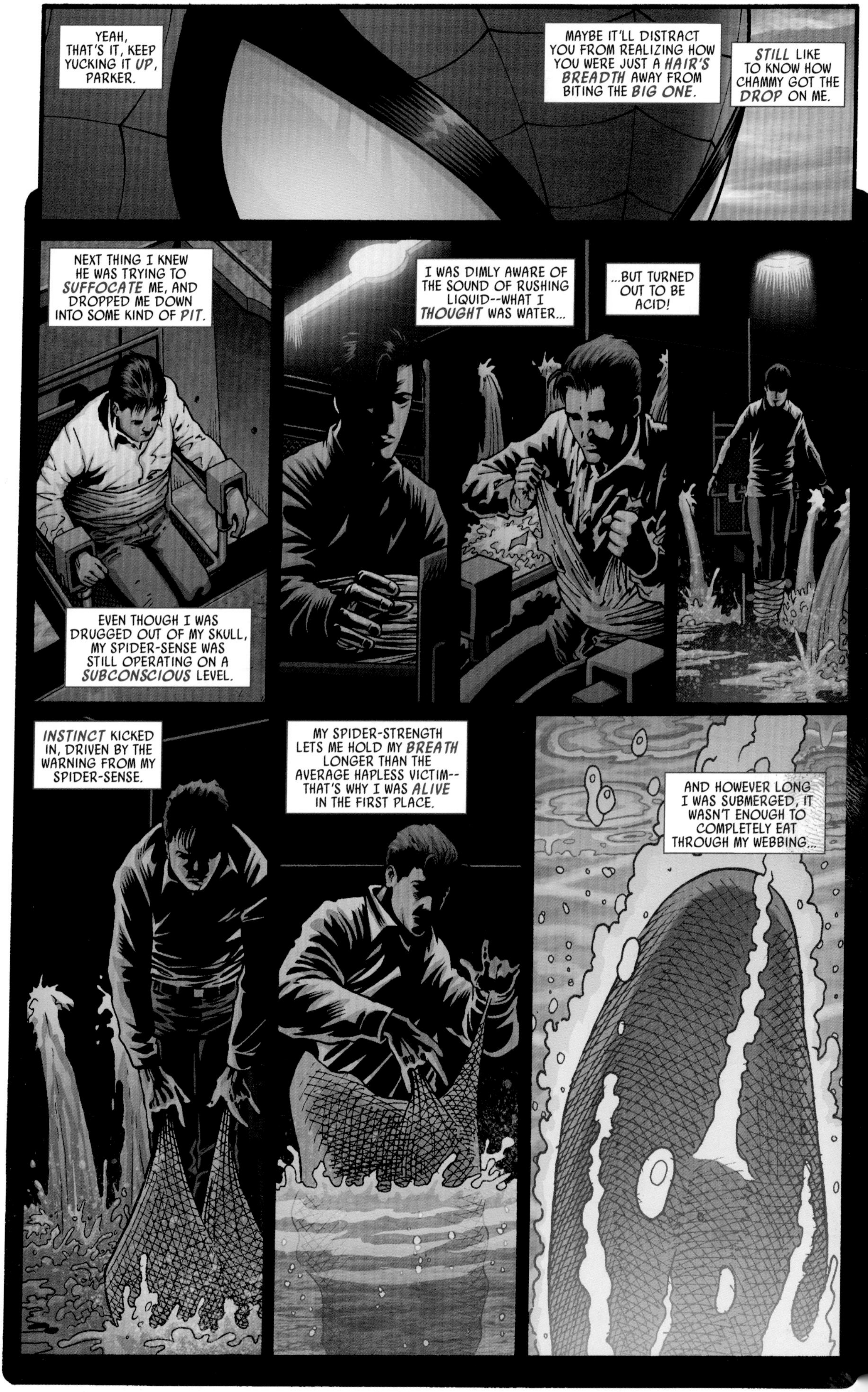

YEAH, THAT'S IT, KEEP YUCKING IT UP, PARKER.
MAYBE IT'LL DISTRACT YOU FROM REALIZING HOW YOU WERE JUST A HAIR'S BREADTH AWAY FROM BITING THE BIG ONE.
STILL LIKE TO KNOW HOW CHAMMY GOT THE DROP ON ME.
NEXT THING I KNEW HE WAS TRYING TO SUFFOCATE ME, AND DROPPED ME DOWN INTO SOME KIND OF PIT.
EVEN THOUGH I WAS DRUGGED OUT OF MY SKULL, MY SPIDER-SENSE WAS STILL OPERATING ON A SUBCONSCIOUS LEVEL.
I WAS DIMLY AWARE OF THE SOUND OF RUSHING LIQUID--WHAT I THOUGHT WAS WATER...
...BUT TURNED OUT TO BE ACID!
INSTINCT KICKED IN, DRIVEN BY THE WARNING FROM MY SPIDER-SENSE.
MY SPIDER-STRENGTH LETS ME HOLD MY BREATH LONGER THAN THE AVERAGE HAPLESS VICTIM--THAT'S WHY I WAS ALIVE IN THE FIRST PLACE.
AND HOWEVER LONG I WAS SUBMERGED, IT WASN'T ENOUGH TO COMPLETELY EAT THROUGH MY WEBBING...

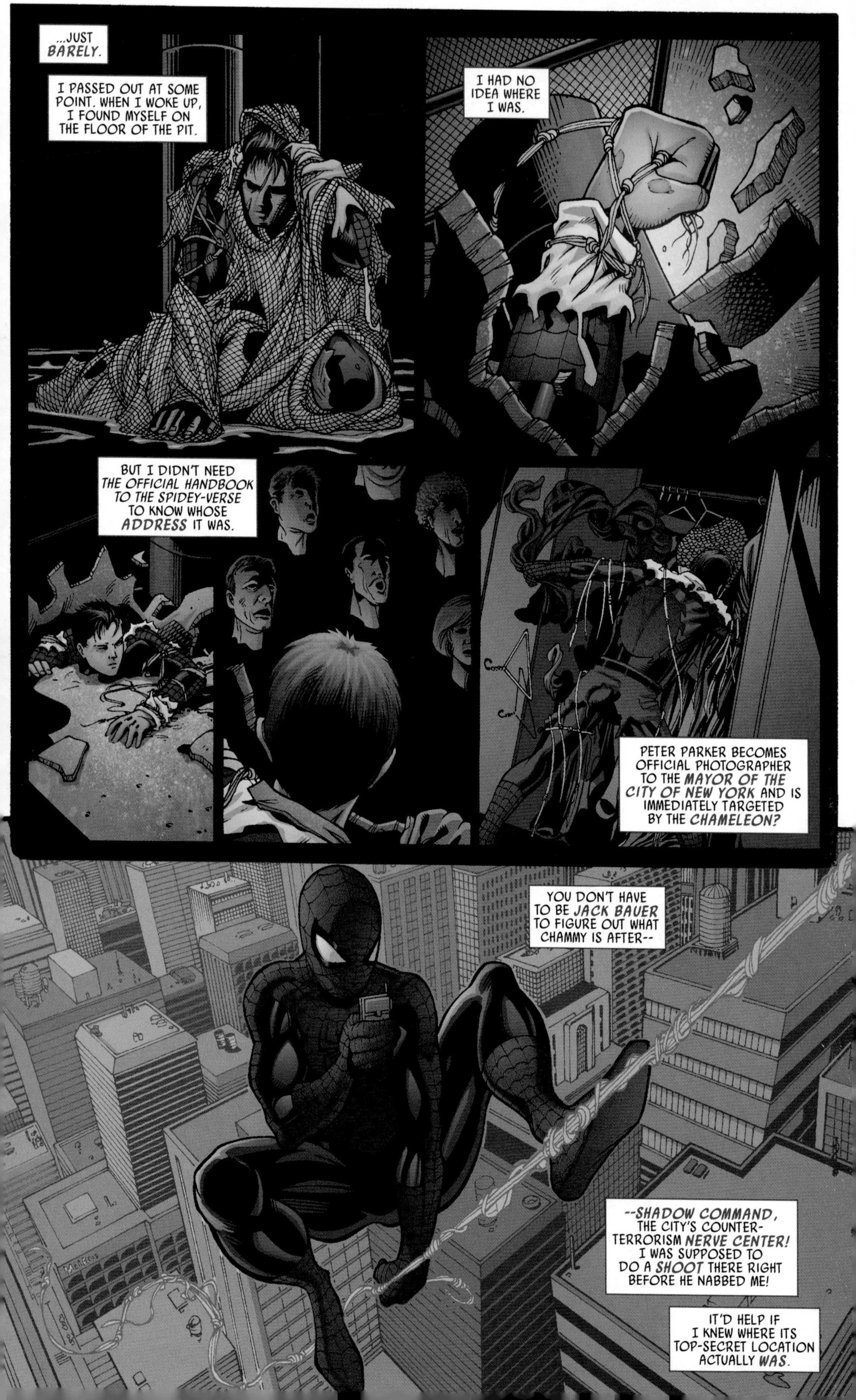

...JUST BARELY.
I PASSED OUT AT SOME POINT. WHEN I WOKE UP, I FOUND MYSELF ON THE FLOOR OF THE PIT.
I HAD NO IDEA WHERE I WAS.
BUT I DIDN'T NEED THE OFFICIAL HANDBOOK TO THE SPIDEY-VERSE TO KNOW WHOSE ADDRESS IT WAS.
PETER PARKER BECOMES OFFICIAL PHOTOGRAPHER TO THE MAYOR OF THE CITY OF NEW YORK AND IS IMMEDIATELY TARGETED BY THE CHAMELEON?
YOU DON'T HAVE TO BE JACK BAUER TO FIGURE OUT WHAT CHAMMY IS AFTER--
--SHADOW COMMAND, THE CITY'S COUNTER-TERRORISM NERVE CENTER! I WAS SUPPOSED TO DO A SHOOT THERE RIGHT BEFORE HE NABBED ME!
IT'D HELP IF I KNEW WHERE ITS TOP-SECRET LOCATION ACTUALLY WAS.

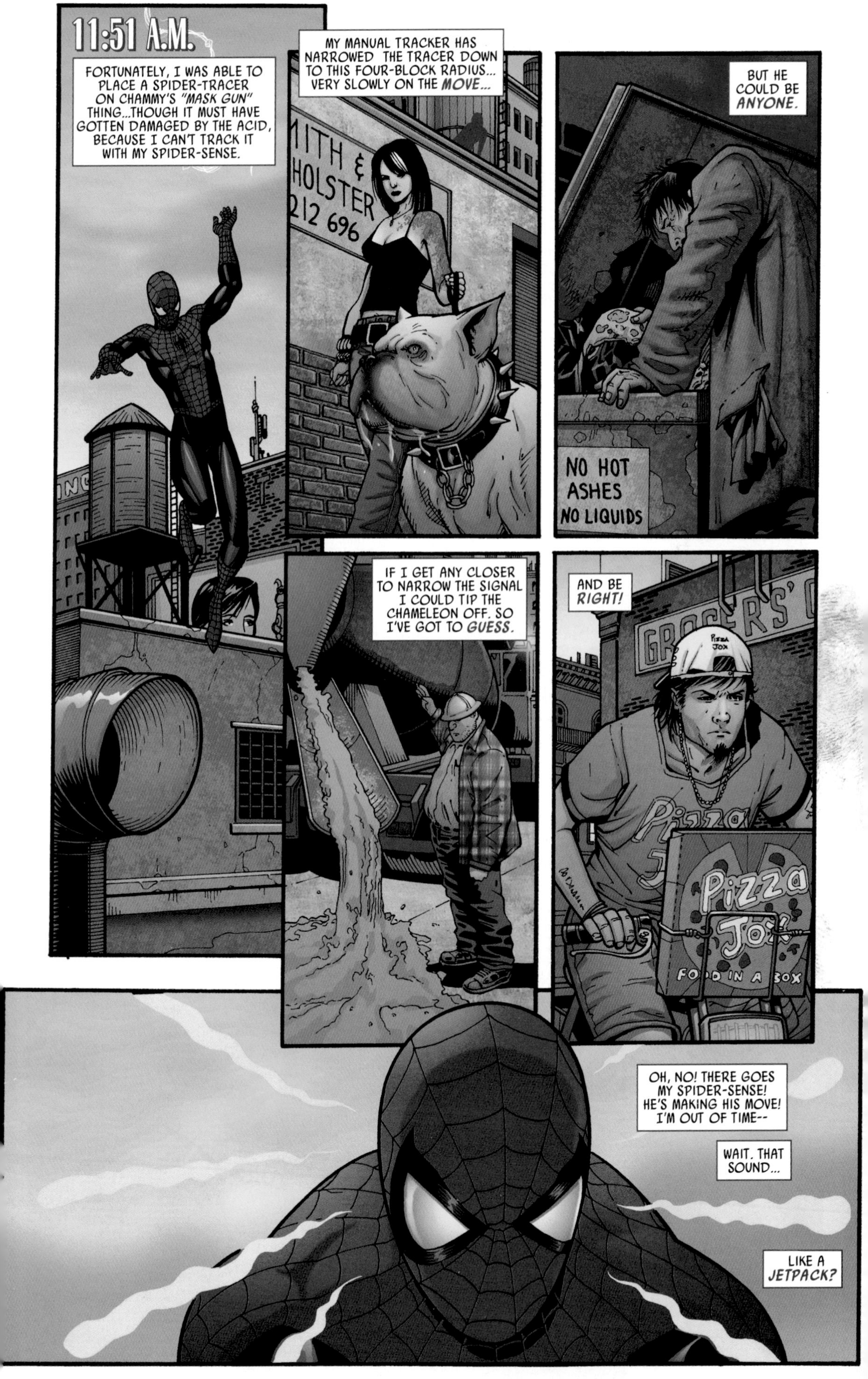
11:51 A.M.
FORTUNATELY, I WAS ABLE TO PLACE A SPIDER-TRACER ON CHAMMY'S "MASK GUN" THING...THOUGH IT MUST HAVE GOTTEN DAMAGED BY THE ACID, BECAUSE I CAN'T TRACK IT WITH MY SPIDER-SENSE.
MY MANUAL TRACKER HAS NARROWED THE TRACER DOWN TO THIS FOUR-BLOCK RADIUS... VERY SLOWLY ON THE MOVE...
MITH & HOLSTER 212 696
BUT HE COULD BE ANYONE.
NO HOT ASHES NO LIQUIDS
IF I GET ANY CLOSER TO NARROW THE SIGNAL I COULD TIP THE CHAMELEON OFF. SO I'VE GOT TO GUESS.
AND BE RIGHT!
PIZZA JOX
FOOD IN A BOX
OH, NO! THERE GOES MY SPIDER-SENSE! HE'S MAKING HIS MOVE! I'M OUT OF TIME--
WAIT. THAT SOUND...
LIKE A JETPACK?

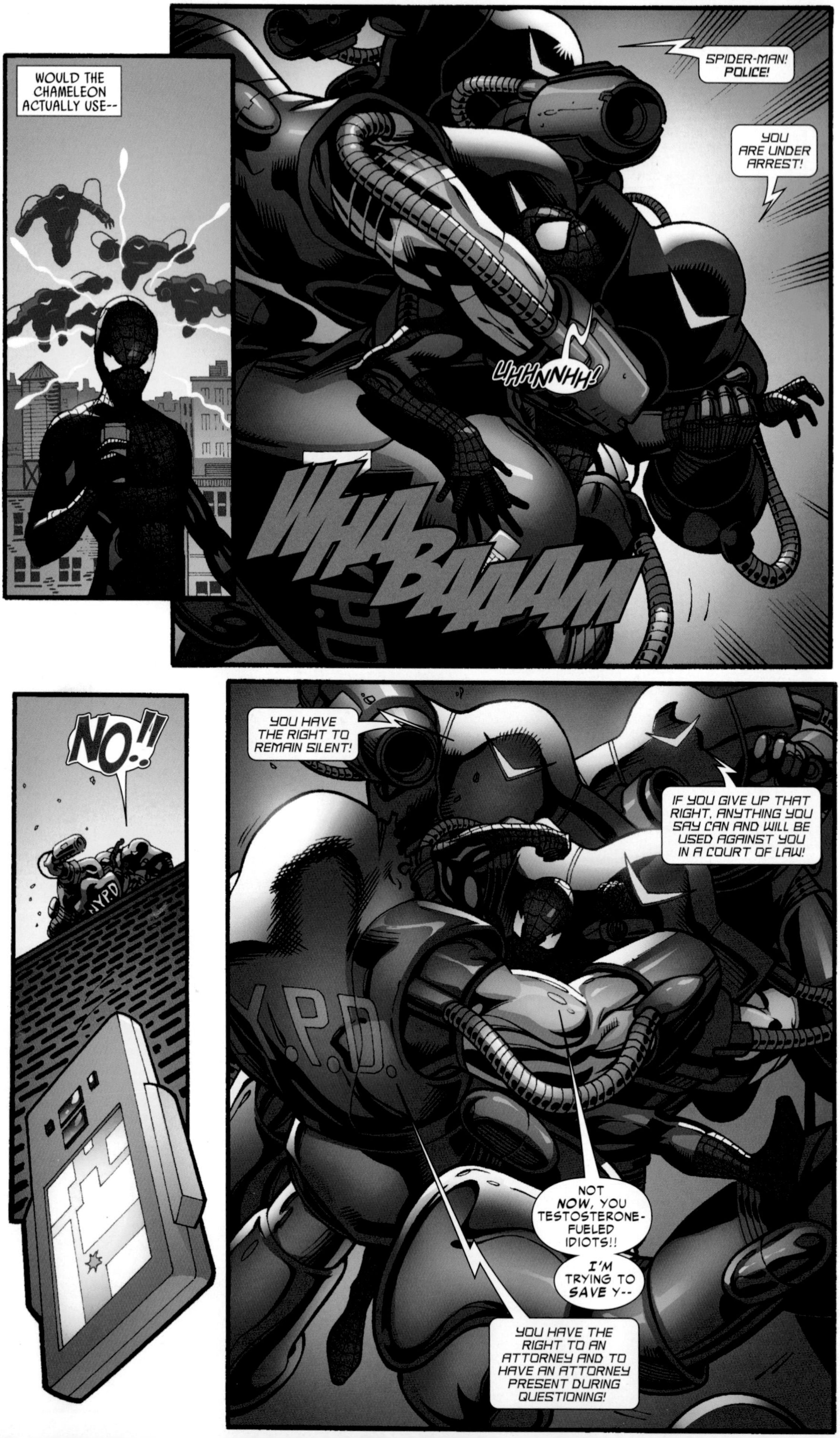

WOULD THE CHAMELEON ACTUALLY USE--
SPIDER-MAN! POLICE!
YOU ARE UNDER ARREST!
UHHNNHH!
WHABAAAM
NO!!
YOU HAVE THE RIGHT TO REMAIN SILENT!
IF YOU GIVE UP THAT RIGHT, ANYTHING YOU SAY CAN AND WILL BE USED AGAINST YOU IN A COURT OF LAW!
NOT NOW, YOU TESTOSTERONE-FUELED IDIOTS!!
I'M TRYING TO SAVE Y--
YOU HAVE THE RIGHT TO AN ATTORNEY AND TO HAVE AN ATTORNEY PRESENT DURING QUESTIONING!

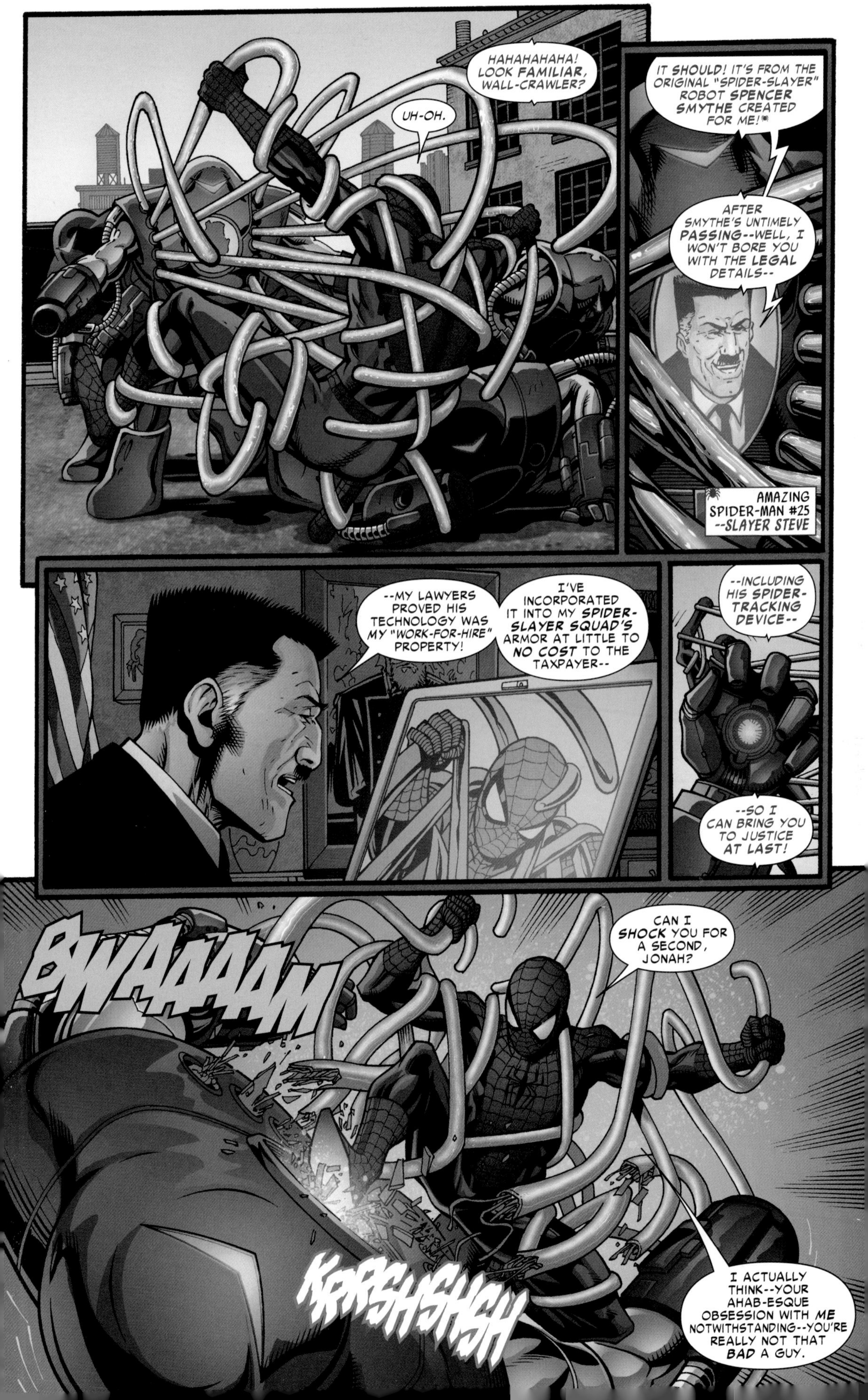
HAHAHAHAHA! LOOK FAMILIAR, WALL-CRAWLER?
UH-OH.
IT SHOULD! IT'S FROM THE ORIGINAL "SPIDER-SLAYER" ROBOT SPENCER SMYTHE CREATED FOR ME!*
AFTER SMYTHE'S UNTIMELY PASSING--WELL, I WON'T BORE YOU WITH THE LEGAL DETAILS--
*AMAZING SPIDER-MAN #25 --SLAYER STEVE
--MY LAWYERS PROVED HIS TECHNOLOGY WAS MY "WORK-FOR-HIRE" PROPERTY!
I'VE INCORPORATED IT INTO MY SPIDER-SLAYER SQUAD'S ARMOR AT LITTLE TO NO COST TO THE TAXPAYER--
--INCLUDING HIS SPIDER-TRACKING DEVICE--
--SO I CAN BRING YOU TO JUSTICE AT LAST!
BWAAAAM
CAN I SHOCK YOU FOR A SECOND, JONAH?
KRRSHSHSH
I ACTUALLY THINK--YOUR AHAB-ESQUE OBSESSION WITH ME NOTWITHSTANDING--YOU'RE REALLY NOT THAT BAD A GUY.

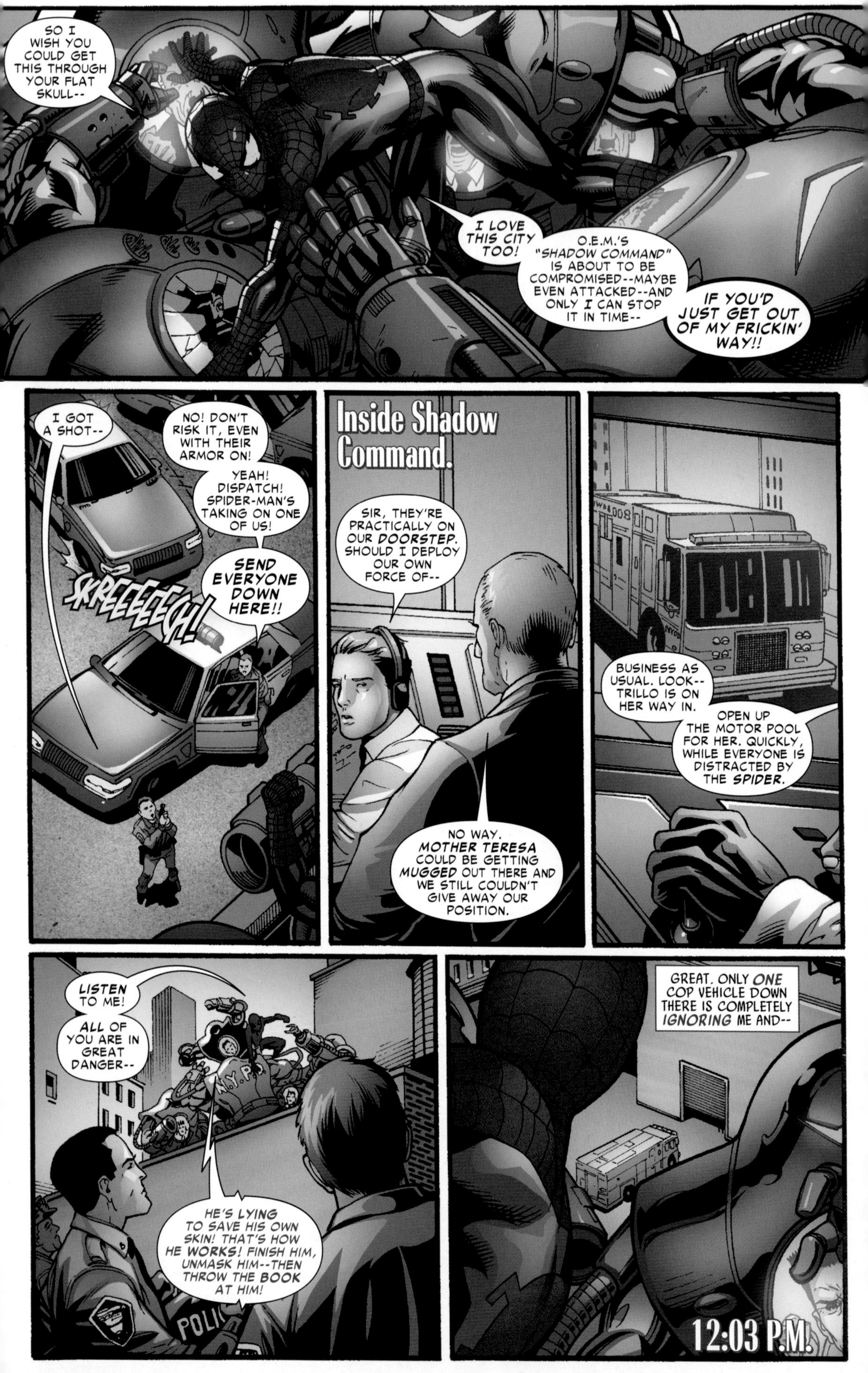

SO I WISH YOU COULD GET THIS THROUGH YOUR FLAT SKULL--
I LOVE THIS CITY TOO!
O.E.M.'S "SHADOW COMMAND" IS ABOUT TO BE COMPROMISED--MAYBE EVEN ATTACKED--AND ONLY I CAN STOP IT IN TIME--
IF YOU'D JUST GET OUT OF MY FRICKIN' WAY!!
I GOT A SHOT--
NO! DON'T RISK IT, EVEN WITH THEIR ARMOR ON!
YEAH! DISPATCH! SPIDER-MAN'S TAKING ON ONE OF US!
SEND EVERYONE DOWN HERE!!
SKREEEEECH!
Inside Shadow Command.
SIR, THEY'RE PRACTICALLY ON OUR DOORSTEP. SHOULD I DEPLOY OUR OWN FORCE OF--
NO WAY. MOTHER TERESA COULD BE GETTING MUGGED OUT THERE AND WE STILL COULDN'T GIVE AWAY OUR POSITION.
BUSINESS AS USUAL. LOOK-- TRILLO IS ON HER WAY IN.
OPEN UP THE MOTOR POOL FOR HER. QUICKLY, WHILE EVERYONE IS DISTRACTED BY THE SPIDER.
LISTEN TO ME!
ALL OF YOU ARE IN GREAT DANGER--
HE'S LYING TO SAVE HIS OWN SKIN! THAT'S HOW HE WORKS! FINISH HIM, UNMASK HIM--THEN THROW THE BOOK AT HIM!
GREAT. ONLY ONE COP VEHICLE DOWN THERE IS COMPLETELY IGNORING ME AND--
12:03 P.M.

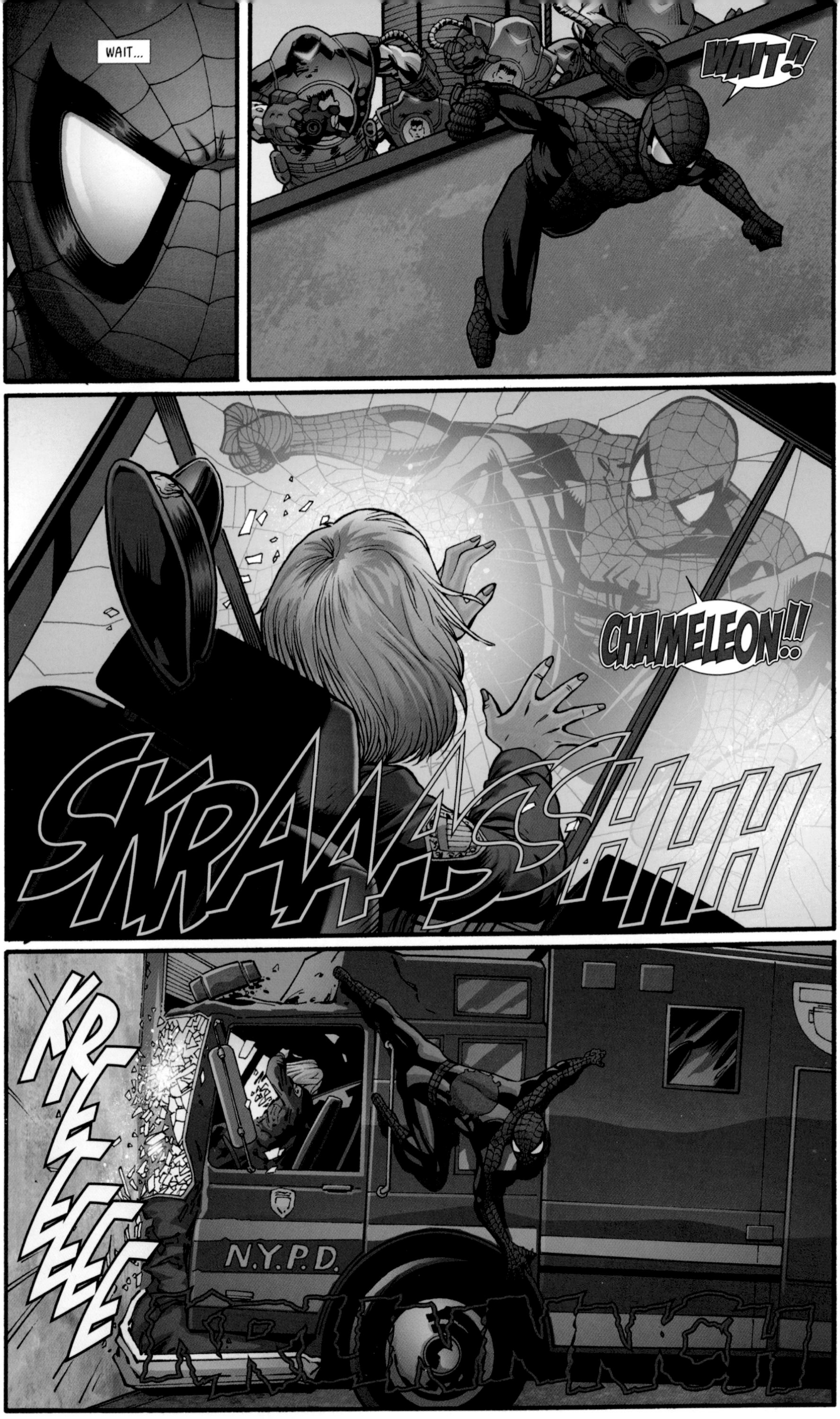
WAIT...
WAIT!!
CHAMELEON!!
SKRAAASSHHH
KREEEEEE
N.Y.P.D.

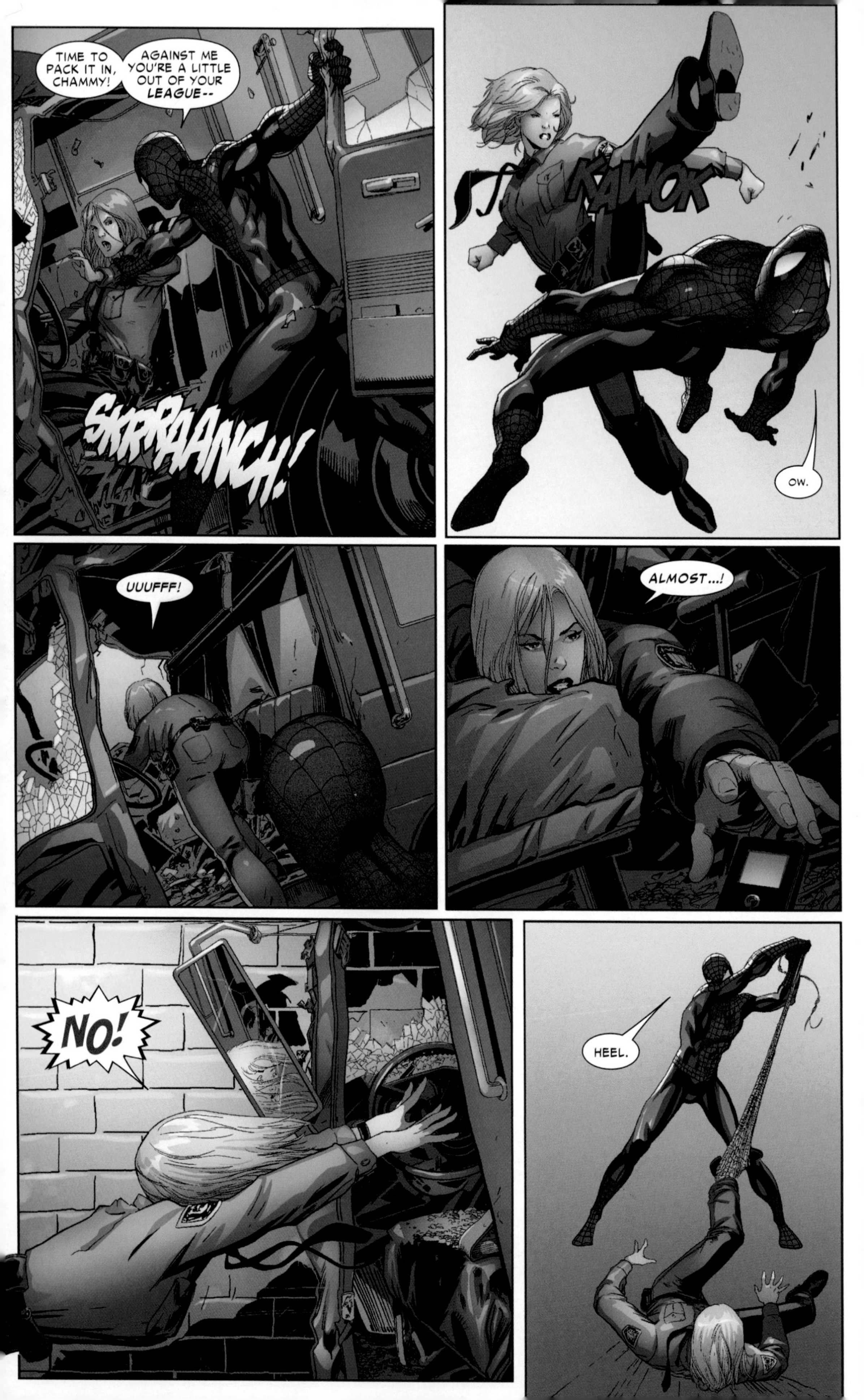
TIME TO PACK IT IN, CHAMMY!
AGAINST ME YOU'RE A LITTLE OUT OF YOUR LEAGUE--
SKRRAANCH!
KAWOK
OW.
UUUFFF!
ALMOST...!
NO!
HEEL.

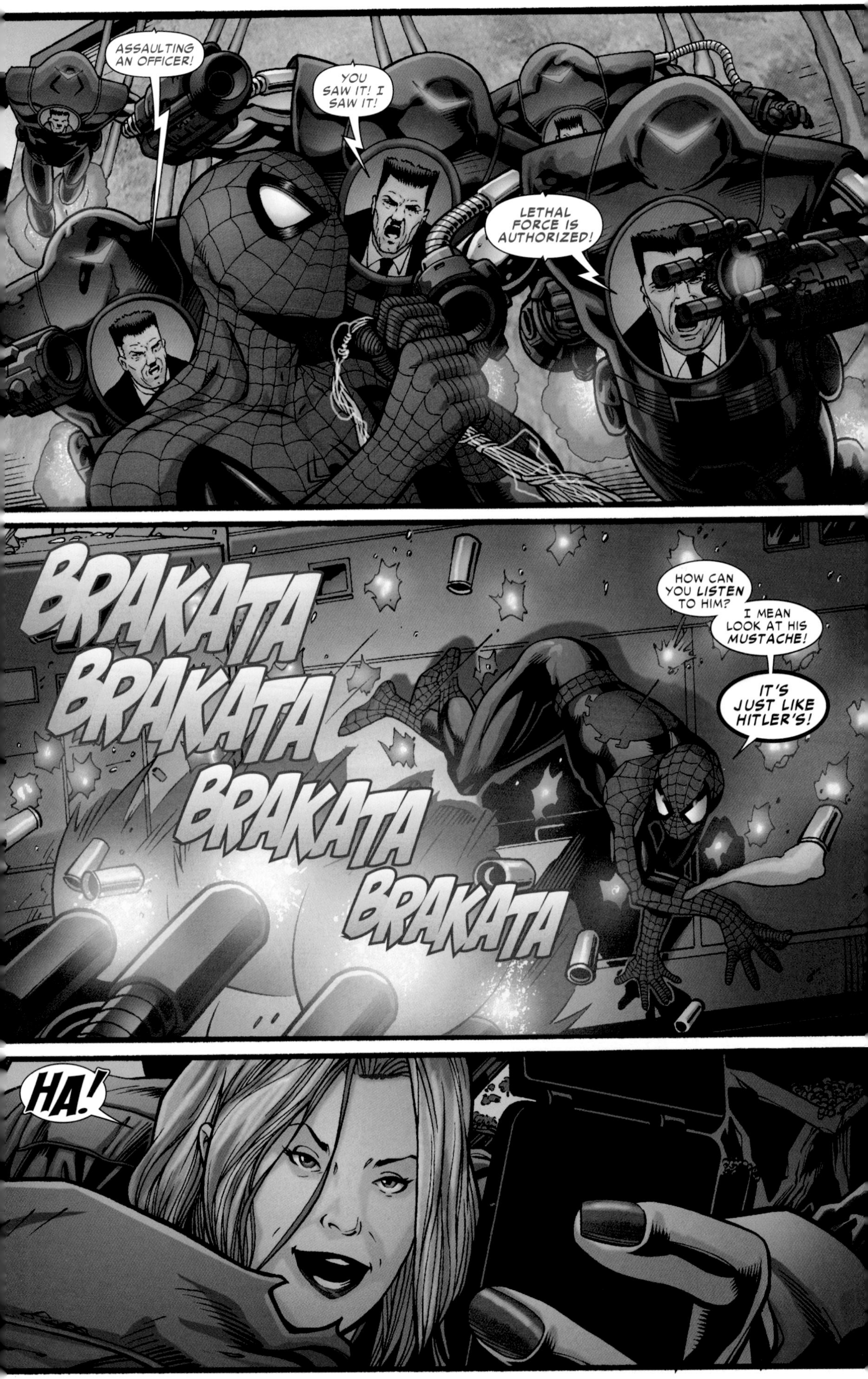
ASSAULTING AN OFFICER!
YOU SAW IT! I SAW IT!
LETHAL FORCE IS AUTHORIZED!
BRAKATA BRAKATA BRAKATA BRAKATA
HOW CAN YOU LISTEN TO HIM?
I MEAN LOOK AT HIS MUSTACHE!
IT'S JUST LIKE HITLER'S!
HA!

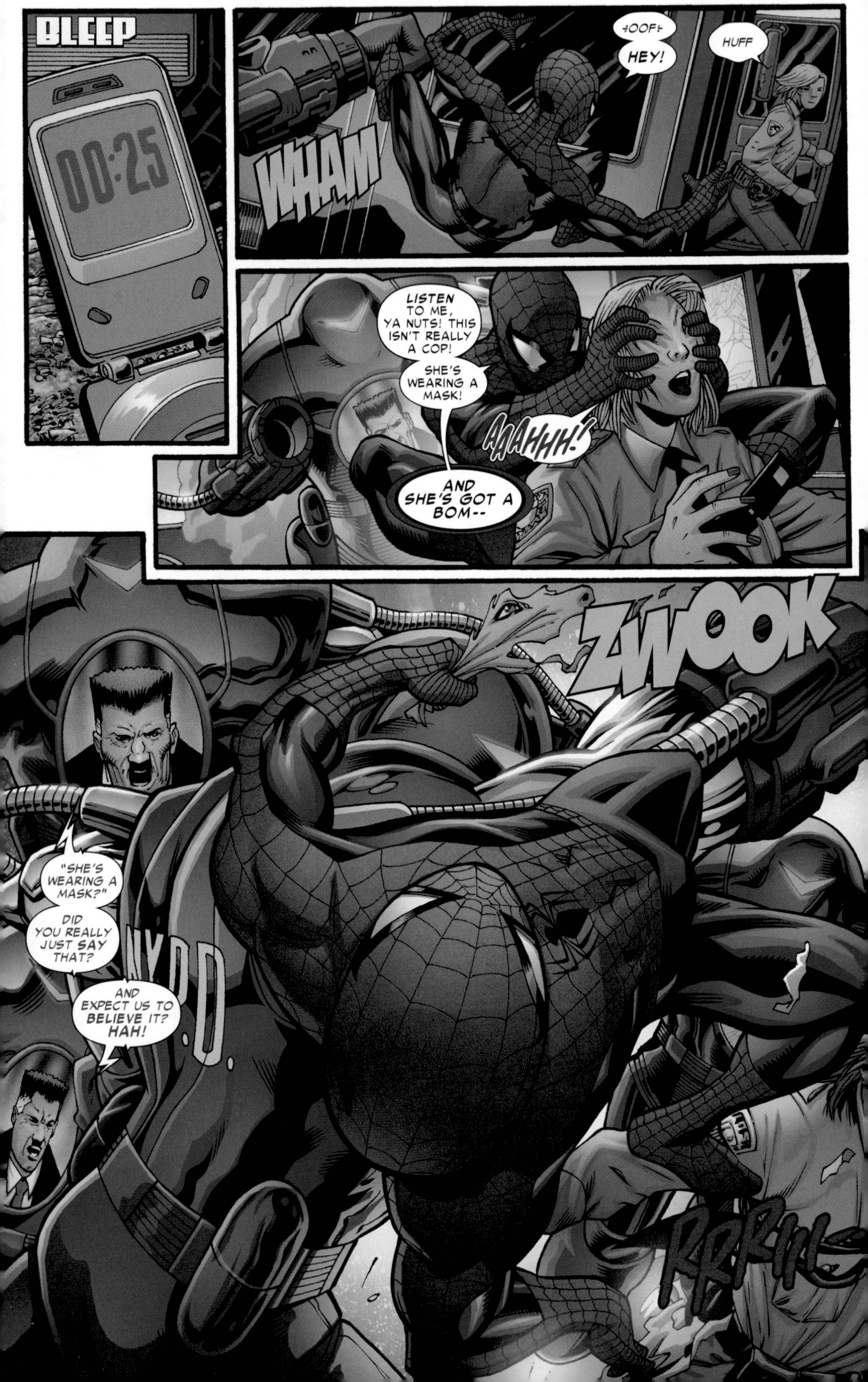
BLEEP
00:25
WHAM
OOF
HEY!
HUFF
LISTEN TO ME, YA NUTS! THIS ISN'T REALLY A COP!
SHE'S WEARING A MASK!
AAAHHH!
AND SHE'S GOT A BOM--
ZWOOK
"SHE'S WEARING A MASK?"
DID YOU REALLY JUST SAY THAT?
AND EXPECT US TO BELIEVE IT? HAH!
NYPD
RRRIIP

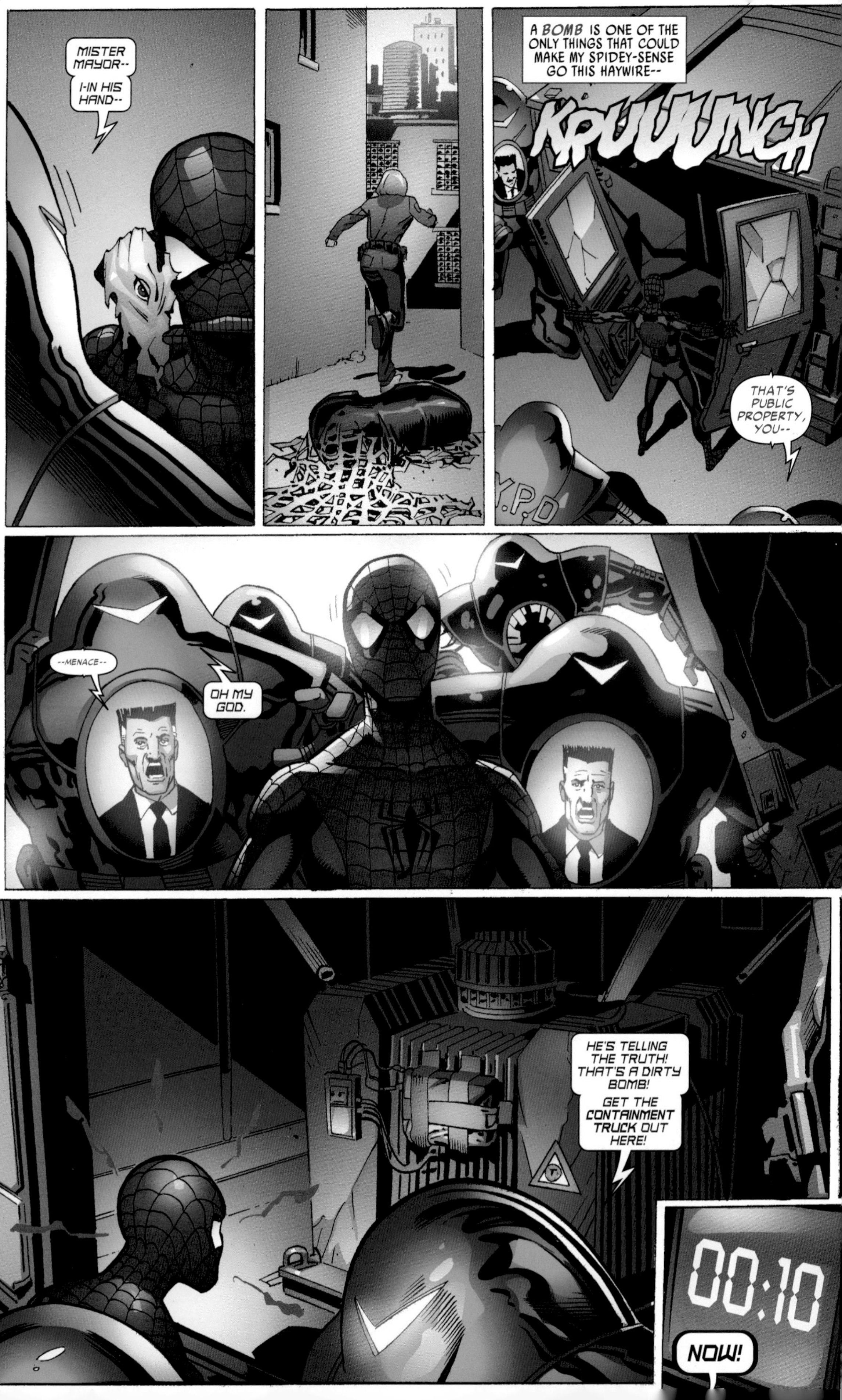

MISTER MAYOR--
I-IN HIS HAND--
A BOMB IS ONE OF THE ONLY THINGS THAT COULD MAKE MY SPIDEY-SENSE GO THIS HAYWIRE--
KRUUUNCH
THAT'S PUBLIC PROPERTY, YOU--
--MENACE--
OH MY GOD.
HE'S TELLING THE TRUTH! THAT'S A DIRTY BOMB!
GET THE CONTAINMENT TRUCK OUT HERE!
00:10
NOW!

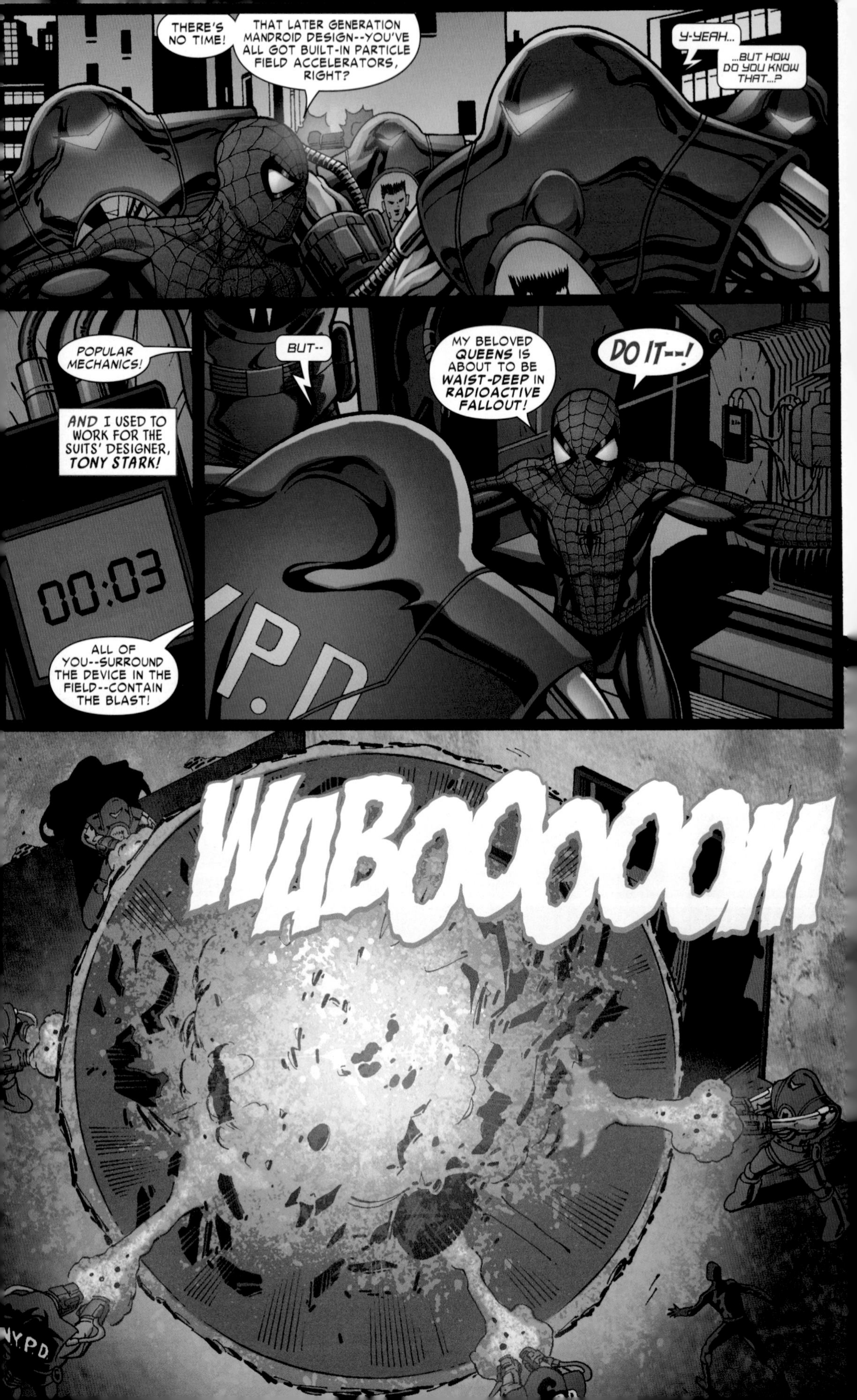
THERE'S NO TIME!
THAT LATER GENERATION MANDROID DESIGN--YOU'VE ALL GOT BUILT-IN PARTICLE FIELD ACCELERATORS, RIGHT?
Y-YEAH...
...BUT HOW DO YOU KNOW THAT...?
POPULAR MECHANICS!
AND I USED TO WORK FOR THE SUITS' DESIGNER, TONY STARK!
00:03
ALL OF YOU--SURROUND THE DEVICE IN THE FIELD--CONTAIN THE BLAST!
BUT--
MY BELOVED QUEENS IS ABOUT TO BE WAIST-DEEP IN RADIOACTIVE FALLOUT!
DO IT--!
N.Y.P.D.
WABOOOOOM
N.Y.P.D.

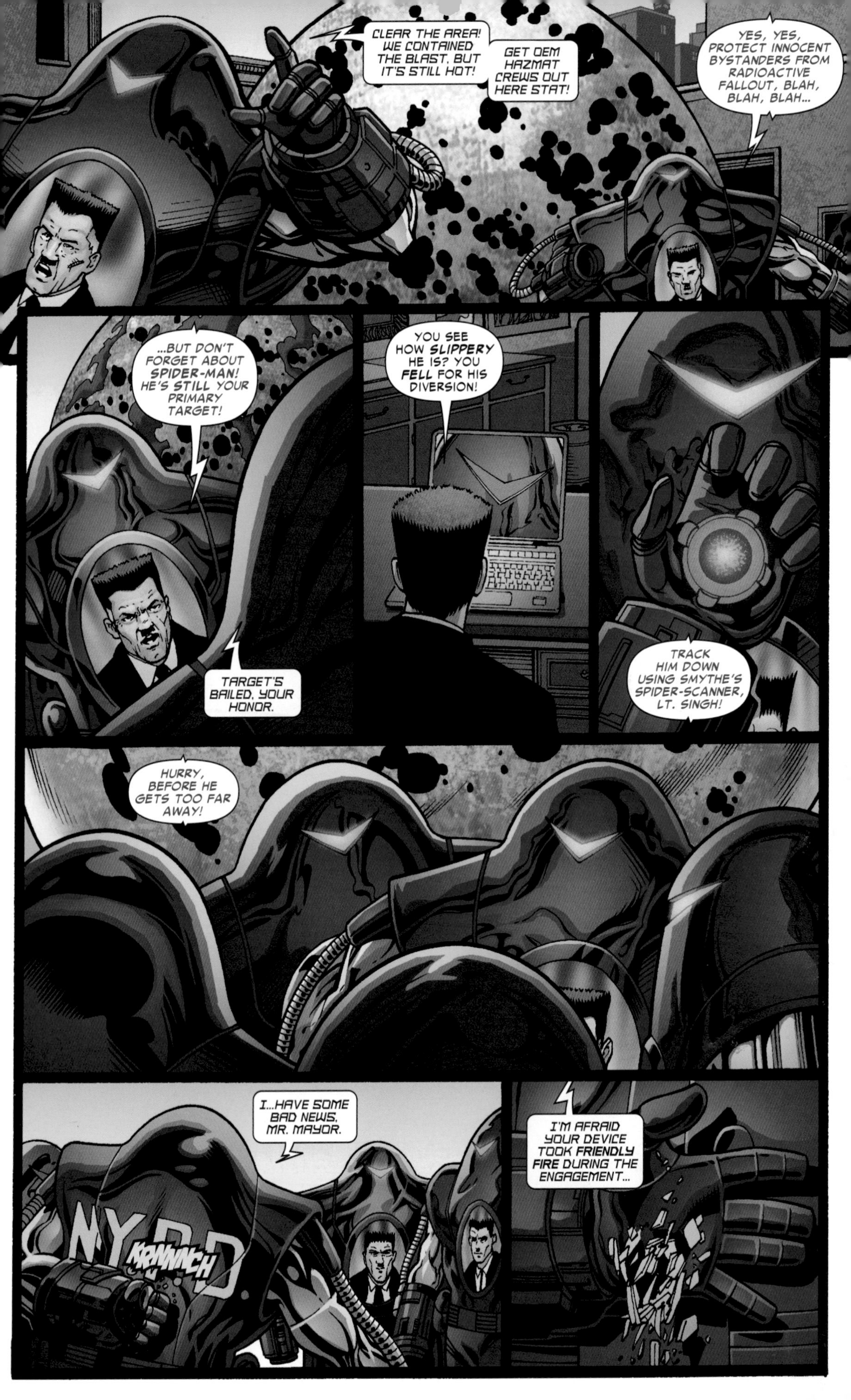
CLEAR THE AREA! WE CONTAINED THE BLAST, BUT IT'S STILL HOT!
GET OEM HAZMAT CREWS OUT HERE STAT!
YES, YES, PROTECT INNOCENT BYSTANDERS FROM RADIOACTIVE FALLOUT, BLAH, BLAH, BLAH...
...BUT DON'T FORGET ABOUT SPIDER-MAN! HE'S STILL YOUR PRIMARY TARGET!
TARGET'S BAILED, YOUR HONOR.
YOU SEE HOW SLIPPERY HE IS? YOU FELL FOR HIS DIVERSION!
TRACK HIM DOWN USING SMYTHE'S SPIDER-SCANNER, LT. SINGH!
HURRY, BEFORE HE GETS TOO FAR AWAY!
I...HAVE SOME BAD NEWS, MR. MAYOR.
NYPD
KRNNNCH
I'M AFRAID YOUR DEVICE TOOK FRIENDLY FIRE DURING THE ENGAGEMENT...

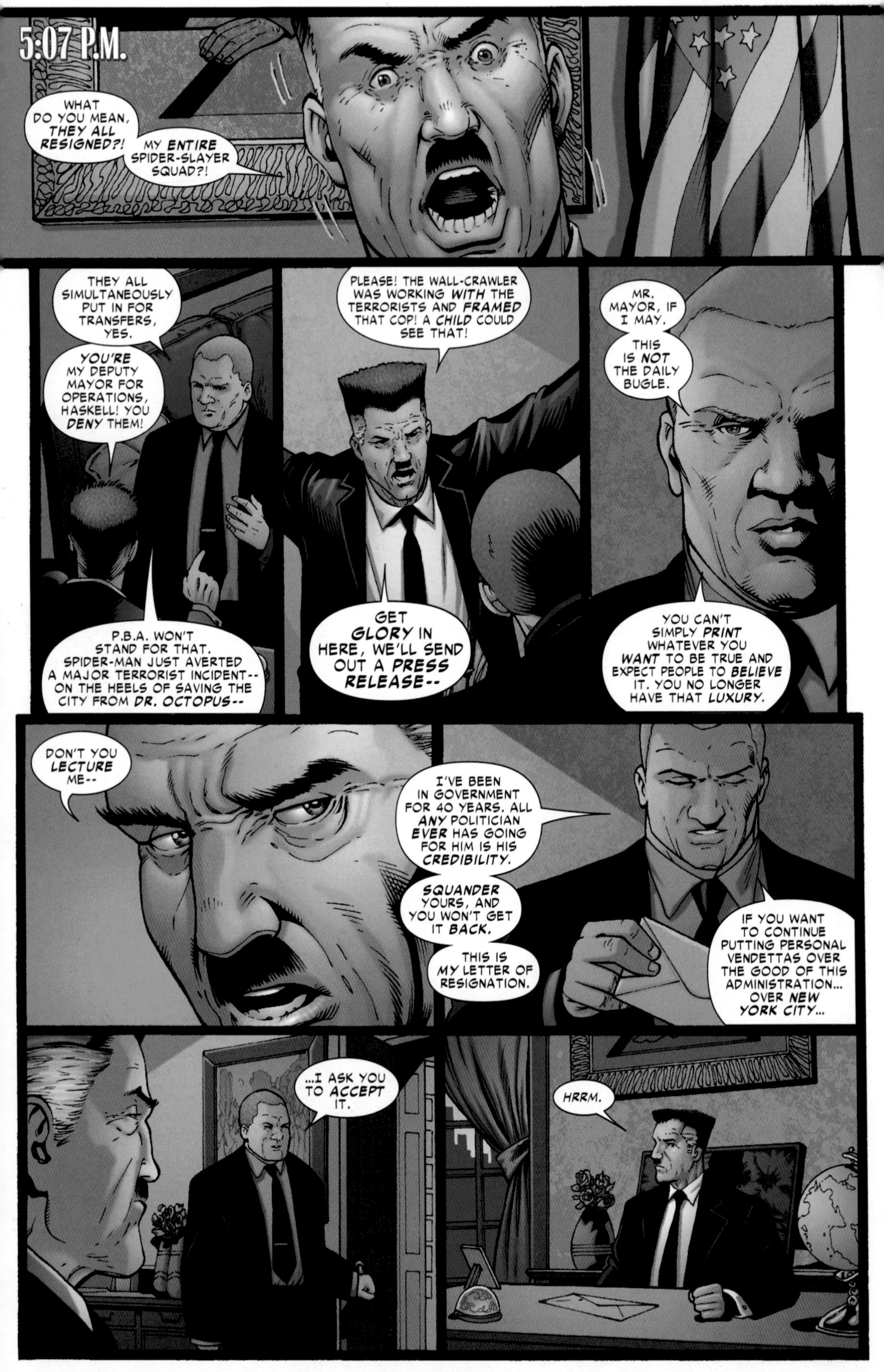
5:07 P.M.
WHAT DO YOU MEAN, THEY ALL RESIGNED?!
MY ENTIRE SPIDER-SLAYER SQUAD?!
THEY ALL SIMULTANEOUSLY PUT IN FOR TRANSFERS, YES.
YOU'RE MY DEPUTY MAYOR FOR OPERATIONS, HASKELL! YOU DENY THEM!
P.B.A. WON'T STAND FOR THAT. SPIDER-MAN JUST AVERTED A MAJOR TERRORIST INCIDENT-- ON THE HEELS OF SAVING THE CITY FROM DR. OCTOPUS--
PLEASE! THE WALL-CRAWLER WAS WORKING WITH THE TERRORISTS AND FRAMED THAT COP! A CHILD COULD SEE THAT!
GET GLORY IN HERE, WE'LL SEND OUT A PRESS RELEASE--
MR. MAYOR, IF I MAY.
THIS IS NOT THE DAILY BUGLE.
YOU CAN'T SIMPLY PRINT WHATEVER YOU WANT TO BE TRUE AND EXPECT PEOPLE TO BELIEVE IT. YOU NO LONGER HAVE THAT LUXURY.
DON'T YOU LECTURE ME--
I'VE BEEN IN GOVERNMENT FOR 40 YEARS. ALL ANY POLITICIAN EVER HAS GOING FOR HIM IS HIS CREDIBILITY.
SQUANDER YOURS, AND YOU WON'T GET IT BACK.
THIS IS MY LETTER OF RESIGNATION.
IF YOU WANT TO CONTINUE PUTTING PERSONAL VENDETTAS OVER THE GOOD OF THIS ADMINISTRATION... OVER NEW YORK CITY...
...I ASK YOU TO ACCEPT IT.
HRRM.

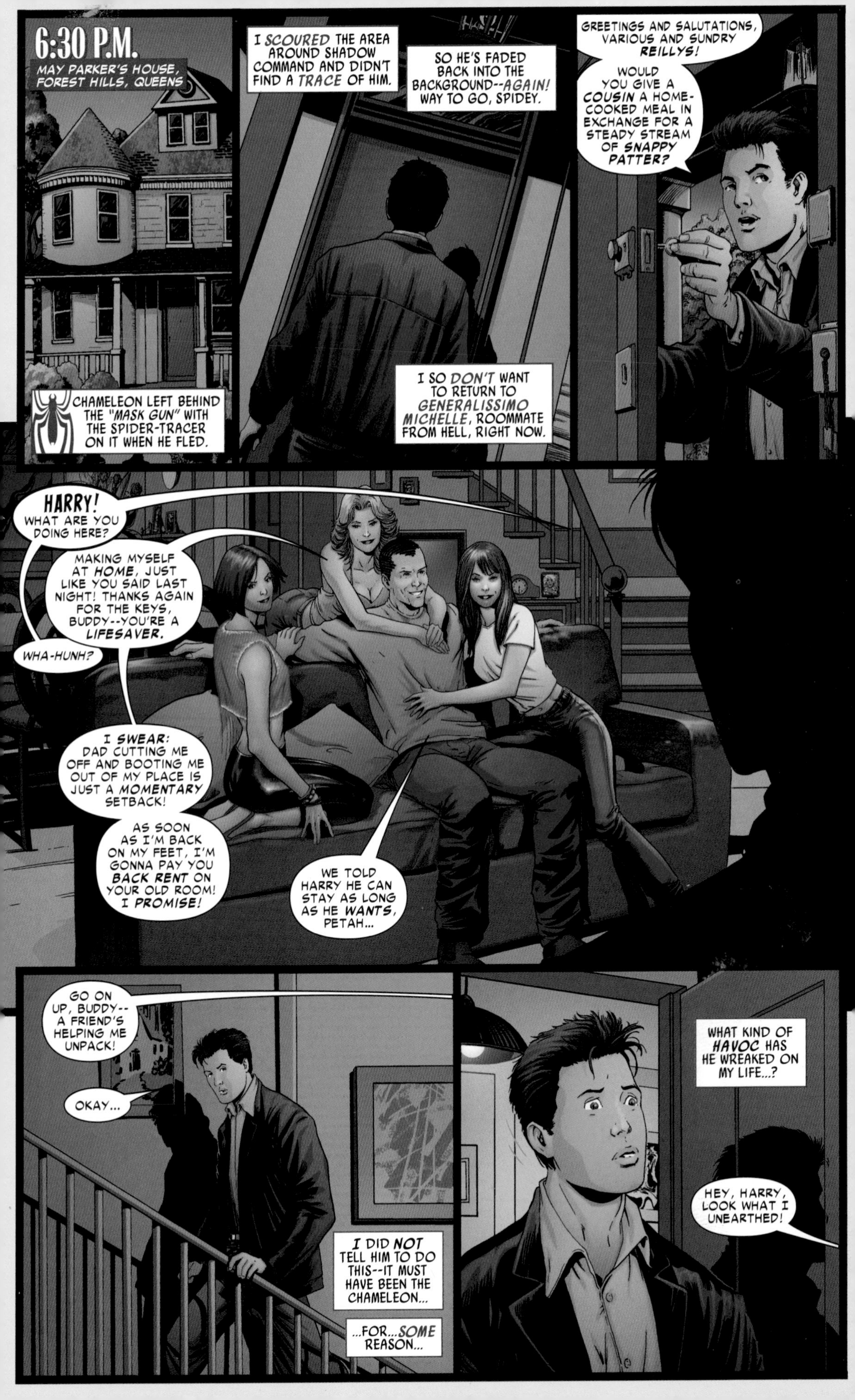
6:30 P.M.
MAY PARKER'S HOUSE, FOREST HILLS, QUEENS
CHAMELEON LEFT BEHIND THE "MASK GUN" WITH THE SPIDER-TRACER ON IT WHEN HE FLED.
I SCOURED THE AREA AROUND SHADOW COMMAND AND DIDN'T FIND A TRACE OF HIM.
SO HE'S FADED BACK INTO THE BACKGROUND--AGAIN! WAY TO GO, SPIDEY.
I SO DON'T WANT TO RETURN TO GENERALISSIMO MICHELLE, ROOMMATE FROM HELL, RIGHT NOW.
GREETINGS AND SALUTATIONS, VARIOUS AND SUNDRY REILLYS!
WOULD YOU GIVE A COUSIN A HOME-COOKED MEAL IN EXCHANGE FOR A STEADY STREAM OF SNAPPY PATTER?
HARRY! WHAT ARE YOU DOING HERE?
MAKING MYSELF AT HOME, JUST LIKE YOU SAID LAST NIGHT! THANKS AGAIN FOR THE KEYS, BUDDY--YOU'RE A LIFESAVER.
WHA-HUNH?
I SWEAR: DAD CUTTING ME OFF AND BOOTING ME OUT OF MY PLACE IS JUST A MOMENTARY SETBACK!
AS SOON AS I'M BACK ON MY FEET, I'M GONNA PAY YOU BACK RENT ON YOUR OLD ROOM! I PROMISE!
WE TOLD HARRY HE CAN STAY AS LONG AS HE WANTS, PETAH...
GO ON UP, BUDDY-- A FRIEND'S HELPING ME UNPACK!
OKAY...
I DID NOT TELL HIM TO DO THIS--IT MUST HAVE BEEN THE CHAMELEON...
...FOR...SOME REASON...
WHAT KIND OF HAVOC HAS HE WREAKED ON MY LIFE...?
HEY, HARRY, LOOK WHAT I UNEARTHED!

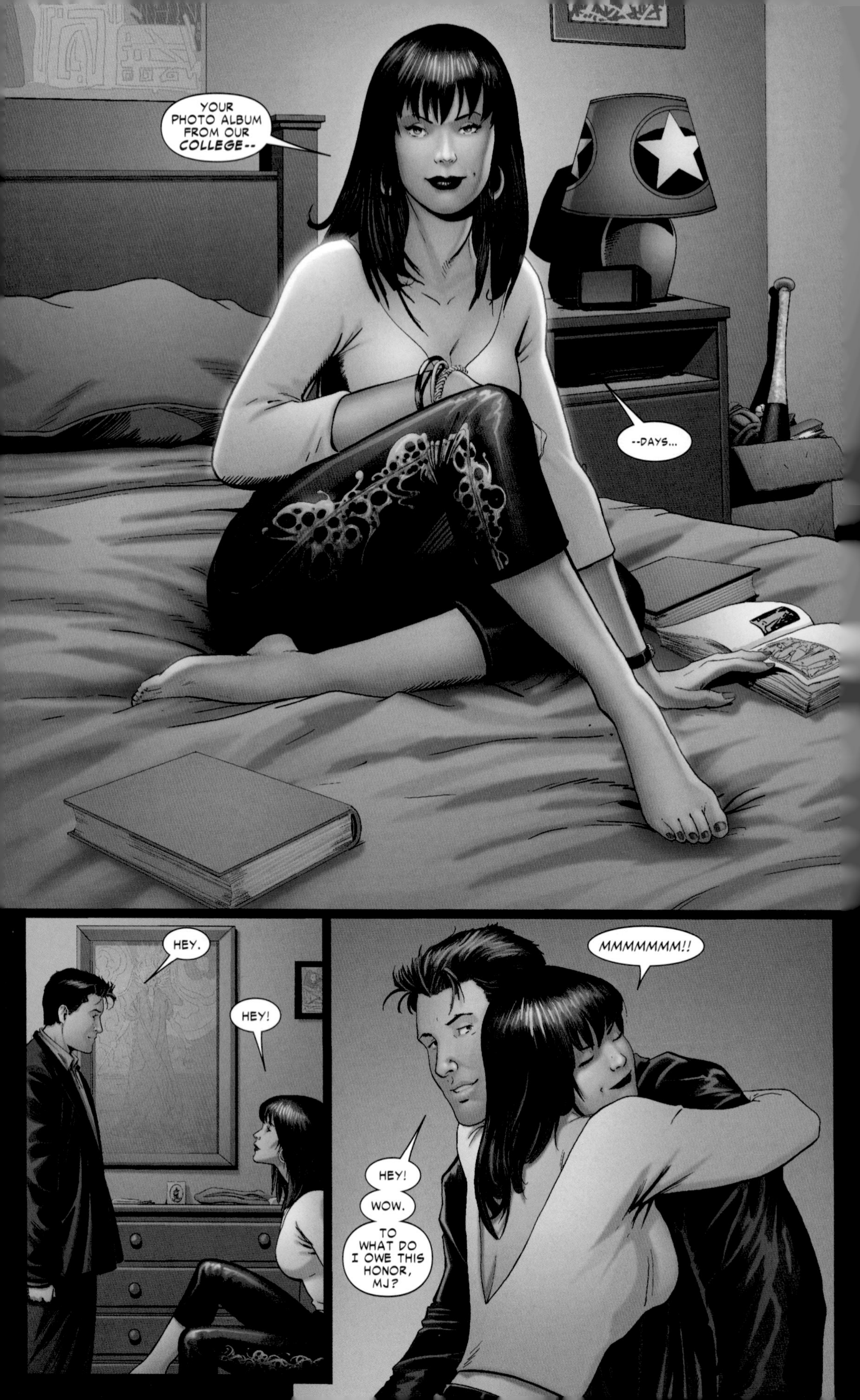
YOUR PHOTO ALBUM FROM OUR COLLEGE--
--DAYS...
HEY.
HEY!
MMMMMMM!!
HEY!
WOW.
TO WHAT DO I OWE THIS HONOR, MJ?

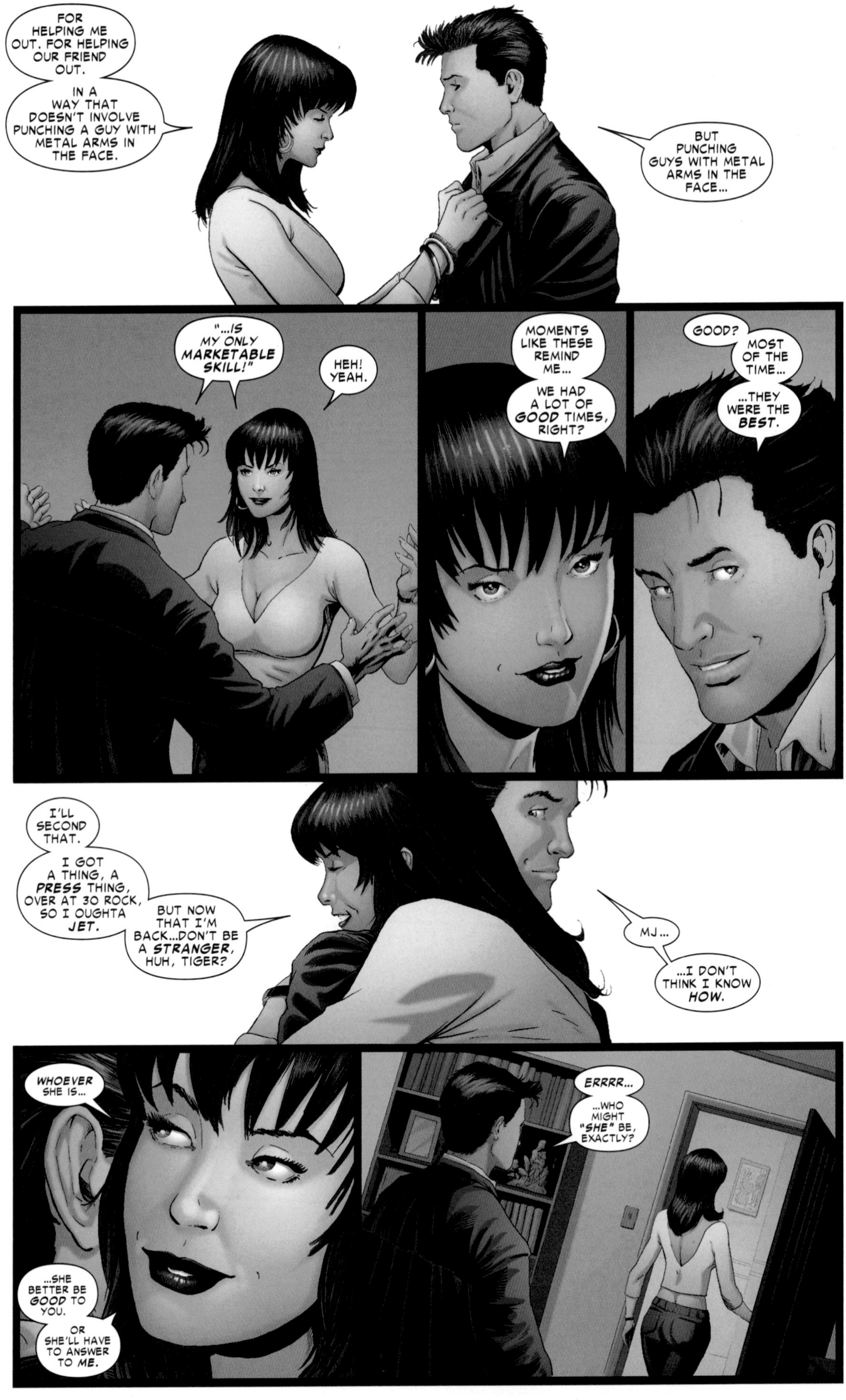

FOR HELPING ME OUT. FOR HELPING OUR FRIEND OUT.
IN A WAY THAT DOESN'T INVOLVE PUNCHING A GUY WITH METAL ARMS IN THE FACE.
BUT PUNCHING GUYS WITH METAL ARMS IN THE FACE...
"...IS MY ONLY MARKETABLE SKILL!"
HEH! YEAH.
MOMENTS LIKE THESE REMIND ME...
WE HAD A LOT OF GOOD TIMES, RIGHT?
GOOD?
MOST OF THE TIME...
...THEY WERE THE BEST.
I'LL SECOND THAT.
I GOT A THING, A PRESS THING, OVER AT 30 ROCK, SO I OUGHTA JET.
BUT NOW THAT I'M BACK...DON'T BE A STRANGER, HUH, TIGER?
MJ...
...I DON'T THINK I KNOW HOW.
WHOEVER SHE IS...
...SHE BETTER BE GOOD TO YOU.
OR SHE'LL HAVE TO ANSWER TO ME.
ERRRR...
...WHO MIGHT "SHE" BE, EXACTLY?

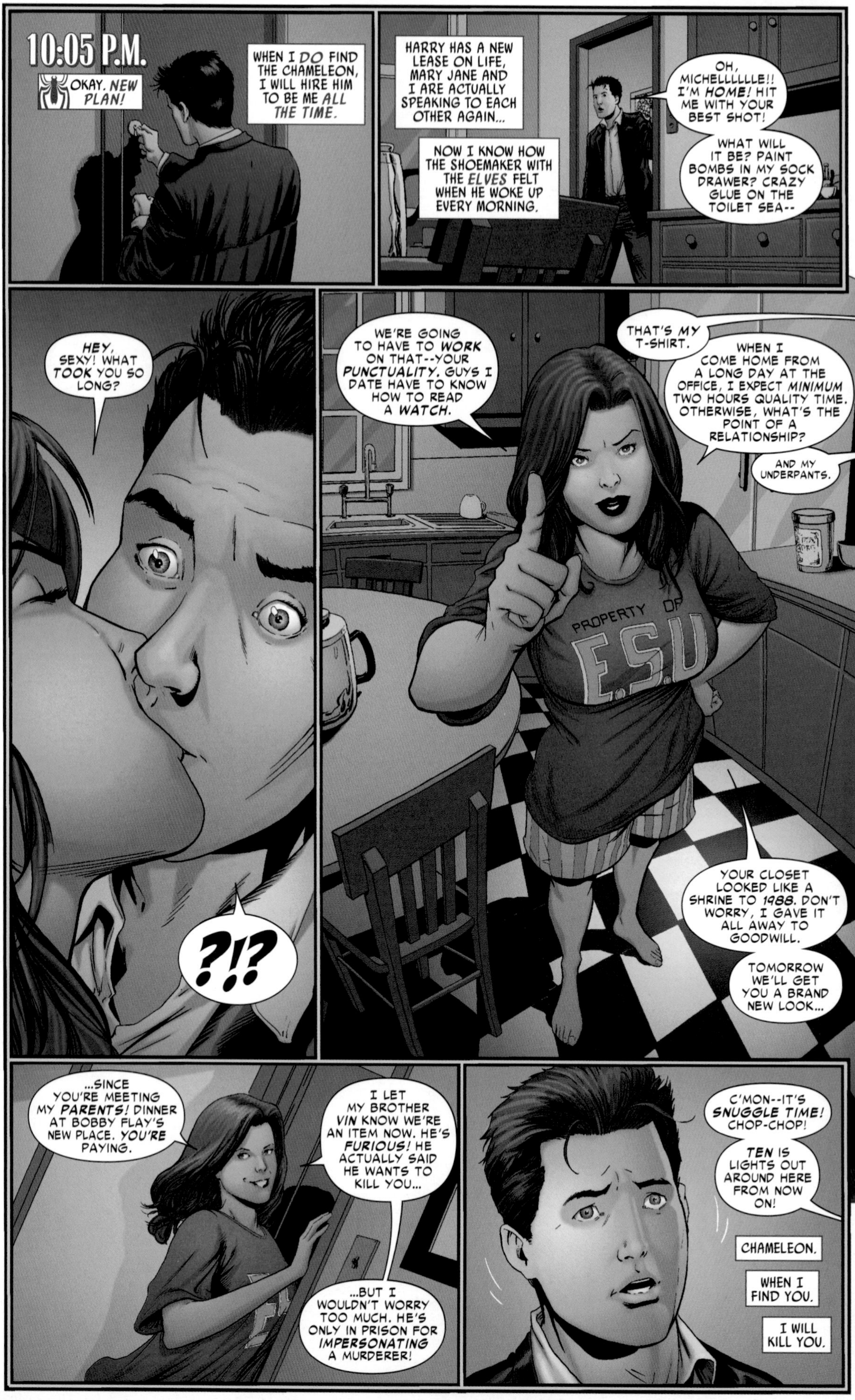
10:05 P.M.
OKAY. NEW PLAN!
WHEN I DO FIND THE CHAMELEON, I WILL HIRE HIM TO BE ME ALL THE TIME.
HARRY HAS A NEW LEASE ON LIFE, MARY JANE AND I ARE ACTUALLY SPEAKING TO EACH OTHER AGAIN...
NOW I KNOW HOW THE SHOEMAKER WITH THE ELVES FELT WHEN HE WOKE UP EVERY MORNING.
OH, MICHELLLLLLLE!! I'M HOME! HIT ME WITH YOUR BEST SHOT!
WHAT WILL IT BE? PAINT BOMBS IN MY SOCK DRAWER? CRAZY GLUE ON THE TOILET SEA--
HEY, SEXY! WHAT TOOK YOU SO LONG?
?!?
WE'RE GOING TO HAVE TO WORK ON THAT--YOUR PUNCTUALITY. GUYS I DATE HAVE TO KNOW HOW TO READ A WATCH.
THAT'S MY T-SHIRT.
WHEN I COME HOME FROM A LONG DAY AT THE OFFICE, I EXPECT MINIMUM TWO HOURS QUALITY TIME. OTHERWISE, WHAT'S THE POINT OF A RELATIONSHIP?
AND MY UNDERPANTS.
PROPERTY OF E.S.U.
YOUR CLOSET LOOKED LIKE A SHRINE TO 1988. DON'T WORRY, I GAVE IT ALL AWAY TO GOODWILL.
TOMORROW WE'LL GET YOU A BRAND NEW LOOK...
...SINCE YOU'RE MEETING MY PARENTS! DINNER AT BOBBY FLAY'S NEW PLACE. YOU'RE PAYING.
I LET MY BROTHER VIN KNOW WE'RE AN ITEM NOW. HE'S FURIOUS! HE ACTUALLY SAID HE WANTS TO KILL YOU...
...BUT I WOULDN'T WORRY TOO MUCH. HE'S ONLY IN PRISON FOR IMPERSONATING A MURDERER!
C'MON--IT'S SNUGGLE TIME! CHOP-CHOP!
TEN IS LIGHTS OUT AROUND HERE FROM NOW ON!
CHAMELEON.
WHEN I FIND YOU.
I WILL KILL YOU.

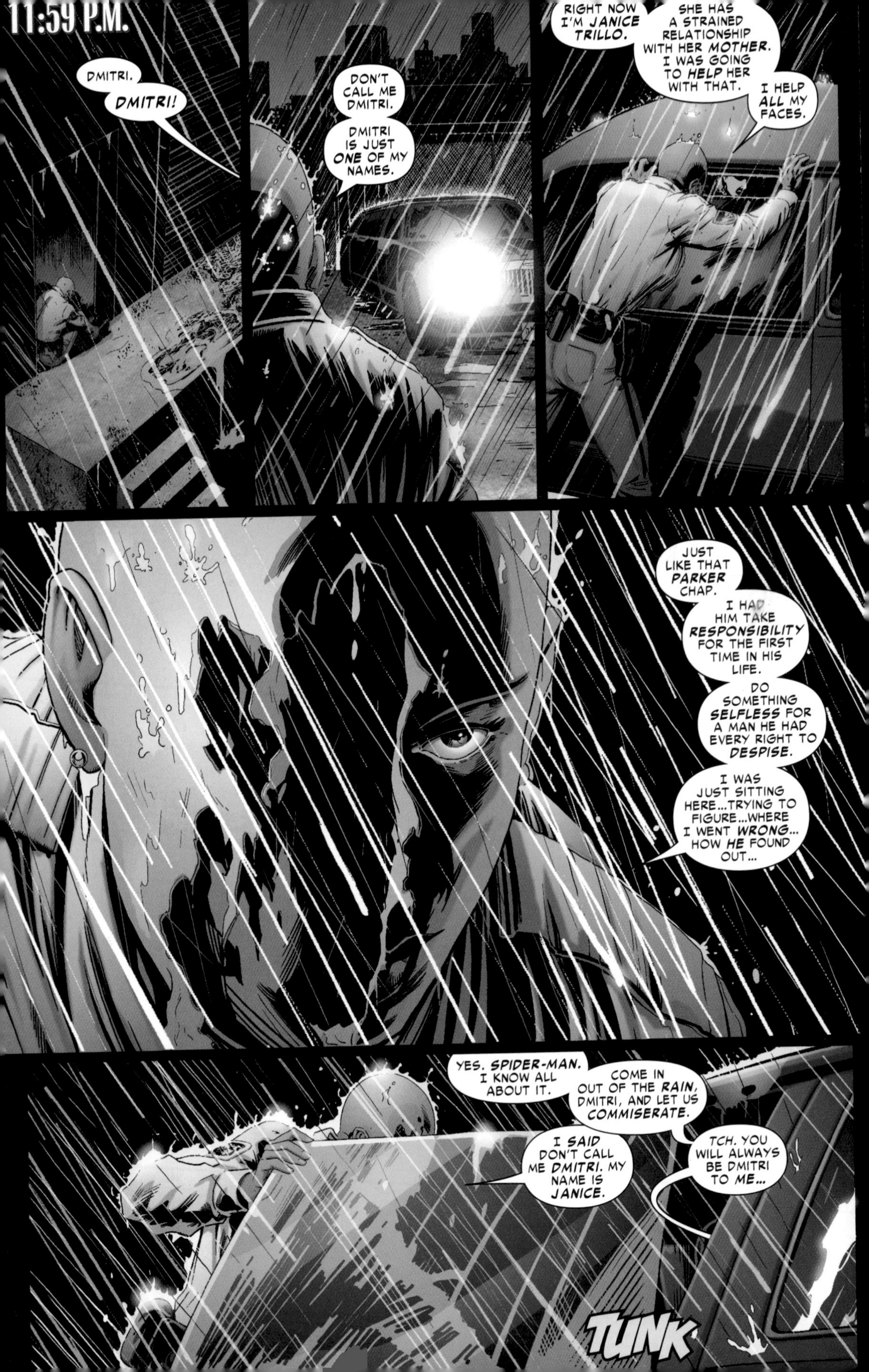
11:59 P.M.
DMITRI.
DMITRI!
DON'T CALL ME DMITRI.
DMITRI IS JUST ONE OF MY NAMES.
RIGHT NOW I'M JANICE TRILLO.
SHE HAS A STRAINED RELATIONSHIP WITH HER MOTHER. I WAS GOING TO HELP HER WITH THAT.
I HELP ALL MY FACES.
JUST LIKE THAT PARKER CHAP.
I HAD HIM TAKE RESPONSIBILITY FOR THE FIRST TIME IN HIS LIFE.
DO SOMETHING SELFLESS FOR A MAN HE HAD EVERY RIGHT TO DESPISE.
I WAS JUST SITTING HERE...TRYING TO FIGURE...WHERE I WENT WRONG... HOW HE FOUND OUT...
YES. SPIDER-MAN. I KNOW ALL ABOUT IT.
COME IN OUT OF THE RAIN, DMITRI, AND LET US COMMISERATE.
I SAID DON'T CALL ME DMITRI. MY NAME IS JANICE.
TCH. YOU WILL ALWAYS BE DMITRI TO ME...
TUNK

THIS IS HOW MY HUSBAND INTRODUCED US.

YOU REMEMBER MY HUSBAND, DON'T YOU, DMITRI?

KRAVEN THE HUNTER.

SPIDER-MAN KILLED HIM. NOW MY DAUGHTER AND I NEED YOUR HELP...

...TO RETURN THE FAVOR.

RED-HEADED STRANGER:

THE ANCIENT GALLER:

FRED VAN LENTE — WRITER

BARRY KITSON — PENCILER

RICK KETCHAM & BARRY KITSON — INKERS

JEROMY COX & ANTONIO FABELA — COLORISTS

VC'S JOE CARAMAGNA — LETTERER

TOM BRENNAN — ASST. EDITOR

STEPHEN WACKER — WILLIE FAN

TOM BREVOORT — EXEC. EDITOR

JOE QUESADA — EDITOR IN CHIEF

DAN BUCKLEY — PUBLISHER

A EXEC.

GALE, GUGGENHEIM, KELLY, SLOTT, VAN LENTE, WAID

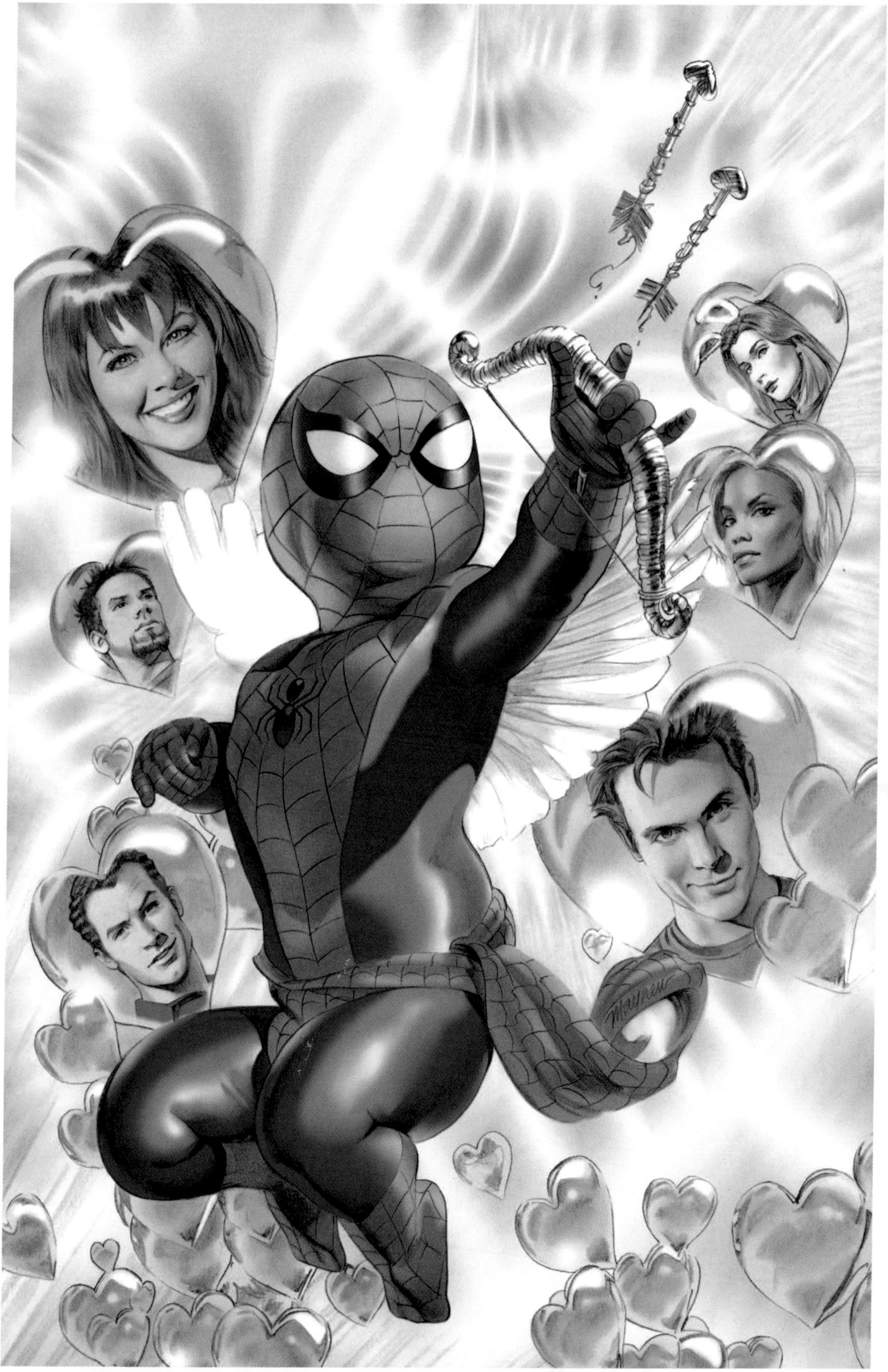
Mayhew

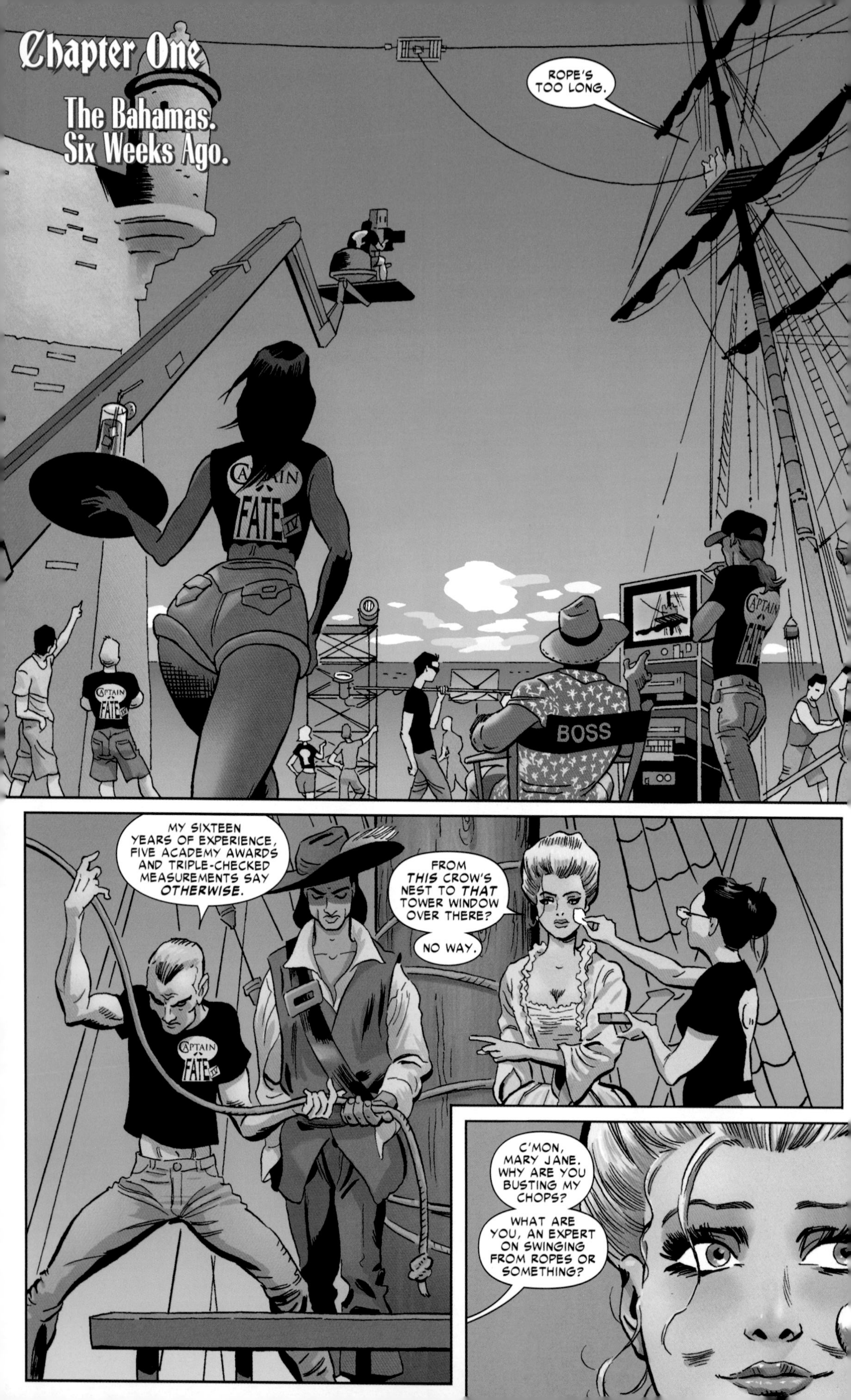
Chapter One
The Bahamas. Six Weeks Ago.
ROPE'S TOO LONG.
CAPTAIN FATE TV
BOSS
MY SIXTEEN YEARS OF EXPERIENCE, FIVE ACADEMY AWARDS AND TRIPLE-CHECKED MEASUREMENTS SAY OTHERWISE.
FROM THIS CROW'S NEST TO THAT TOWER WINDOW OVER THERE?
NO WAY.
C'MON, MARY JANE. WHY ARE YOU BUSTING MY CHOPS?
WHAT ARE YOU, AN EXPERT ON SWINGING FROM ROPES OR SOMETHING?

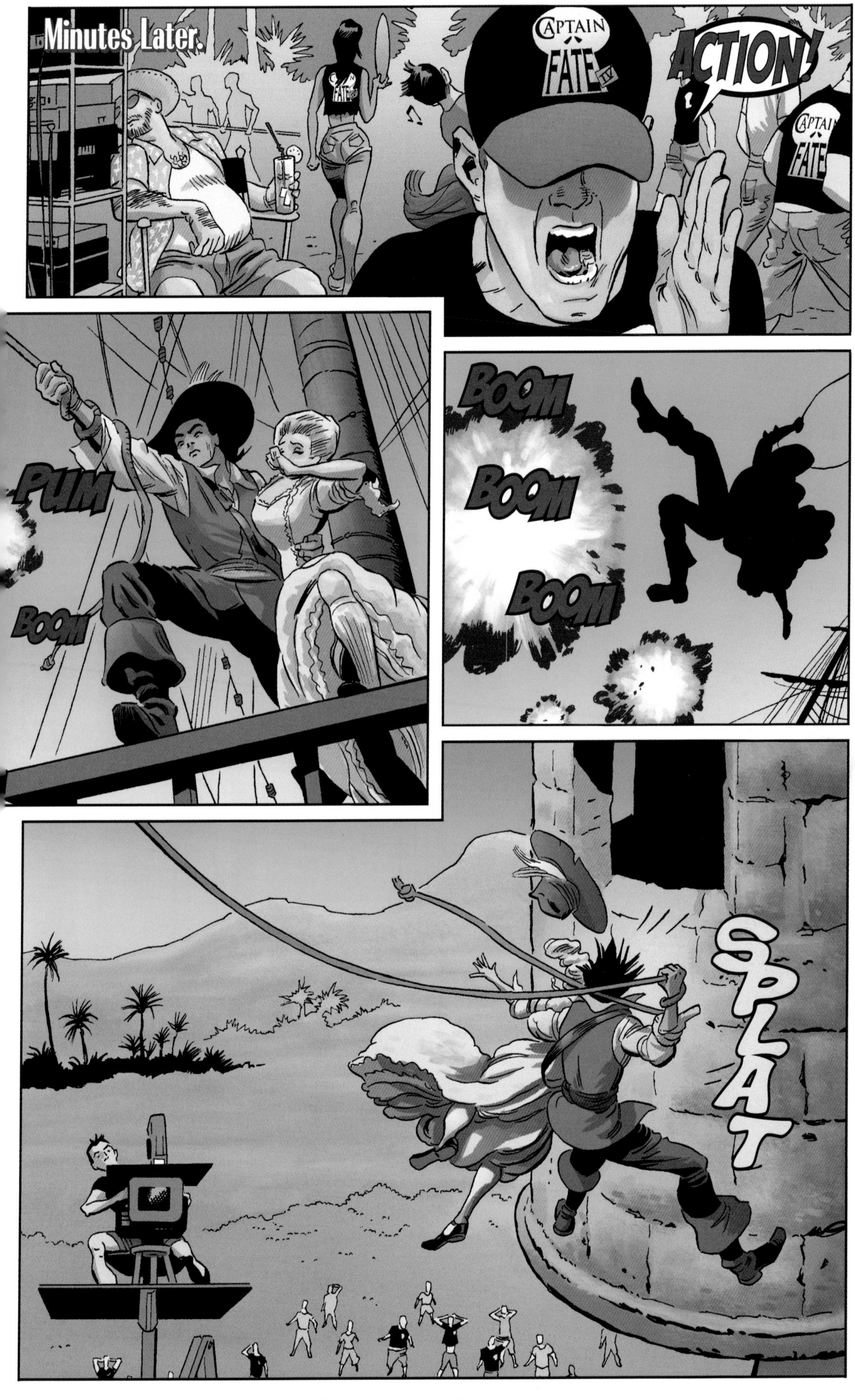
Minutes Later.
CAPTAIN FATE
ACTION!
CAPTAIN FATE
PUM
BOOM
BOOM
BOOM
BOOM
SPLAT

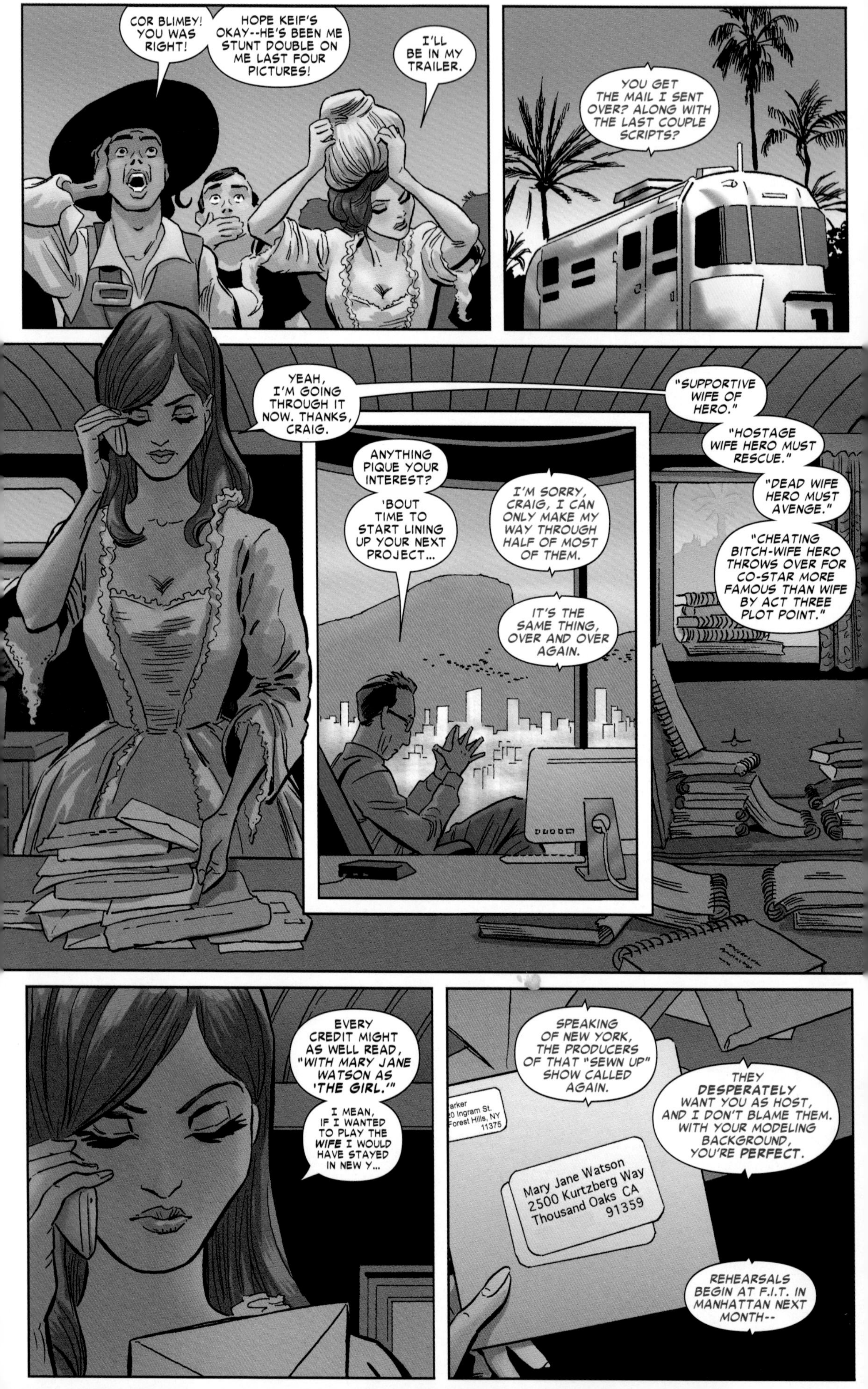
COR BLIMEY! YOU WAS RIGHT!
HOPE KEIF'S OKAY--HE'S BEEN ME STUNT DOUBLE ON ME LAST FOUR PICTURES!
I'LL BE IN MY TRAILER.
YOU GET THE MAIL I SENT OVER? ALONG WITH THE LAST COUPLE SCRIPTS?
YEAH, I'M GOING THROUGH IT NOW. THANKS, CRAIG.
"SUPPORTIVE WIFE OF HERO."
ANYTHING PIQUE YOUR INTEREST?
'BOUT TIME TO START LINING UP YOUR NEXT PROJECT...
I'M SORRY, CRAIG, I CAN ONLY MAKE MY WAY THROUGH HALF OF MOST OF THEM.
IT'S THE SAME THING, OVER AND OVER AGAIN.
"HOSTAGE WIFE HERO MUST RESCUE."
"DEAD WIFE HERO MUST AVENGE."
"CHEATING BITCH-WIFE HERO THROWS OVER FOR CO-STAR MORE FAMOUS THAN WIFE BY ACT THREE PLOT POINT."
EVERY CREDIT MIGHT AS WELL READ, "WITH MARY JANE WATSON AS 'THE GIRL.'"
I MEAN, IF I WANTED TO PLAY THE WIFE I WOULD HAVE STAYED IN NEW Y...
SPEAKING OF NEW YORK, THE PRODUCERS OF THAT "SEWN UP" SHOW CALLED AGAIN.
arker
20 Ingram St.
Forest Hills, NY
11375
Mary Jane Watson
2500 Kurtzberg Way
Thousand Oaks CA
91359
THEY DESPERATELY WANT YOU AS HOST, AND I DON'T BLAME THEM. WITH YOUR MODELING BACKGROUND, YOU'RE PERFECT.
REHEARSALS BEGIN AT F.I.T. IN MANHATTAN NEXT MONTH--

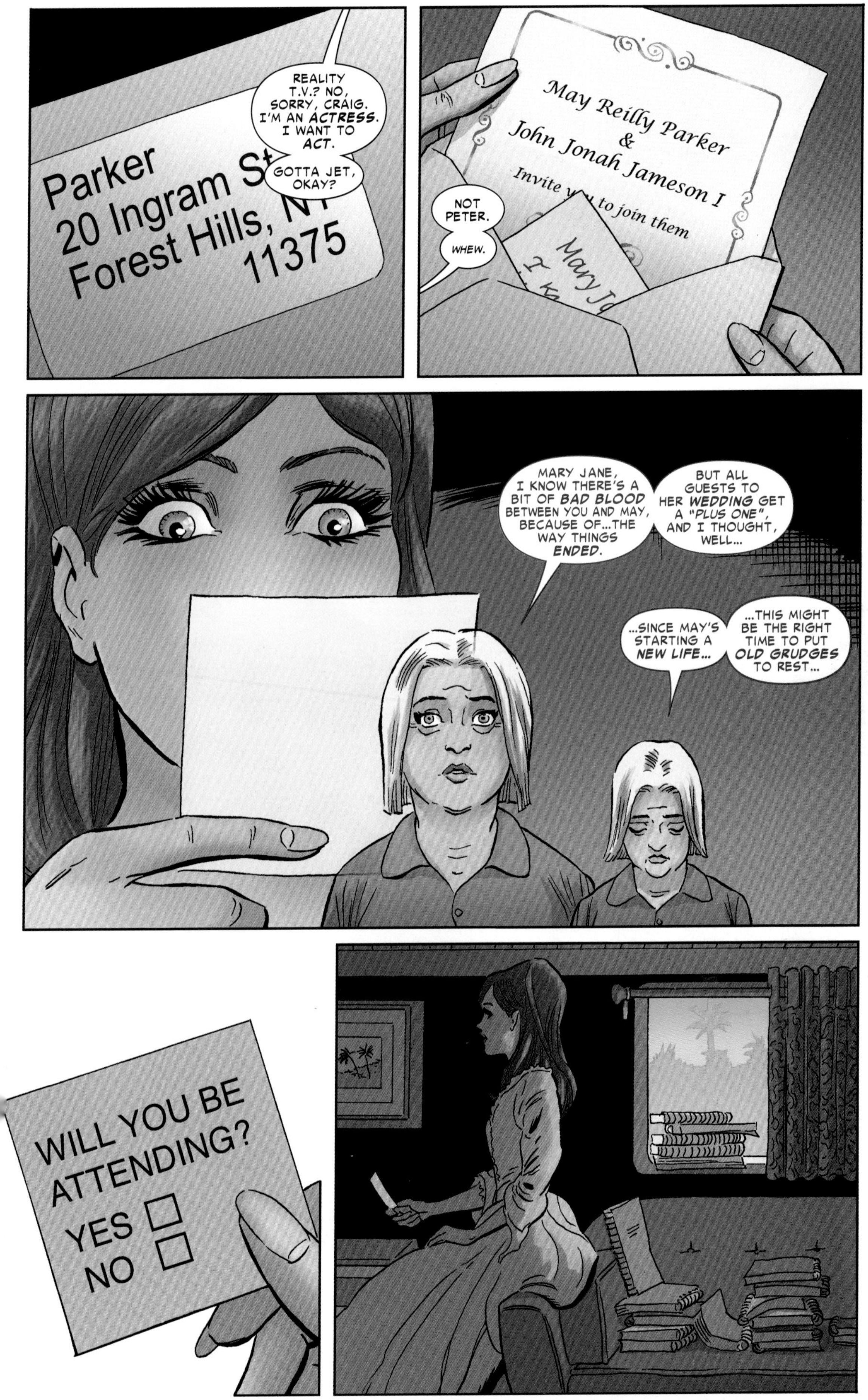
Parker
20 Ingram St
Forest Hills, NY
11375
REALITY T.V.? NO, SORRY, CRAIG. I'M AN ACTRESS. I WANT TO ACT.
GOTTA JET, OKAY?
May Reilly Parker
&
John Jonah Jameson I
Invite you to join them
NOT PETER.
WHEW.
MARY JANE, I KNOW THERE'S A BIT OF BAD BLOOD BETWEEN YOU AND MAY, BECAUSE OF...THE WAY THINGS ENDED.
BUT ALL GUESTS TO HER WEDDING GET A "PLUS ONE", AND I THOUGHT, WELL...
...SINCE MAY'S STARTING A NEW LIFE...
...THIS MIGHT BE THE RIGHT TIME TO PUT OLD GRUDGES TO REST...
WILL YOU BE ATTENDING?
YES
NO

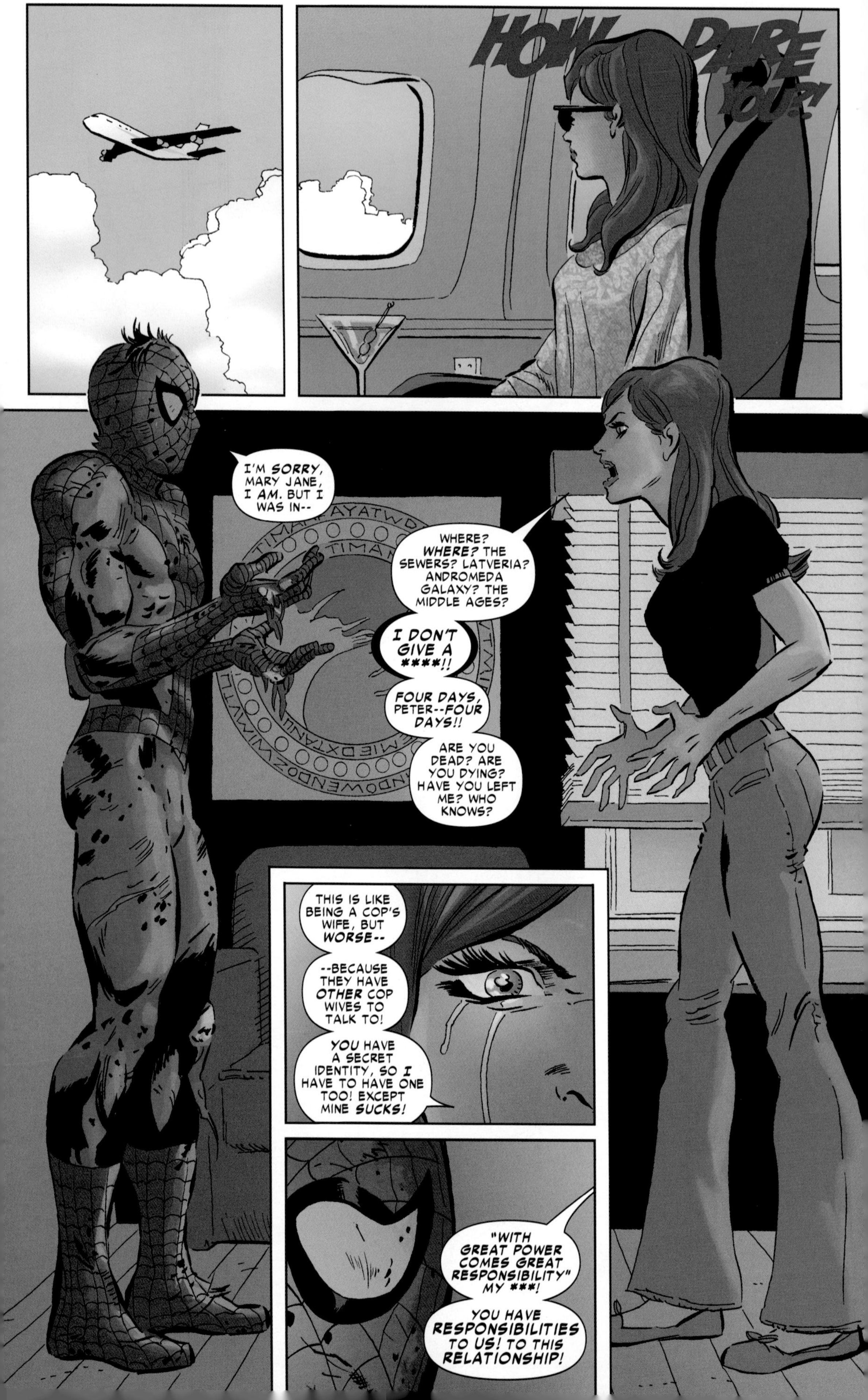
HOW DARE YOU?!
I'M SORRY, MARY JANE, I AM. BUT I WAS IN--
WHERE? WHERE? THE SEWERS? LATVERIA? ANDROMEDA GALAXY? THE MIDDLE AGES?
I DON'T GIVE A ****!!
FOUR DAYS, PETER--FOUR DAYS!!
ARE YOU DEAD? ARE YOU DYING? HAVE YOU LEFT ME? WHO KNOWS?
THIS IS LIKE BEING A COP'S WIFE, BUT WORSE--
--BECAUSE THEY HAVE OTHER COP WIVES TO TALK TO!
YOU HAVE A SECRET IDENTITY, SO I HAVE TO HAVE ONE TOO! EXCEPT MINE SUCKS!
"WITH GREAT POWER COMES GREAT RESPONSIBILITY" MY ***!
YOU HAVE RESPONSIBILITIES TO US! TO THIS RELATIONSHIP!

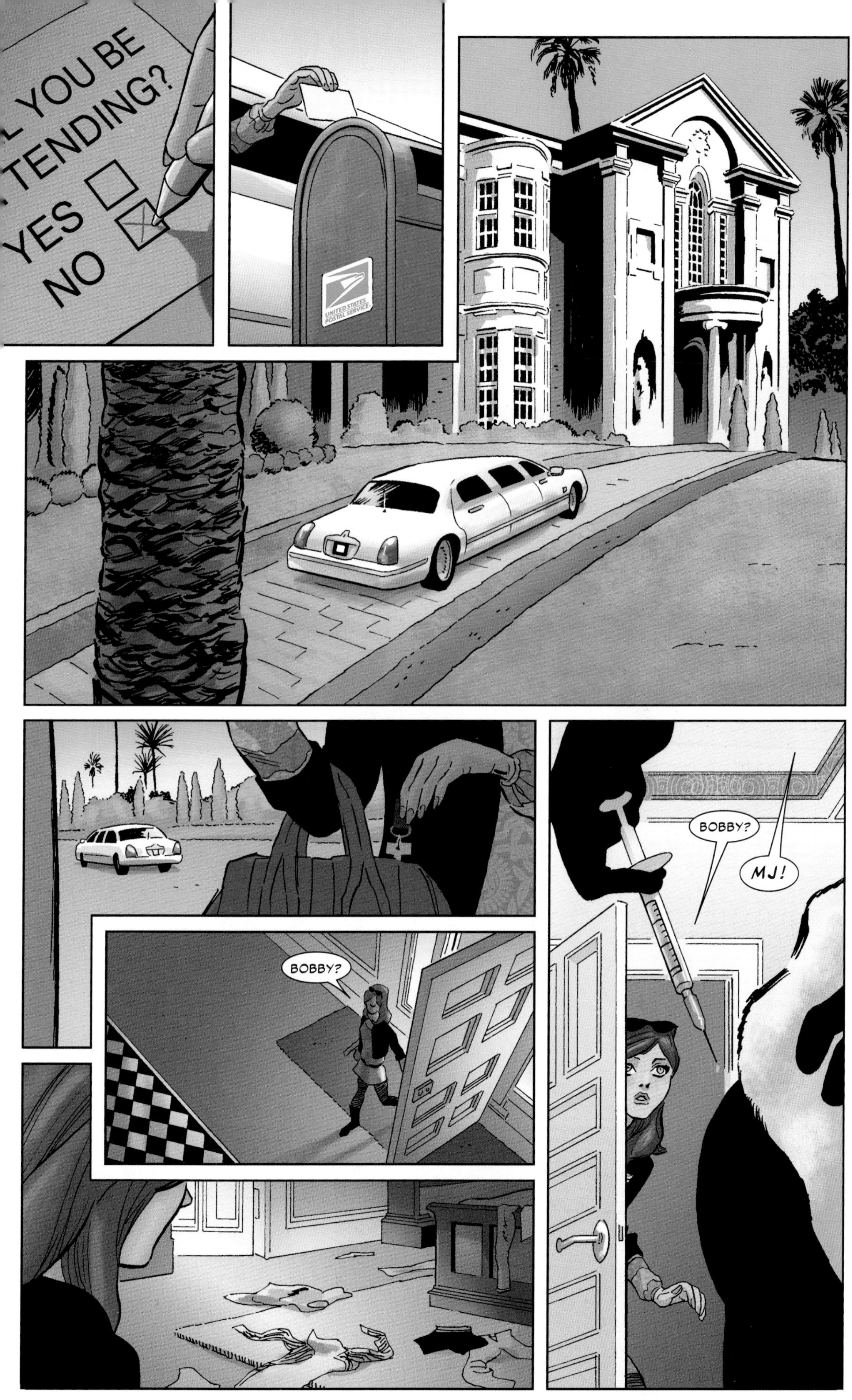
...L YOU BE
...TENDING?
YES
NO
UNITED STATES POSTAL SERVICE
BOBBY?
BOBBY?
MJ!

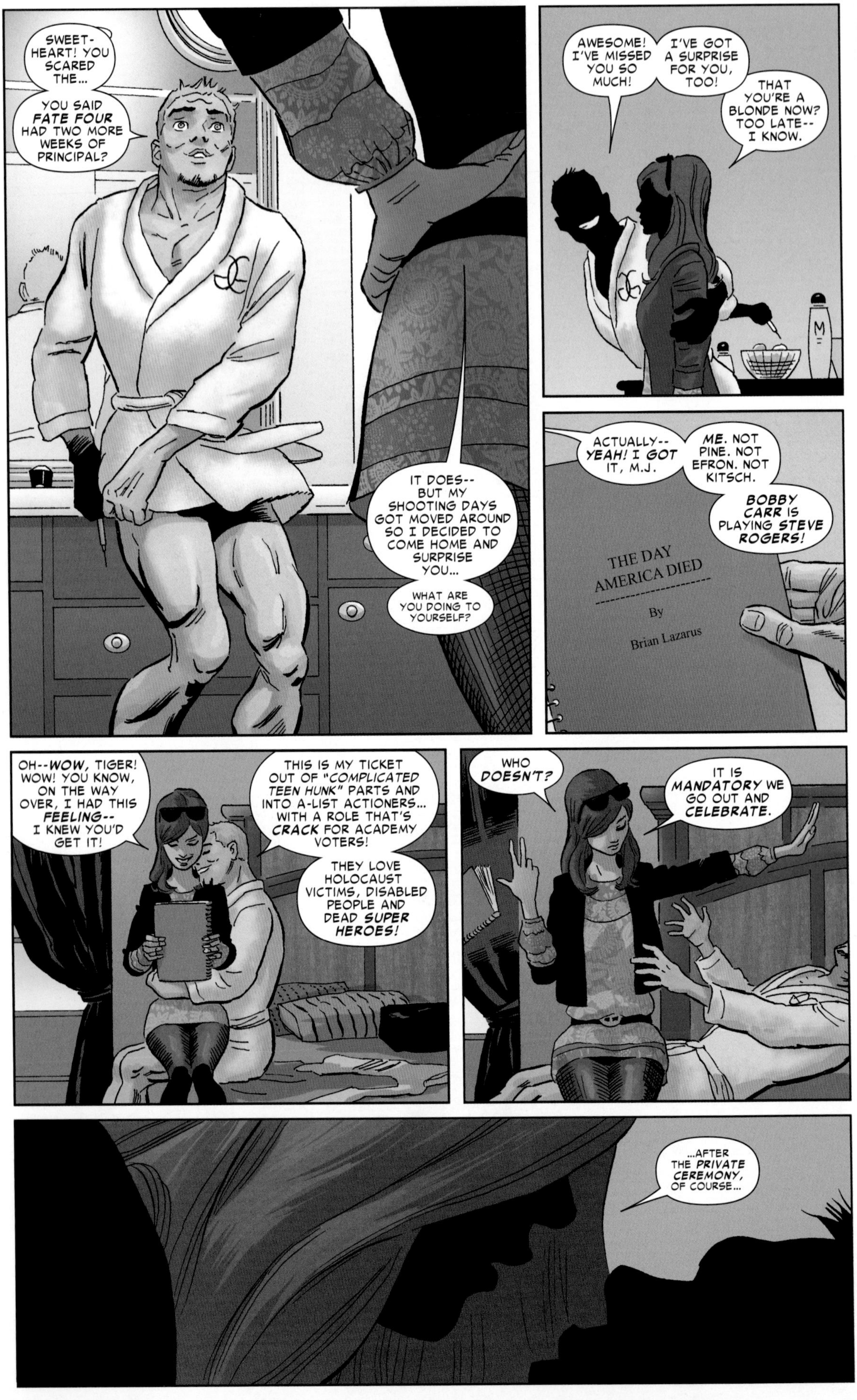
SWEET-HEART! YOU SCARED THE...
YOU SAID FATE FOUR HAD TWO MORE WEEKS OF PRINCIPAL?
IT DOES-- BUT MY SHOOTING DAYS GOT MOVED AROUND SO I DECIDED TO COME HOME AND SURPRISE YOU...
WHAT ARE YOU DOING TO YOURSELF?
AWESOME! I'VE MISSED YOU SO MUCH!
I'VE GOT A SURPRISE FOR YOU, TOO!
THAT YOU'RE A BLONDE NOW? TOO LATE-- I KNOW.
ACTUALLY-- YEAH! I GOT IT, M.J.
ME. NOT PINE. NOT EFRON. NOT KITSCH.
BOBBY CARR IS PLAYING STEVE ROGERS!
THE DAY AMERICA DIED
By
Brian Lazarus
OH--WOW, TIGER! WOW! YOU KNOW, ON THE WAY OVER, I HAD THIS FEELING-- I KNEW YOU'D GET IT!
THIS IS MY TICKET OUT OF "COMPLICATED TEEN HUNK" PARTS AND INTO A-LIST ACTIONERS... WITH A ROLE THAT'S CRACK FOR ACADEMY VOTERS!
THEY LOVE HOLOCAUST VICTIMS, DISABLED PEOPLE AND DEAD SUPER HEROES!
WHO DOESN'T?
IT IS MANDATORY WE GO OUT AND CELEBRATE.
...AFTER THE PRIVATE CEREMONY, OF COURSE...

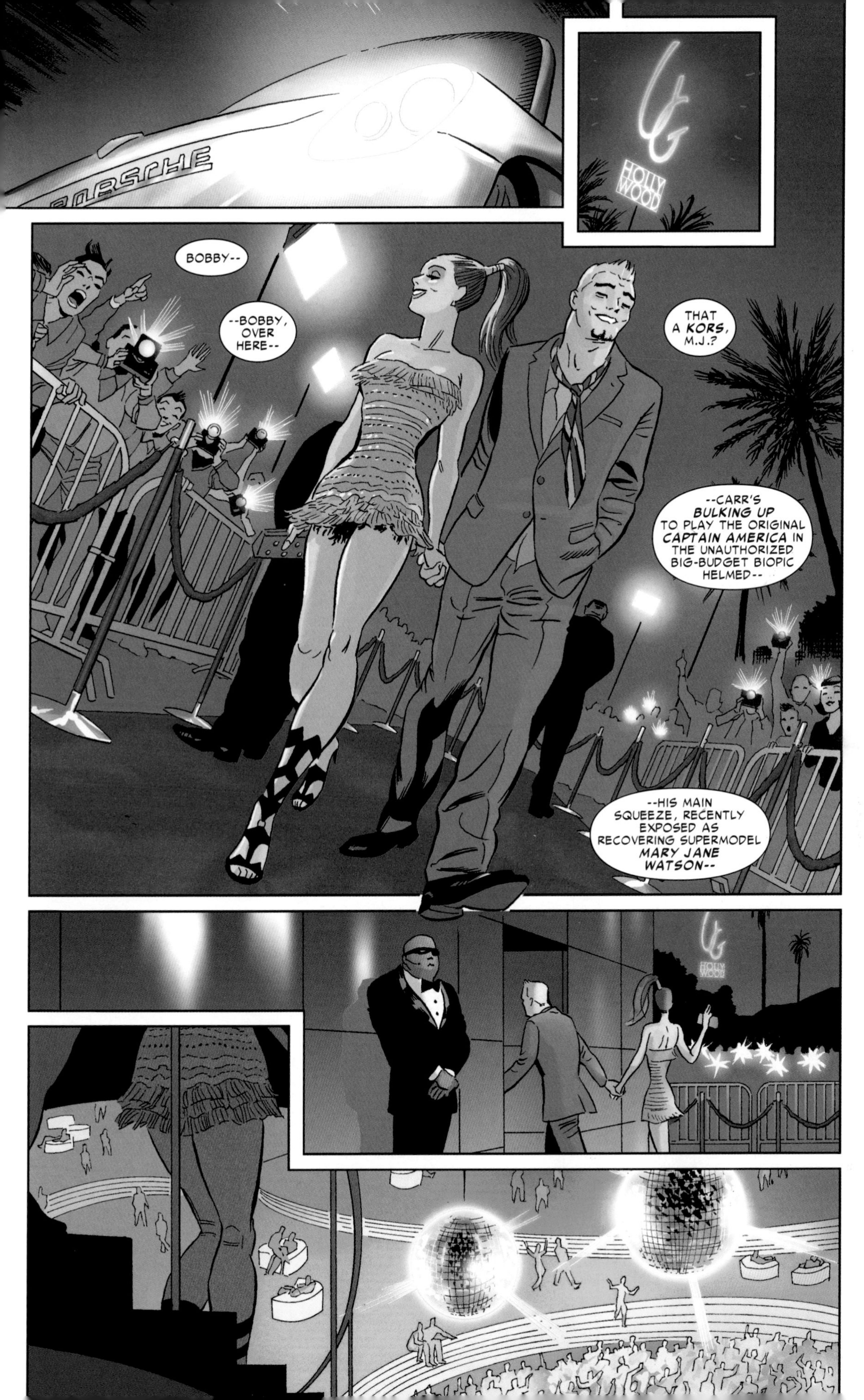
PORSCHE
HOLLY WOOD
BOBBY--
--BOBBY, OVER HERE--
THAT A KORS, M.J.?
--CARR'S BULKING UP TO PLAY THE ORIGINAL CAPTAIN AMERICA IN THE UNAUTHORIZED BIG-BUDGET BIOPIC HELMED--
--HIS MAIN SQUEEZE, RECENTLY EXPOSED AS RECOVERING SUPERMODEL MARY JANE WATSON--
HOLLY WOOD

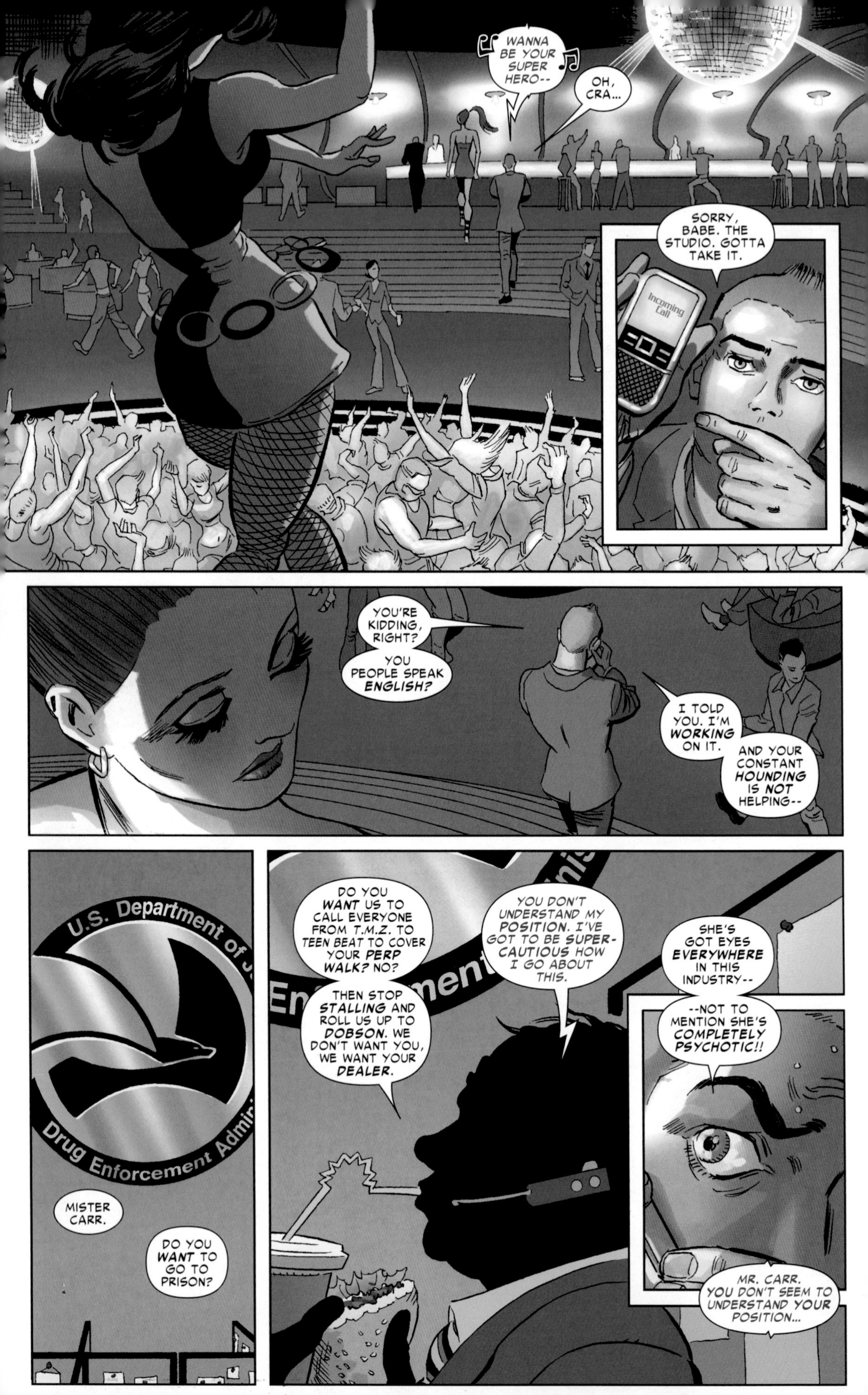
WANNA BE YOUR SUPER HERO--
OH, CRA...
SORRY, BABE. THE STUDIO. GOTTA TAKE IT.
Incoming Call
YOU'RE KIDDING, RIGHT?
YOU PEOPLE SPEAK ENGLISH?
I TOLD YOU. I'M WORKING ON IT.
AND YOUR CONSTANT HOUNDING IS NOT HELPING--
U.S. Department of J
Drug Enforcement Admi
MISTER CARR.
DO YOU WANT TO GO TO PRISON?
DO YOU WANT US TO CALL EVERYONE FROM T.M.Z. TO TEEN BEAT TO COVER YOUR PERP WALK? NO?
THEN STOP STALLING AND ROLL US UP TO DOBSON. WE DON'T WANT YOU, WE WANT YOUR DEALER.
YOU DON'T UNDERSTAND MY POSITION. I'VE GOT TO BE SUPER-CAUTIOUS HOW I GO ABOUT THIS.
SHE'S GOT EYES EVERYWHERE IN THIS INDUSTRY--
--NOT TO MENTION SHE'S COMPLETELY PSYCHOTIC!!
MR. CARR. YOU DON'T SEEM TO UNDERSTAND YOUR POSITION...

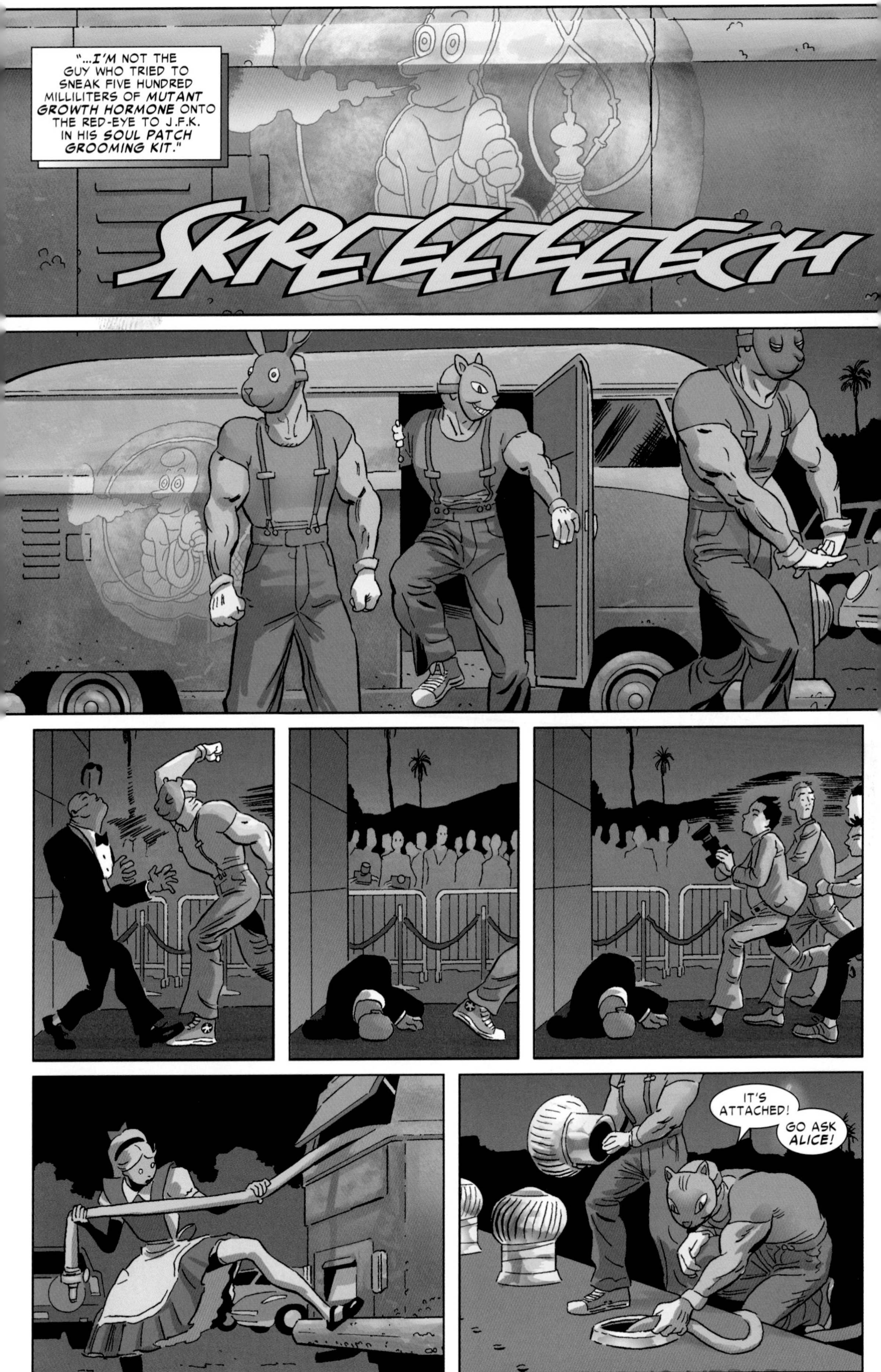
"...I'M NOT THE GUY WHO TRIED TO SNEAK FIVE HUNDRED MILLILITERS OF MUTANT GROWTH HORMONE ONTO THE RED-EYE TO J.F.K. IN HIS SOUL PATCH GROOMING KIT."
SKREEEEEECH
IT'S ATTACHED!
GO ASK ALICE!

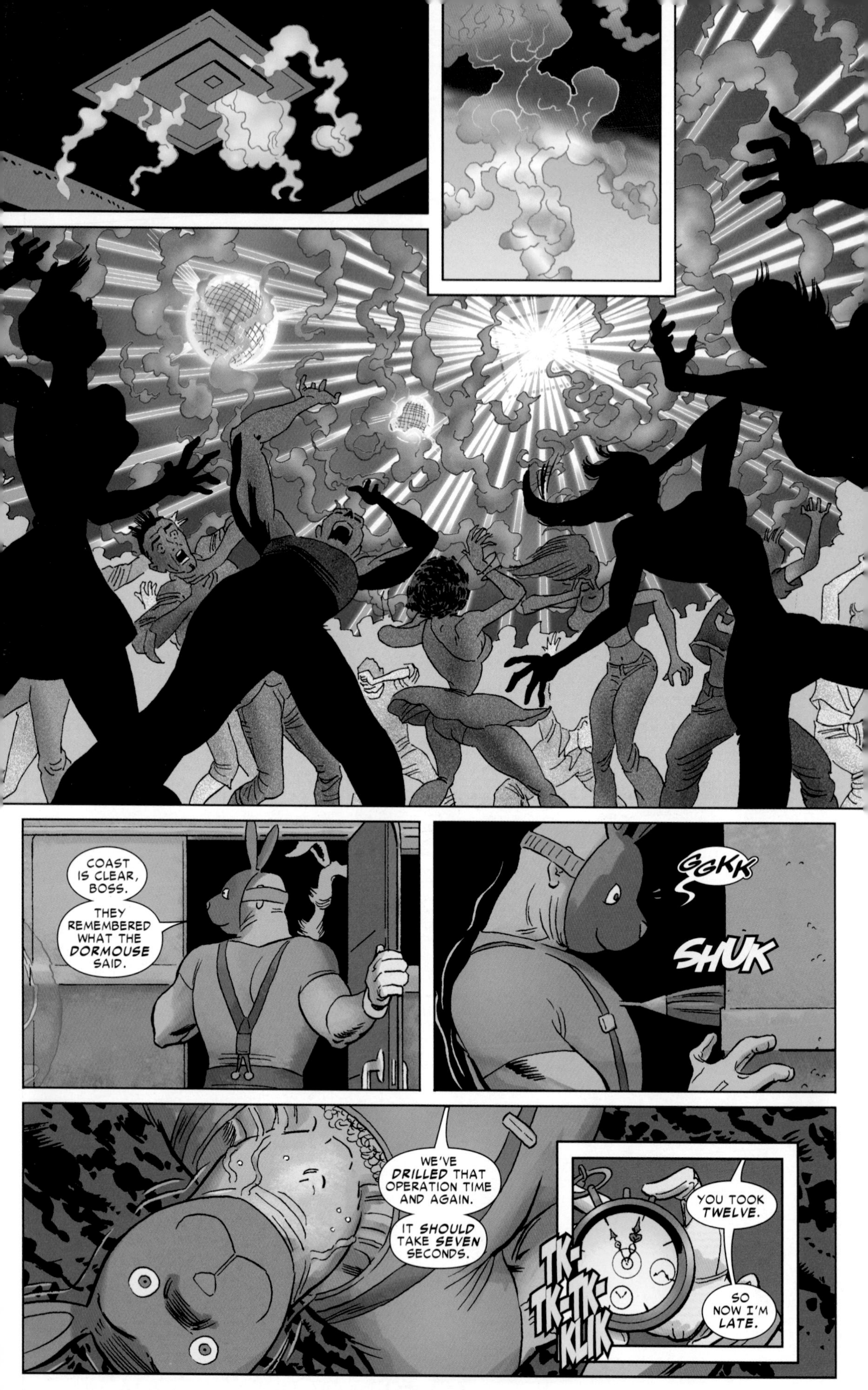
COAST IS CLEAR, BOSS.
THEY REMEMBERED WHAT THE DORMOUSE SAID.
GGKK
SHUK
WE'VE DRILLED THAT OPERATION TIME AND AGAIN.
IT SHOULD TAKE SEVEN SECONDS.
YOU TOOK TWELVE.
SO NOW I'M LATE.
TK-TK-TK-KLIK

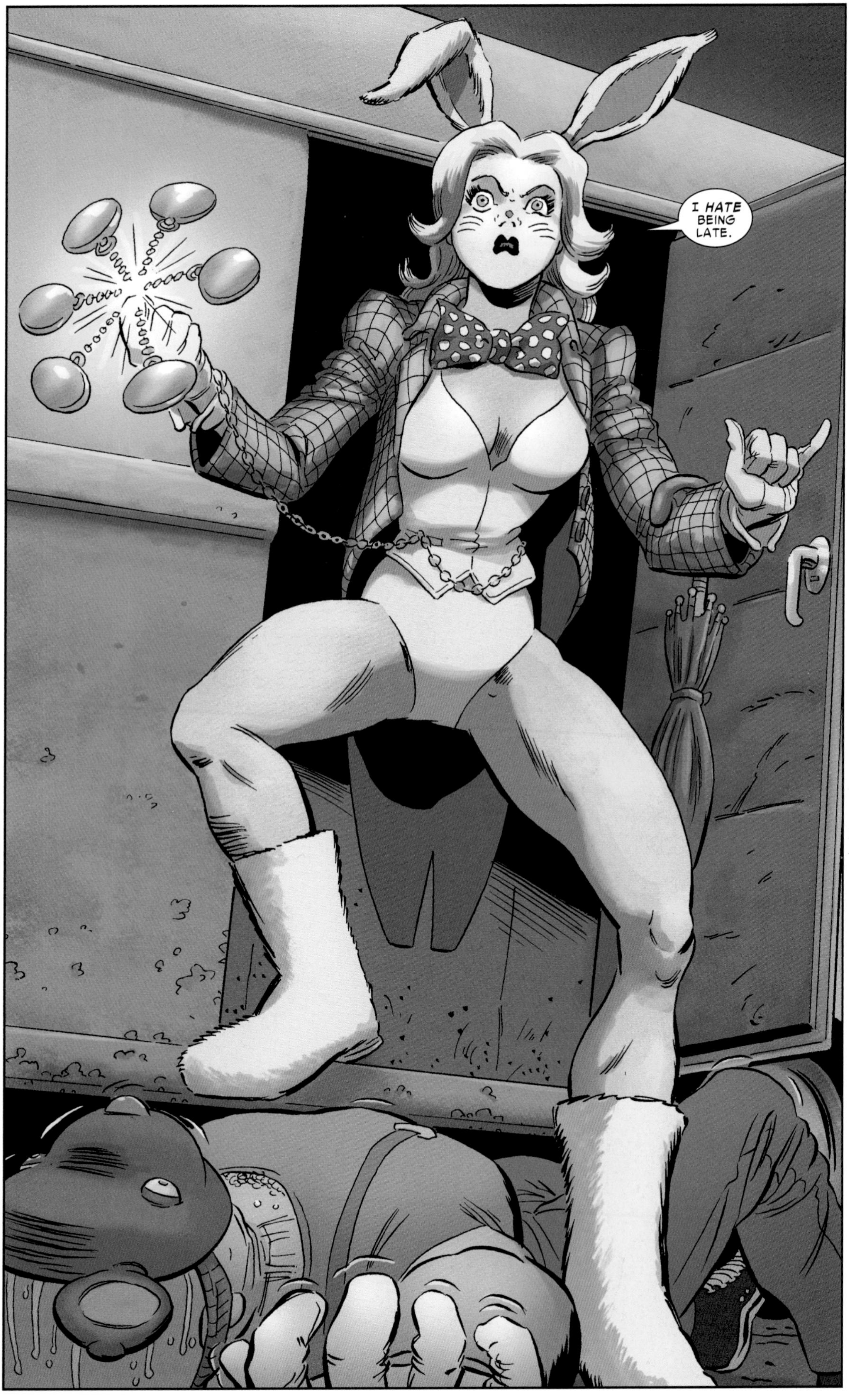
I *HATE* BEING LATE.

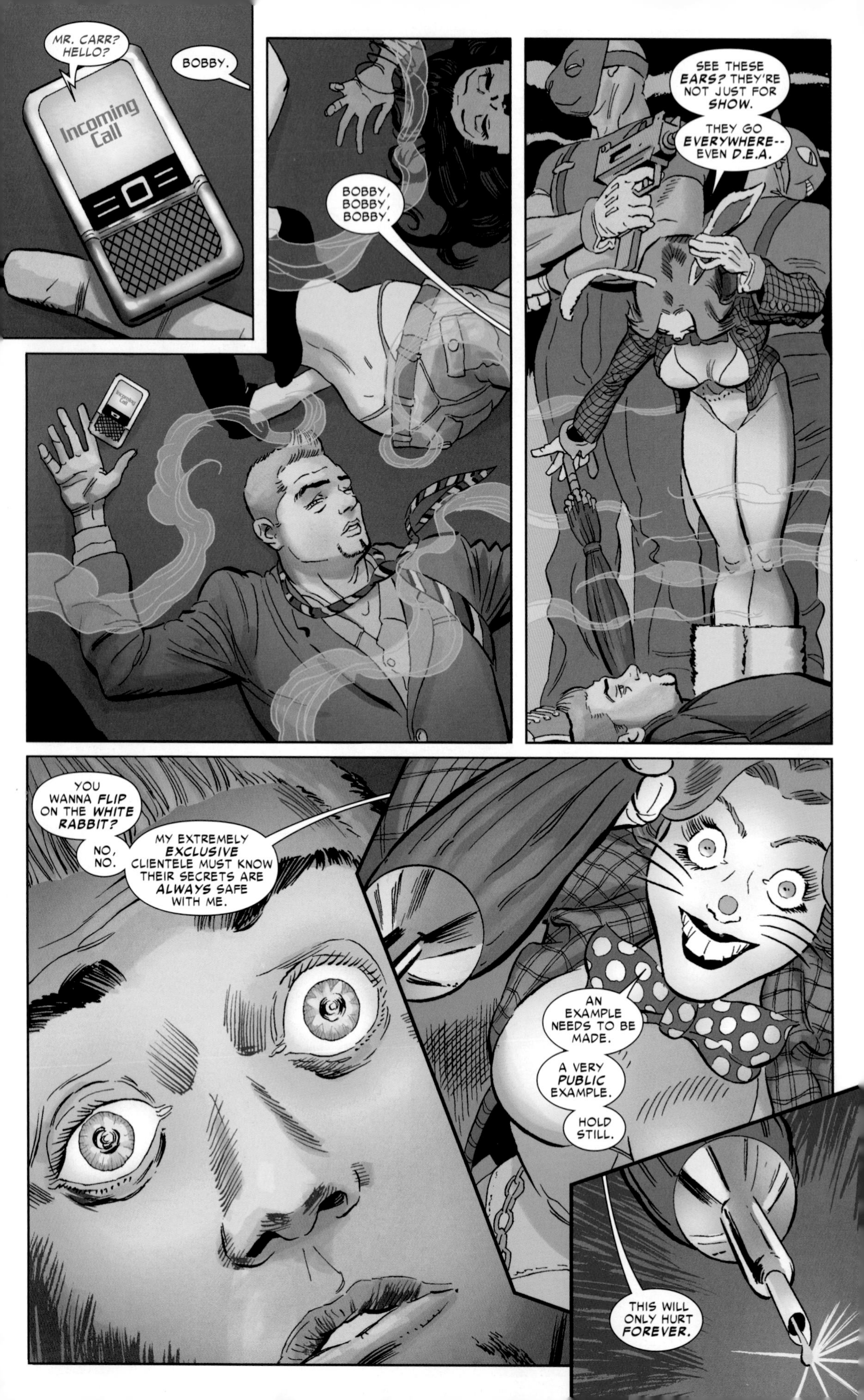

MR. CARR? HELLO?
Incoming Call
BOBBY.
BOBBY, BOBBY, BOBBY.
SEE THESE EARS? THEY'RE NOT JUST FOR SHOW.
THEY GO EVERYWHERE-- EVEN D.E.A.
Incoming Call
YOU WANNA FLIP ON THE WHITE RABBIT?
NO, NO.
MY EXTREMELY EXCLUSIVE CLIENTELE MUST KNOW THEIR SECRETS ARE ALWAYS SAFE WITH ME.
AN EXAMPLE NEEDS TO BE MADE.
A VERY PUBLIC EXAMPLE.
HOLD STILL.
THIS WILL ONLY HURT FOREVER.

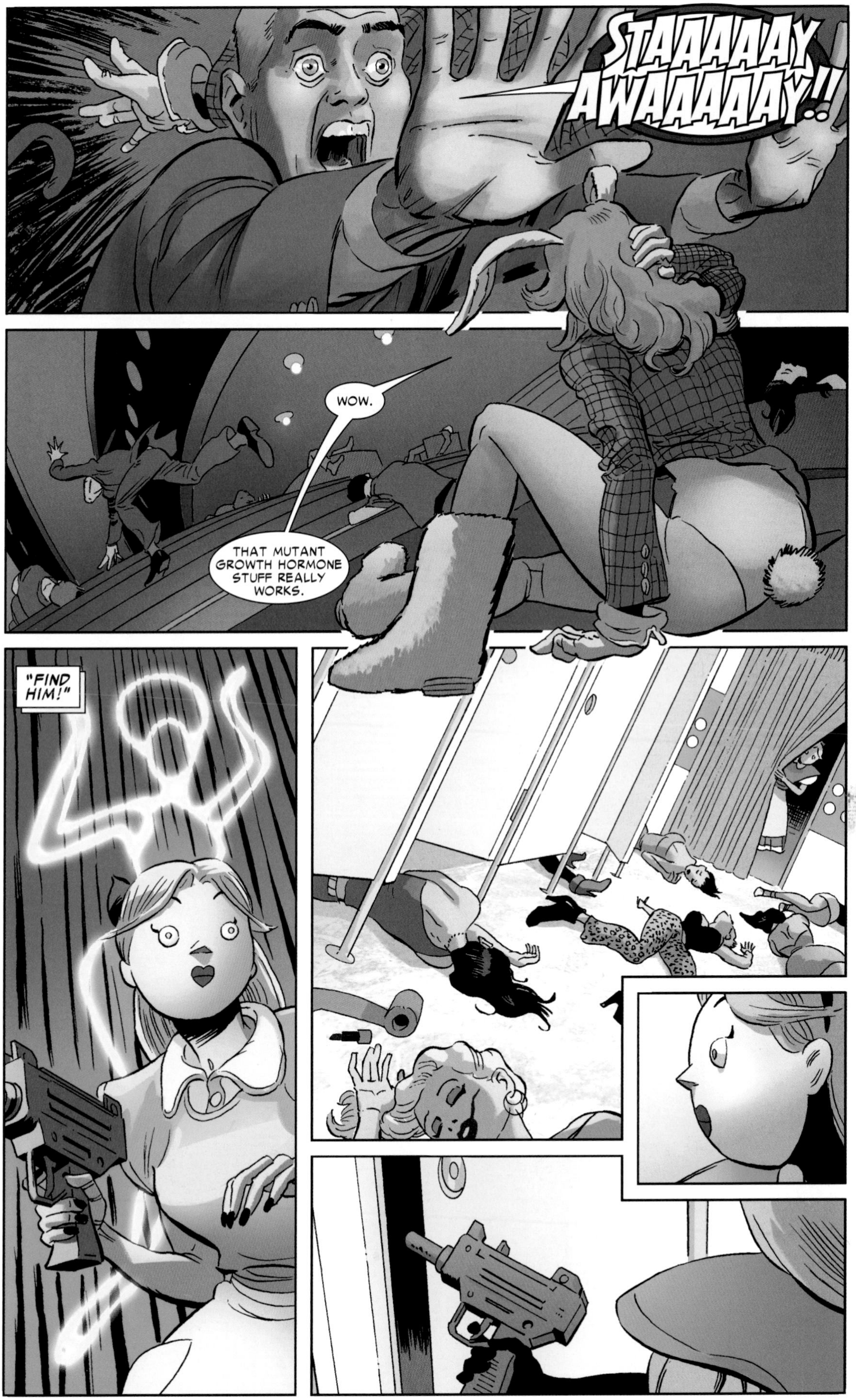
STAAAAAY AWAAAAAY!!
WOW.
THAT MUTANT GROWTH HORMONE STUFF REALLY WORKS.
"FIND HIM!"

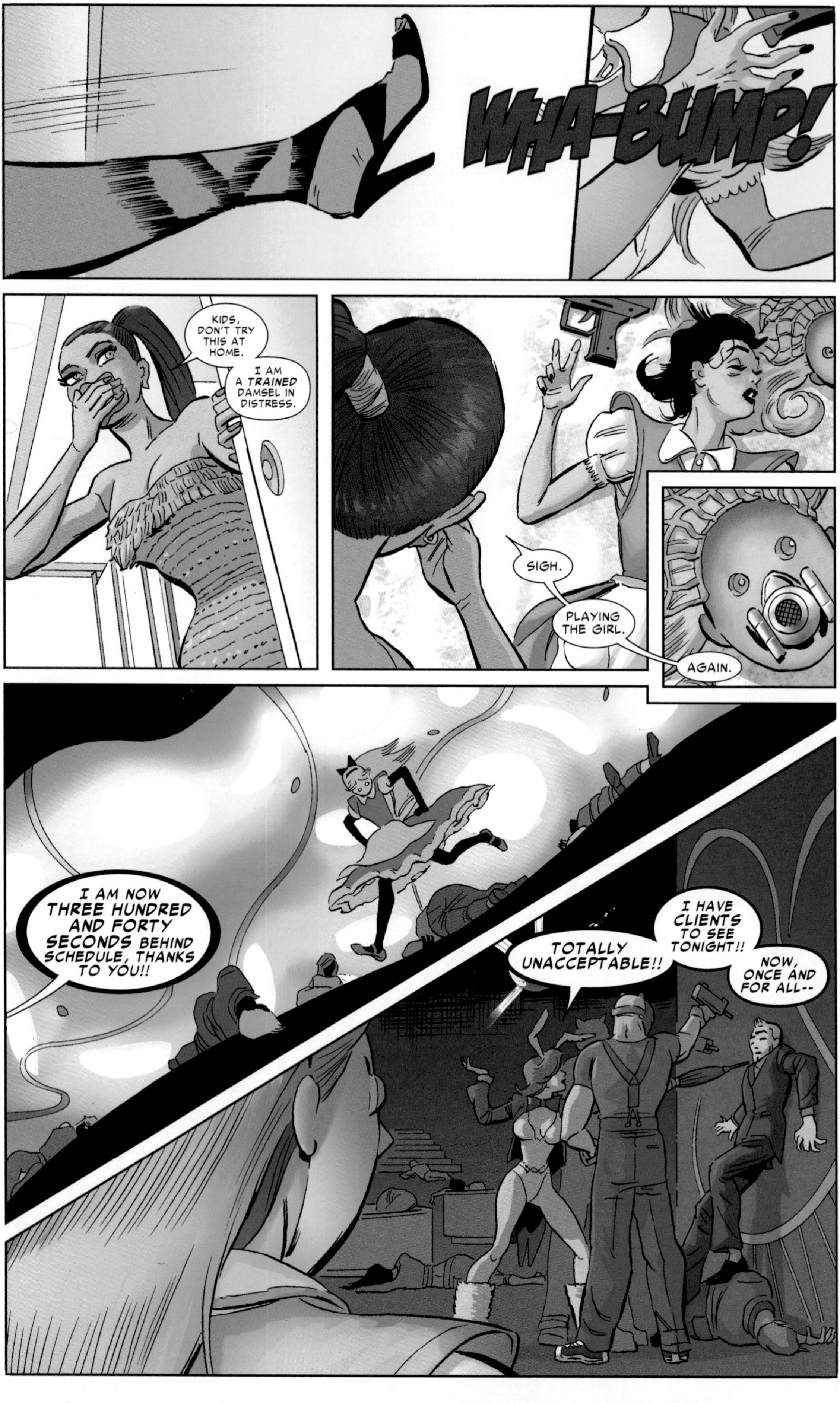
WHA-BUMP!
KIDS, DON'T TRY THIS AT HOME.
I AM A TRAINED DAMSEL IN DISTRESS.
SIGH.
PLAYING THE GIRL.
AGAIN.
I AM NOW THREE HUNDRED AND FORTY SECONDS BEHIND SCHEDULE, THANKS TO YOU!!
TOTALLY UNACCEPTABLE!!
I HAVE CLIENTS TO SEE TONIGHT!!
NOW, ONCE AND FOR ALL--

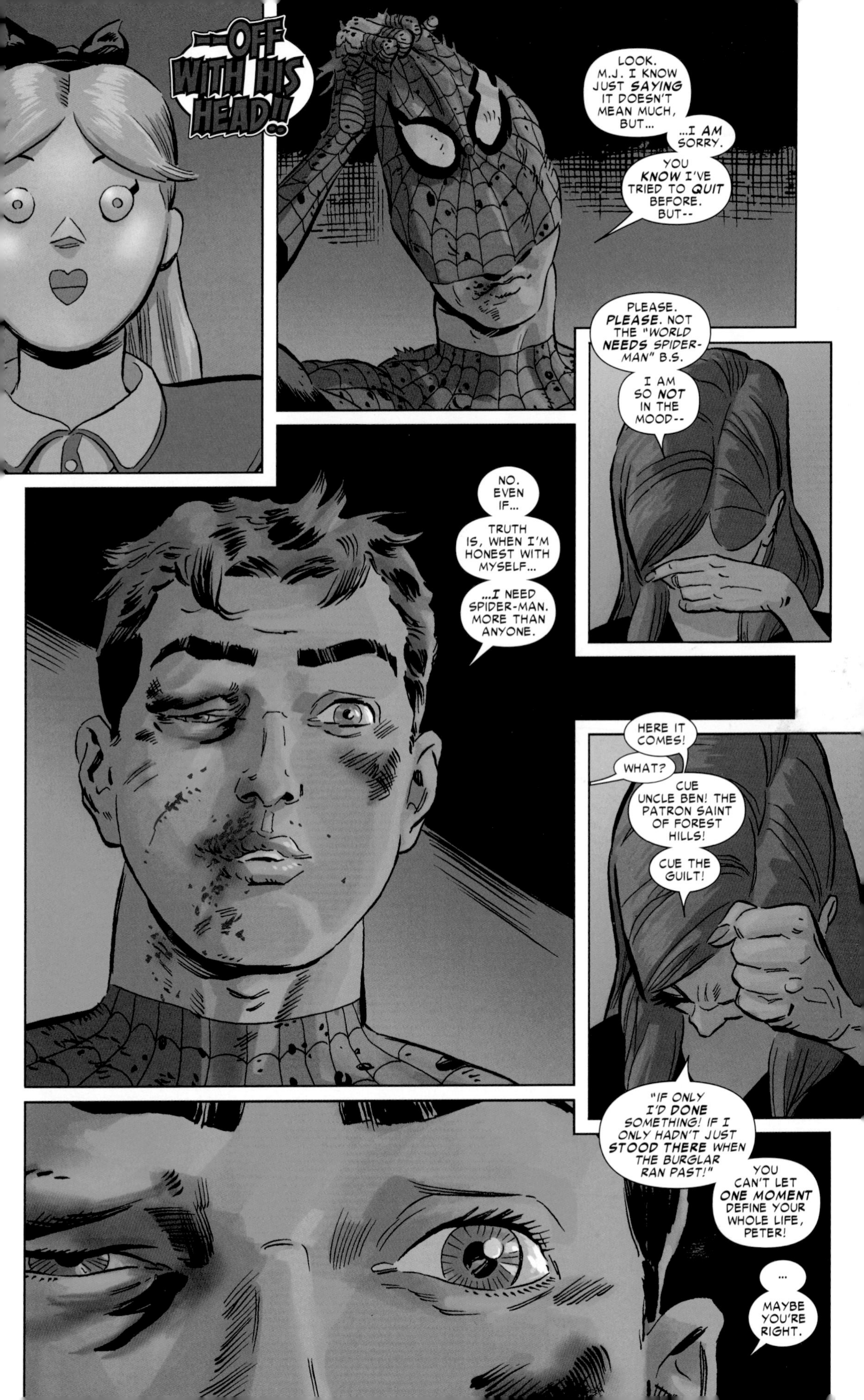
--OFF WITH HIS HEAD!!
LOOK. M.J. I KNOW JUST SAYING IT DOESN'T MEAN MUCH, BUT...
...I AM SORRY.
YOU KNOW I'VE TRIED TO QUIT BEFORE. BUT--
PLEASE. PLEASE. NOT THE "WORLD NEEDS SPIDER-MAN" B.S.
I AM SO NOT IN THE MOOD--
NO. EVEN IF...
TRUTH IS, WHEN I'M HONEST WITH MYSELF...
...I NEED SPIDER-MAN. MORE THAN ANYONE.
HERE IT COMES!
WHAT?
CUE UNCLE BEN! THE PATRON SAINT OF FOREST HILLS!
CUE THE GUILT!
"IF ONLY I'D DONE SOMETHING! IF I ONLY HADN'T JUST STOOD THERE WHEN THE BURGLAR RAN PAST!"
YOU CAN'T LET ONE MOMENT DEFINE YOUR WHOLE LIFE, PETER!
...
MAYBE YOU'RE RIGHT.

...BUT IF YOU EVER FIND YOURSELF *IN* A MOMENT LIKE THAT...

...AND BELIEVE ME, YOU'LL *KNOW* IT WHEN YOU *SEE* IT...

...DON'T DO WHAT I DID.

WHICH WAS *NOTHING.*

BECAUSE I WOULDN'T WISH THIS FEELING ON MY WORST *ENEMY.*

LEAST OF ALL *YOU,* MARY JANE.

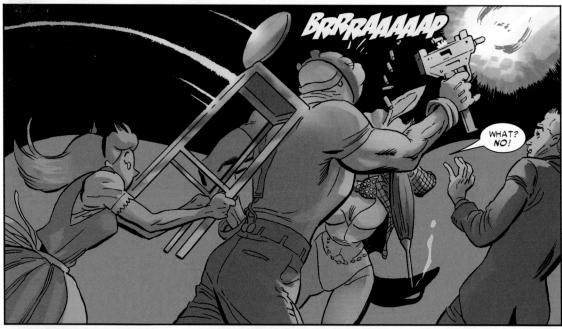

BRRRAAAAAAP

WHAT? NO!

HURRY, BOBBY!

GINNY! WHAT ARE YOU DOING? TRAITOR!

KILL THEM BOTH!!

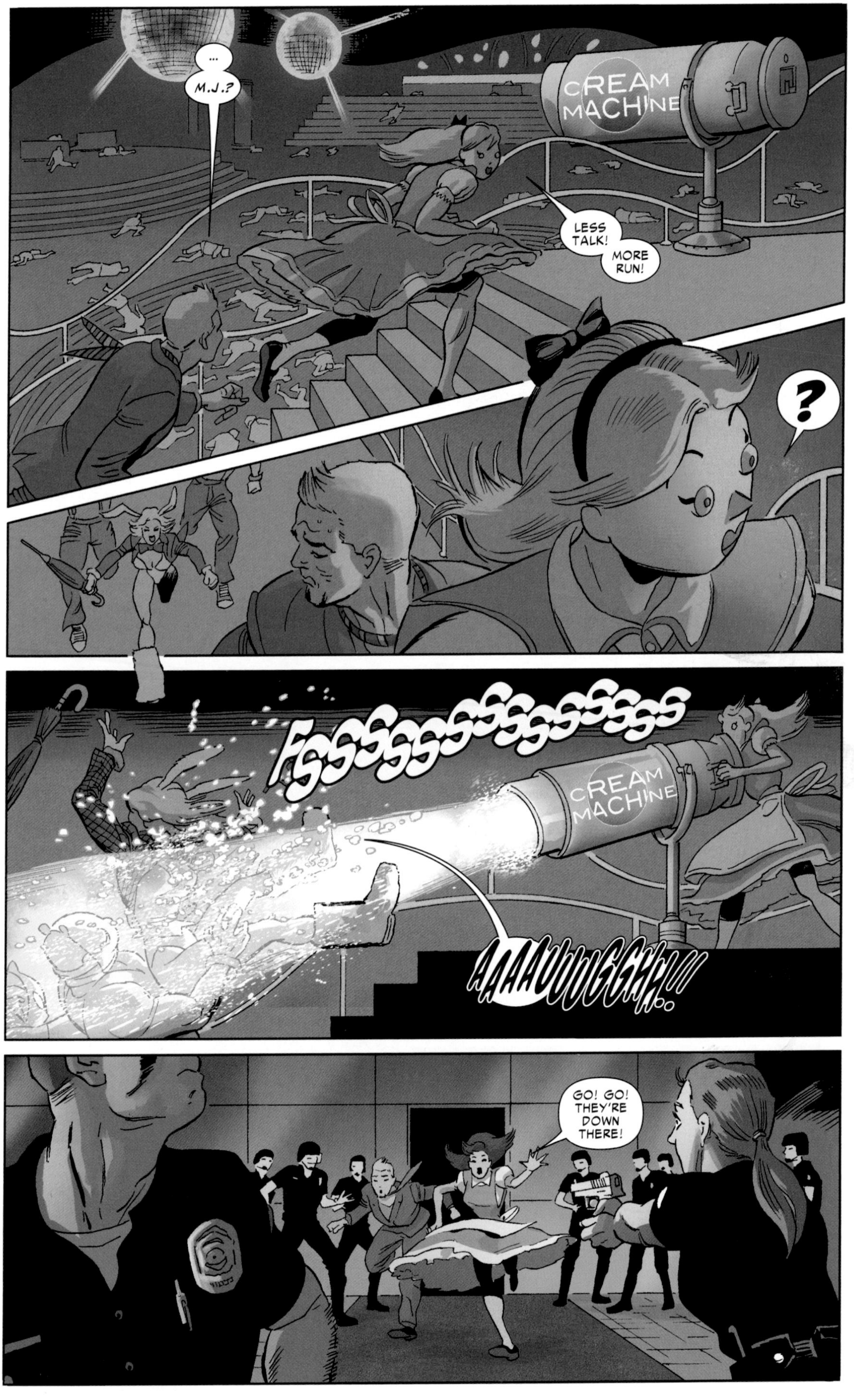
...
M.J.?
LESS TALK! MORE RUN!
CREAM MACHINE
?
FSSSSSSSSSSSSSSS
CREAM MACHINE
AAAAUUUGGHH!!!
GO! GO! THEY'RE DOWN THERE!

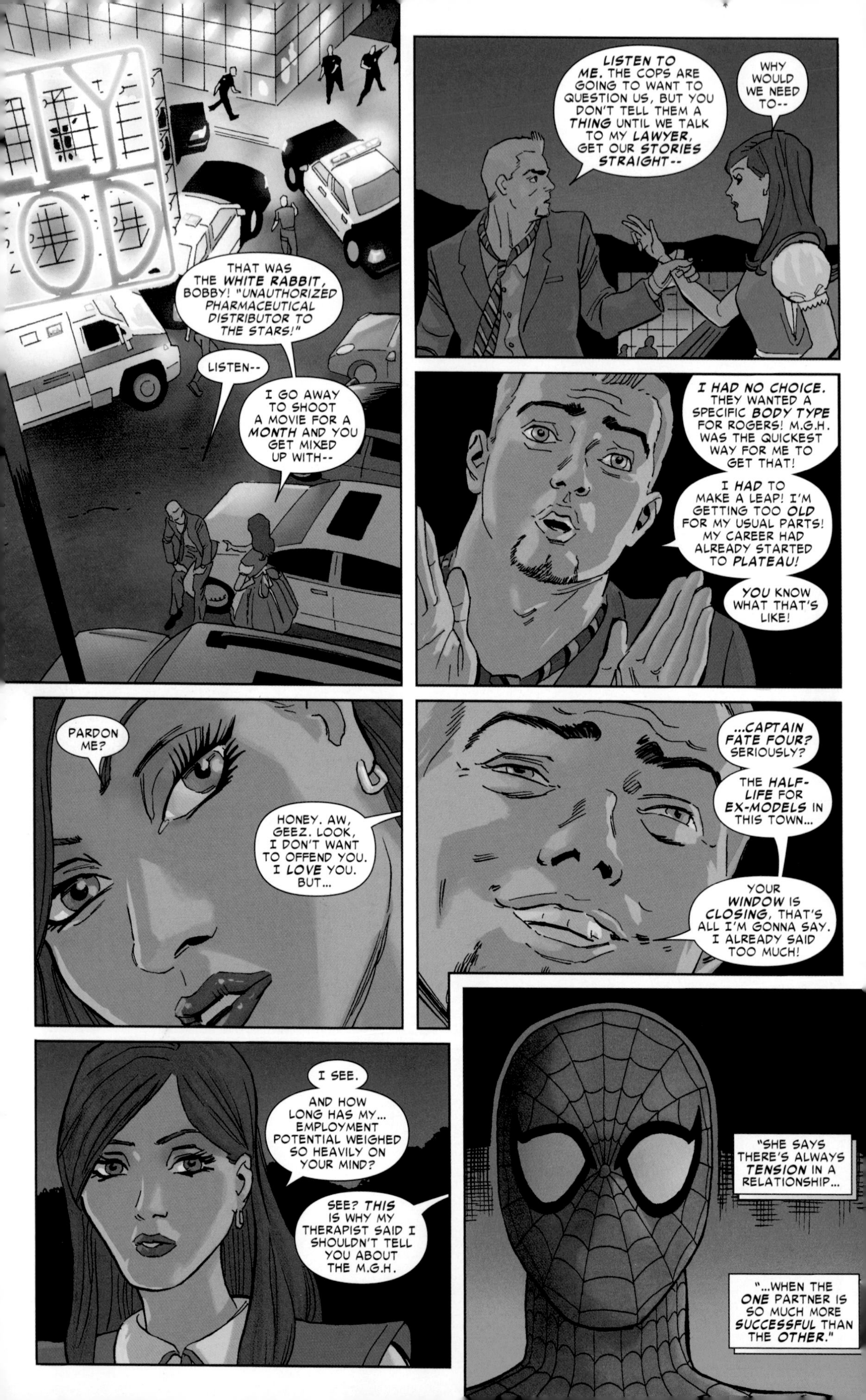
THAT WAS THE WHITE RABBIT, BOBBY! "UNAUTHORIZED PHARMACEUTICAL DISTRIBUTOR TO THE STARS!"
LISTEN--
I GO AWAY TO SHOOT A MOVIE FOR A MONTH AND YOU GET MIXED UP WITH--
LISTEN TO ME. THE COPS ARE GOING TO WANT TO QUESTION US, BUT YOU DON'T TELL THEM A THING UNTIL WE TALK TO MY LAWYER, GET OUR STORIES STRAIGHT--
WHY WOULD WE NEED TO--
I HAD NO CHOICE. THEY WANTED A SPECIFIC BODY TYPE FOR ROGERS! M.G.H. WAS THE QUICKEST WAY FOR ME TO GET THAT!
I HAD TO MAKE A LEAP! I'M GETTING TOO OLD FOR MY USUAL PARTS! MY CAREER HAD ALREADY STARTED TO PLATEAU!
YOU KNOW WHAT THAT'S LIKE!
PARDON ME?
HONEY. AW, GEEZ. LOOK, I DON'T WANT TO OFFEND YOU. I LOVE YOU. BUT...
...CAPTAIN FATE FOUR? SERIOUSLY?
THE HALF-LIFE FOR EX-MODELS IN THIS TOWN...
YOUR WINDOW IS CLOSING, THAT'S ALL I'M GONNA SAY. I ALREADY SAID TOO MUCH!
I SEE.
AND HOW LONG HAS MY... EMPLOYMENT POTENTIAL WEIGHED SO HEAVILY ON YOUR MIND?
SEE? THIS IS WHY MY THERAPIST SAID I SHOULDN'T TELL YOU ABOUT THE M.G.H.
"SHE SAYS THERE'S ALWAYS TENSION IN A RELATIONSHIP...
"...WHEN THE ONE PARTNER IS SO MUCH MORE SUCCESSFUL THAN THE OTHER."

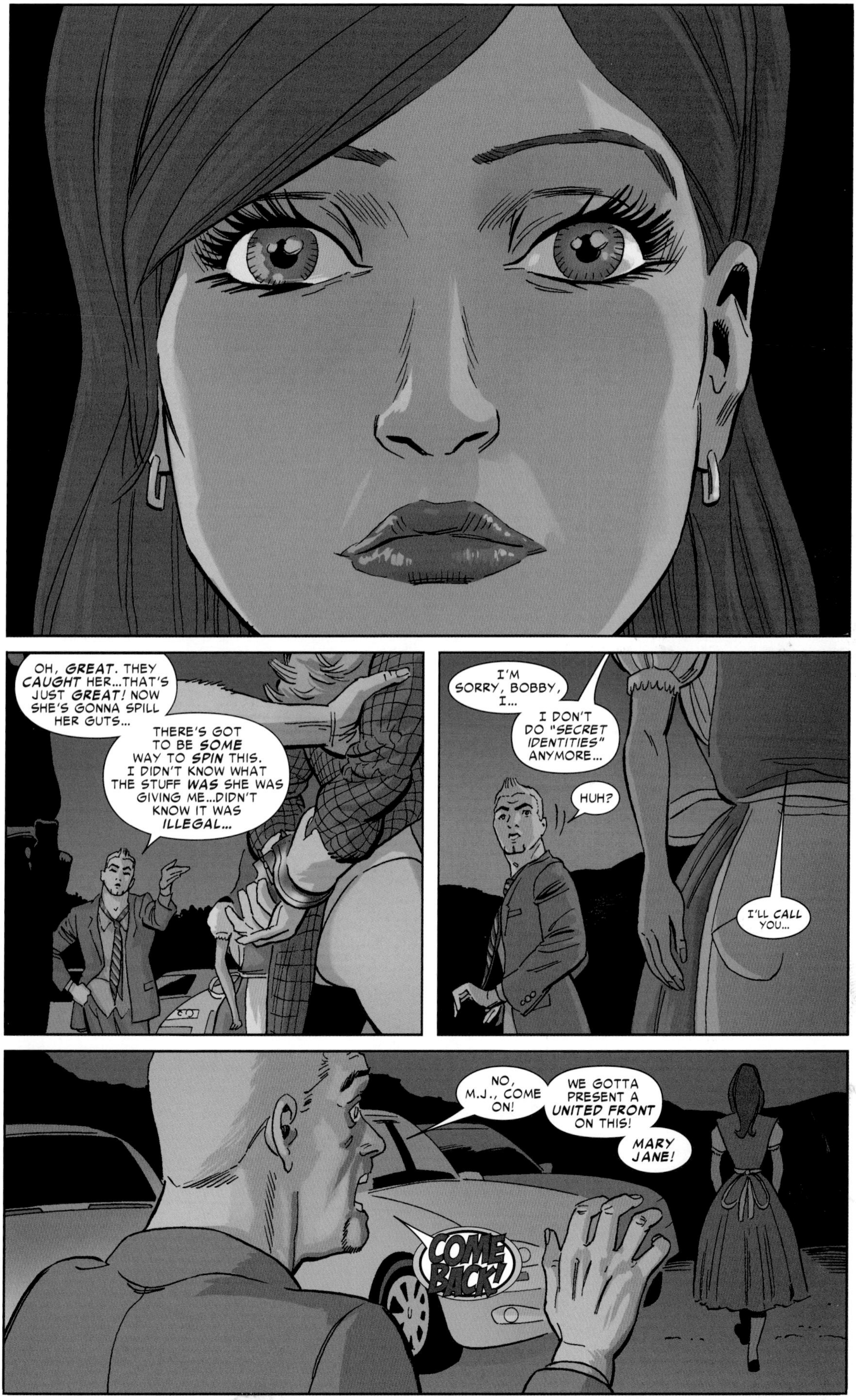
OH, GREAT. THEY CAUGHT HER...THAT'S JUST GREAT! NOW SHE'S GONNA SPILL HER GUTS...
THERE'S GOT TO BE SOME WAY TO SPIN THIS. I DIDN'T KNOW WHAT THE STUFF WAS SHE WAS GIVING ME...DIDN'T KNOW IT WAS ILLEGAL...
I'M SORRY, BOBBY, I...
I DON'T DO "SECRET IDENTITIES" ANYMORE...
HUH?
I'LL CALL YOU...
NO, M.J., COME ON!
WE GOTTA PRESENT A UNITED FRONT ON THIS!
MARY JANE!
COME BACK!

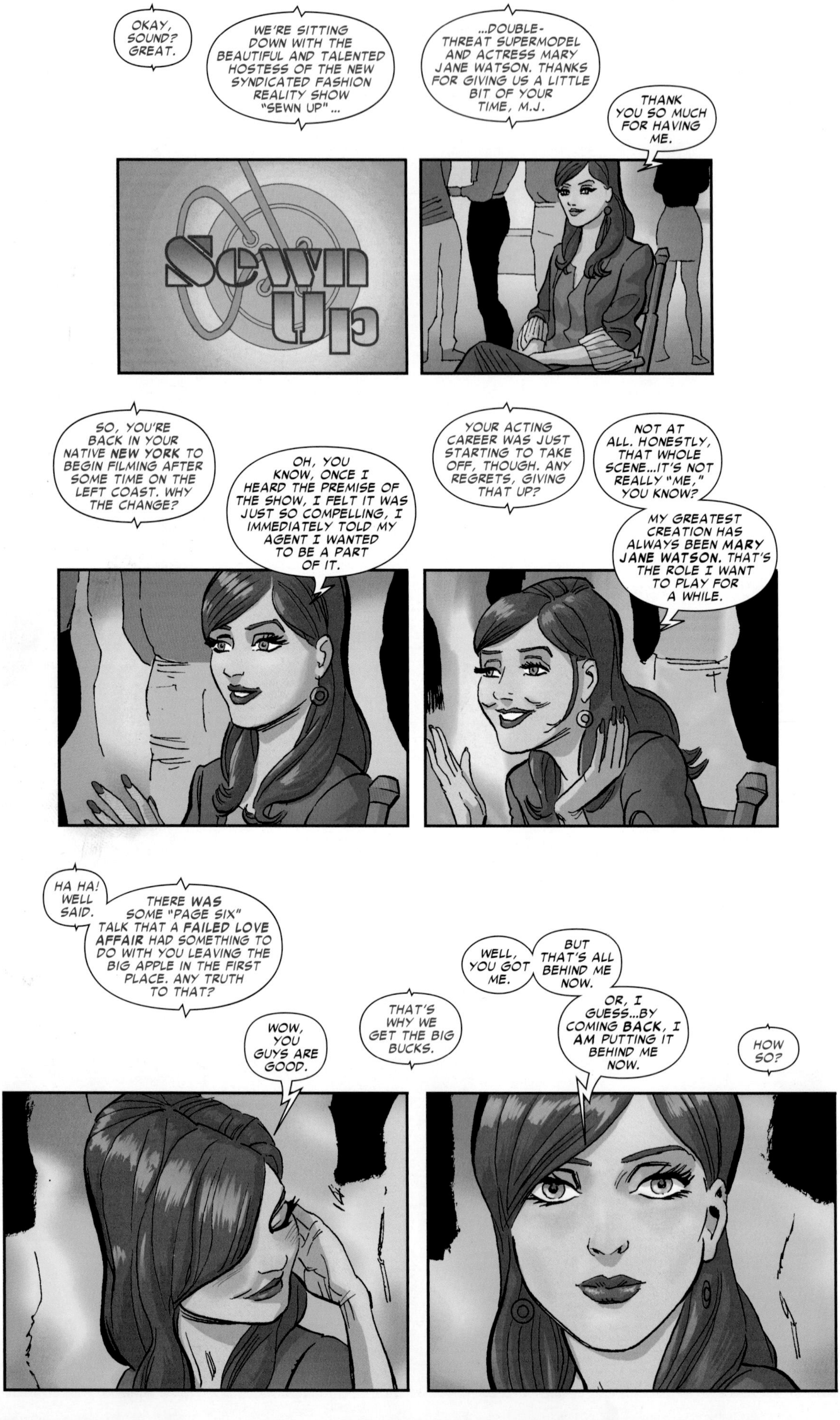
OKAY, SOUND? GREAT.
WE'RE SITTING DOWN WITH THE BEAUTIFUL AND TALENTED HOSTESS OF THE NEW SYNDICATED FASHION REALITY SHOW "SEWN UP"...
...DOUBLE-THREAT SUPERMODEL AND ACTRESS MARY JANE WATSON. THANKS FOR GIVING US A LITTLE BIT OF YOUR TIME, M.J.
THANK YOU SO MUCH FOR HAVING ME.
Sewn Up
SO, YOU'RE BACK IN YOUR NATIVE NEW YORK TO BEGIN FILMING AFTER SOME TIME ON THE LEFT COAST. WHY THE CHANGE?
OH, YOU KNOW, ONCE I HEARD THE PREMISE OF THE SHOW, I FELT IT WAS JUST SO COMPELLING, I IMMEDIATELY TOLD MY AGENT I WANTED TO BE A PART OF IT.
YOUR ACTING CAREER WAS JUST STARTING TO TAKE OFF, THOUGH. ANY REGRETS, GIVING THAT UP?
NOT AT ALL. HONESTLY, THAT WHOLE SCENE...IT'S NOT REALLY "ME," YOU KNOW?
MY GREATEST CREATION HAS ALWAYS BEEN MARY JANE WATSON. THAT'S THE ROLE I WANT TO PLAY FOR A WHILE.
HA HA! WELL SAID.
THERE WAS SOME "PAGE SIX" TALK THAT A FAILED LOVE AFFAIR HAD SOMETHING TO DO WITH YOU LEAVING THE BIG APPLE IN THE FIRST PLACE. ANY TRUTH TO THAT?
WOW, YOU GUYS ARE GOOD.
THAT'S WHY WE GET THE BIG BUCKS.
WELL, YOU GOT ME.
BUT THAT'S ALL BEHIND ME NOW.
OR, I GUESS...BY COMING BACK, I AM PUTTING IT BEHIND ME NOW.
HOW SO?

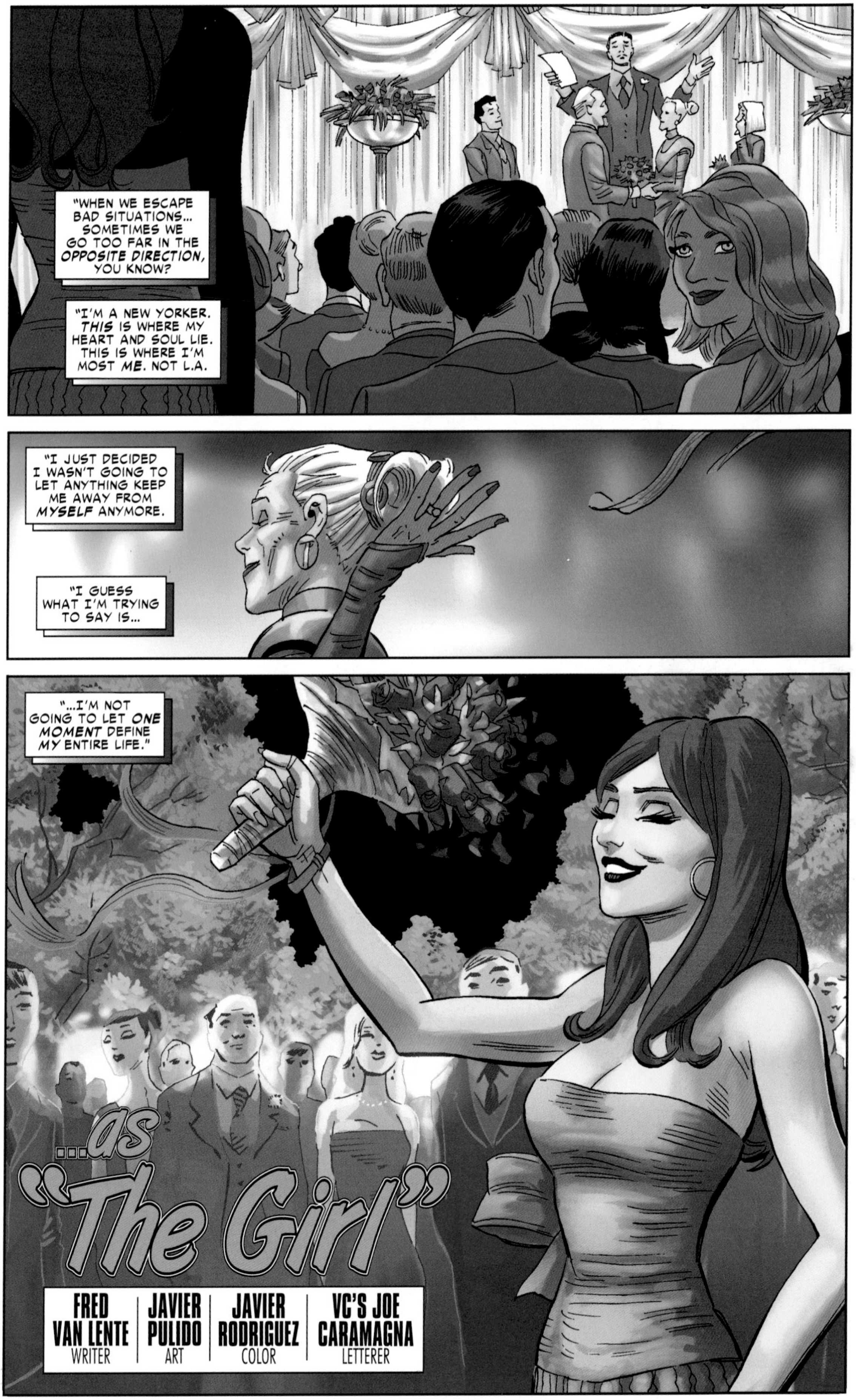
"WHEN WE ESCAPE BAD SITUATIONS... SOMETIMES WE GO TOO FAR IN THE OPPOSITE DIRECTION, YOU KNOW?
"I'M A NEW YORKER. THIS IS WHERE MY HEART AND SOUL LIE. THIS IS WHERE I'M MOST ME. NOT L.A.
"I JUST DECIDED I WASN'T GOING TO LET ANYTHING KEEP ME AWAY FROM MYSELF ANYMORE.
"I GUESS WHAT I'M TRYING TO SAY IS...
"...I'M NOT GOING TO LET ONE MOMENT DEFINE MY ENTIRE LIFE."
...as "The Girl"
FRED VAN LENTE WRITER
JAVIER PULIDO ART
JAVIER RODRIGUEZ COLOR
VC'S JOE CARAMAGNA LETTERER

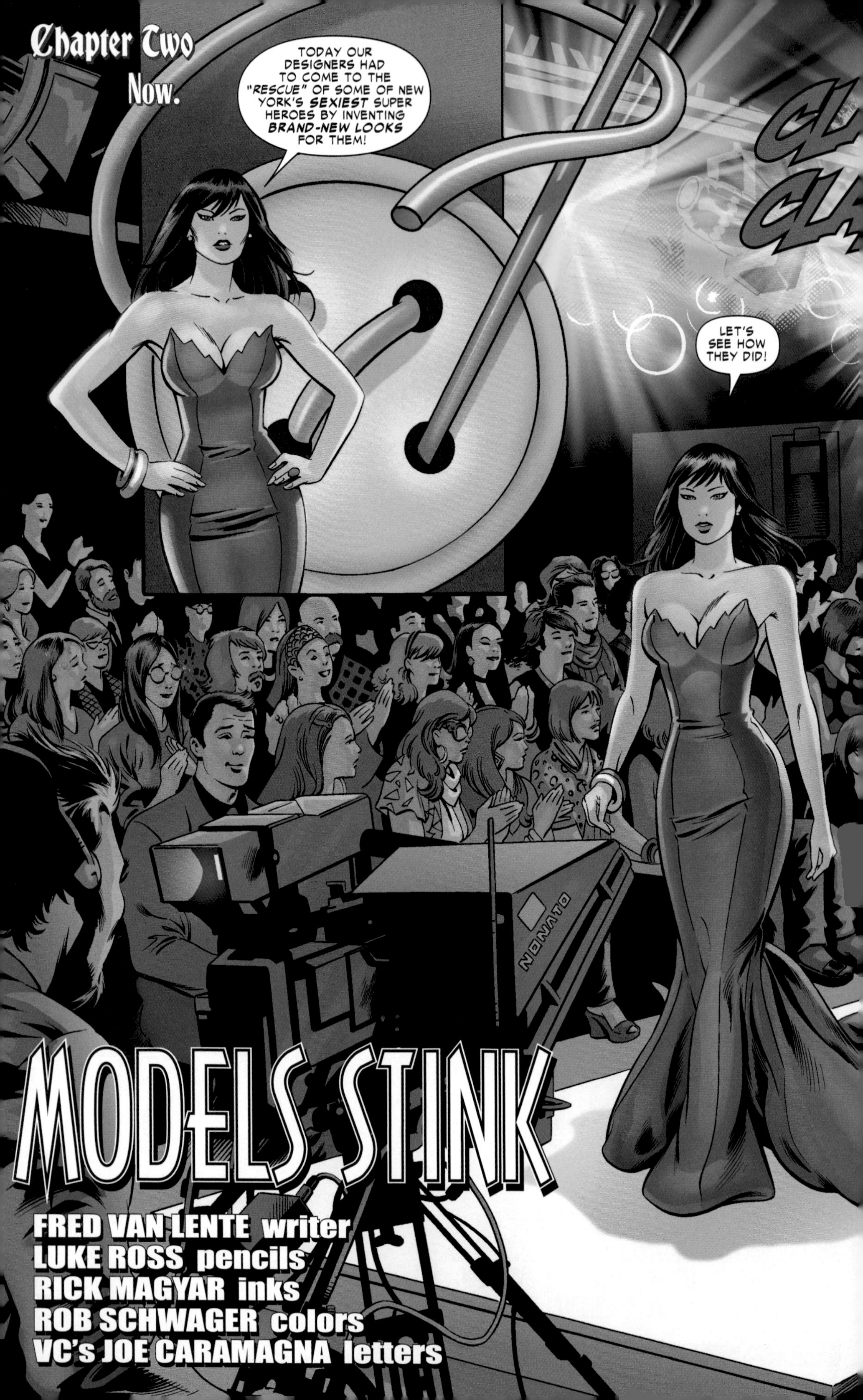

Chapter Two
Now.
TODAY OUR DESIGNERS HAD TO COME TO THE "RESCUE" OF SOME OF NEW YORK'S SEXIEST SUPER HEROES BY INVENTING BRAND-NEW LOOKS FOR THEM!
LET'S SEE HOW THEY DID!
NONATO
MODELS STINK
FRED VAN LENTE writer
LUKE ROSS pencils
RICK MAGYAR inks
ROB SCHWAGER colors
VC's JOE CARAMAGNA letters

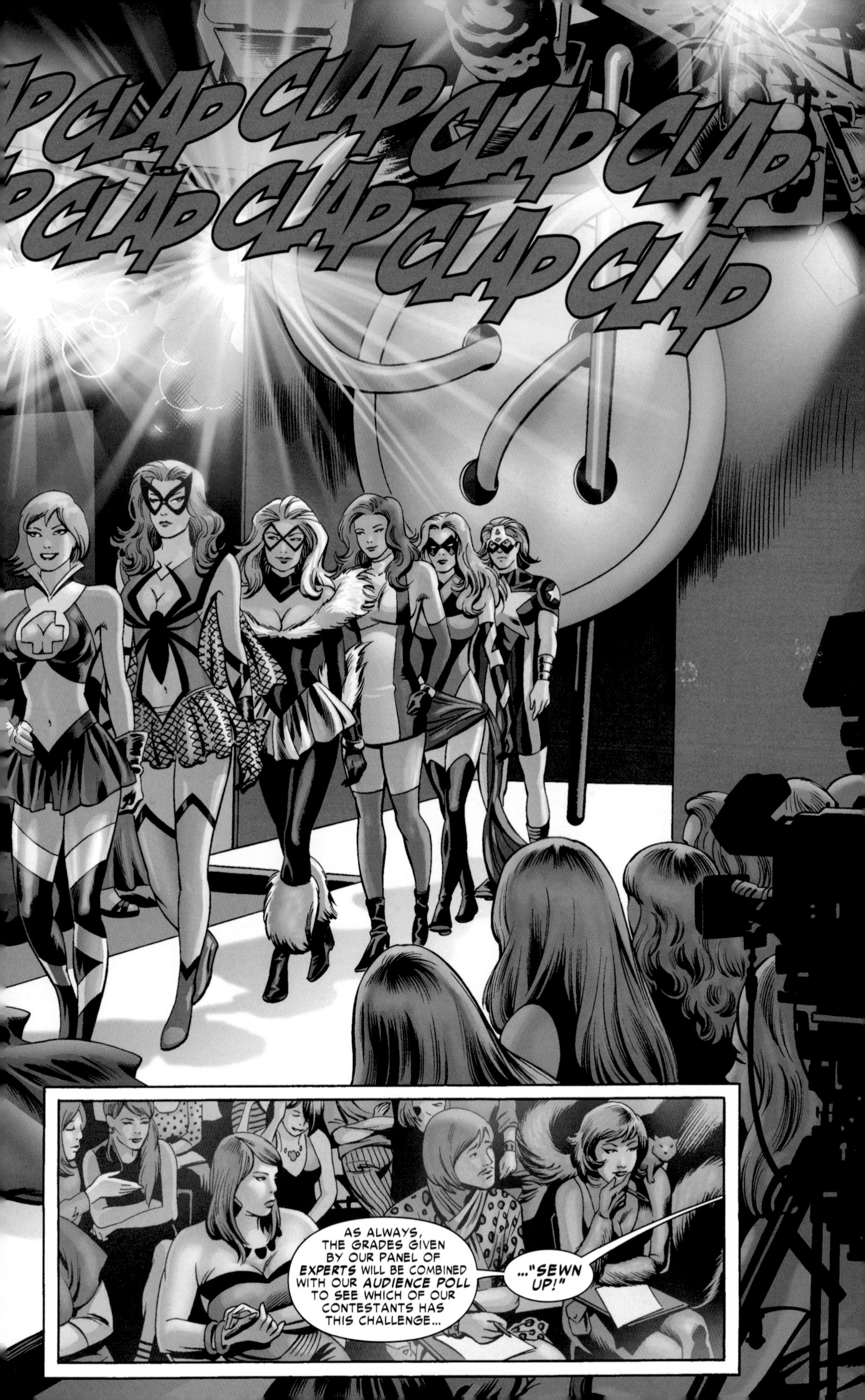

CLAP CLAP CLAP CLAP CLAP CLAP CLAP CLAP
AS ALWAYS, THE GRADES GIVEN BY OUR PANEL OF EXPERTS WILL BE COMBINED WITH OUR AUDIENCE POLL TO SEE WHICH OF OUR CONTESTANTS HAS THIS CHALLENGE...
..."SEWN UP!"

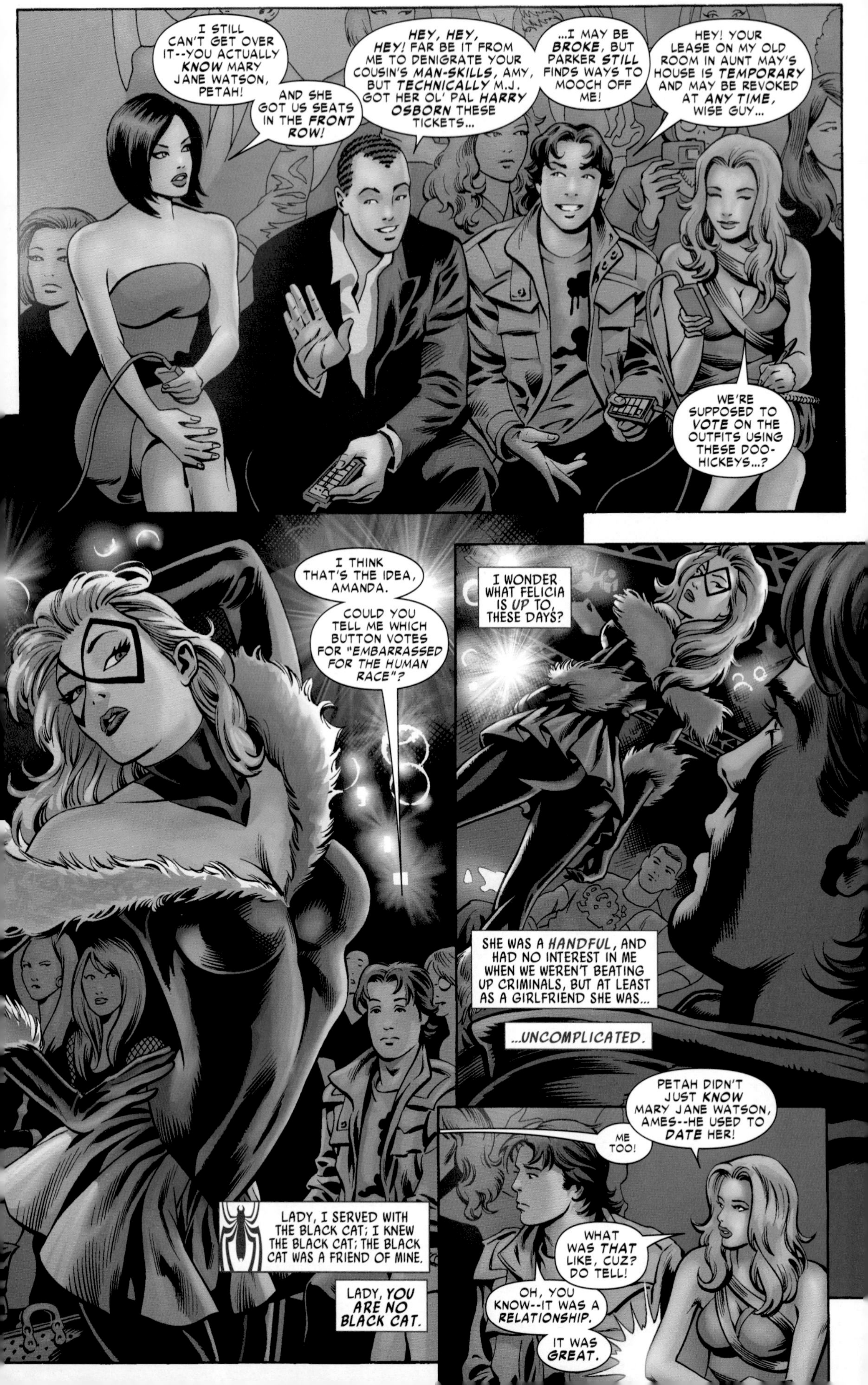
I STILL CAN'T GET OVER IT--YOU ACTUALLY KNOW MARY JANE WATSON, PETAH!
AND SHE GOT US SEATS IN THE FRONT ROW!
HEY, HEY, HEY! FAR BE IT FROM ME TO DENIGRATE YOUR COUSIN'S MAN-SKILLS, AMY, BUT TECHNICALLY M.J. GOT HER OL' PAL HARRY OSBORN THESE TICKETS...
...I MAY BE BROKE, BUT PARKER STILL FINDS WAYS TO MOOCH OFF ME!
HEY! YOUR LEASE ON MY OLD ROOM IN AUNT MAY'S HOUSE IS TEMPORARY AND MAY BE REVOKED AT ANY TIME, WISE GUY...
WE'RE SUPPOSED TO VOTE ON THE OUTFITS USING THESE DOO-HICKEYS...?
I THINK THAT'S THE IDEA, AMANDA.
COULD YOU TELL ME WHICH BUTTON VOTES FOR "EMBARRASSED FOR THE HUMAN RACE"?
LADY, I SERVED WITH THE BLACK CAT; I KNEW THE BLACK CAT; THE BLACK CAT WAS A FRIEND OF MINE.
LADY, YOU ARE NO BLACK CAT.
I WONDER WHAT FELICIA IS UP TO, THESE DAYS?
SHE WAS A HANDFUL, AND HAD NO INTEREST IN ME WHEN WE WEREN'T BEATING UP CRIMINALS, BUT AT LEAST AS A GIRLFRIEND SHE WAS...
...UNCOMPLICATED.
PETAH DIDN'T JUST KNOW MARY JANE WATSON, AMES--HE USED TO DATE HER!
ME TOO!
WHAT WAS THAT LIKE, CUZ? DO TELL!
OH, YOU KNOW--IT WAS A RELATIONSHIP.
IT WAS GREAT.

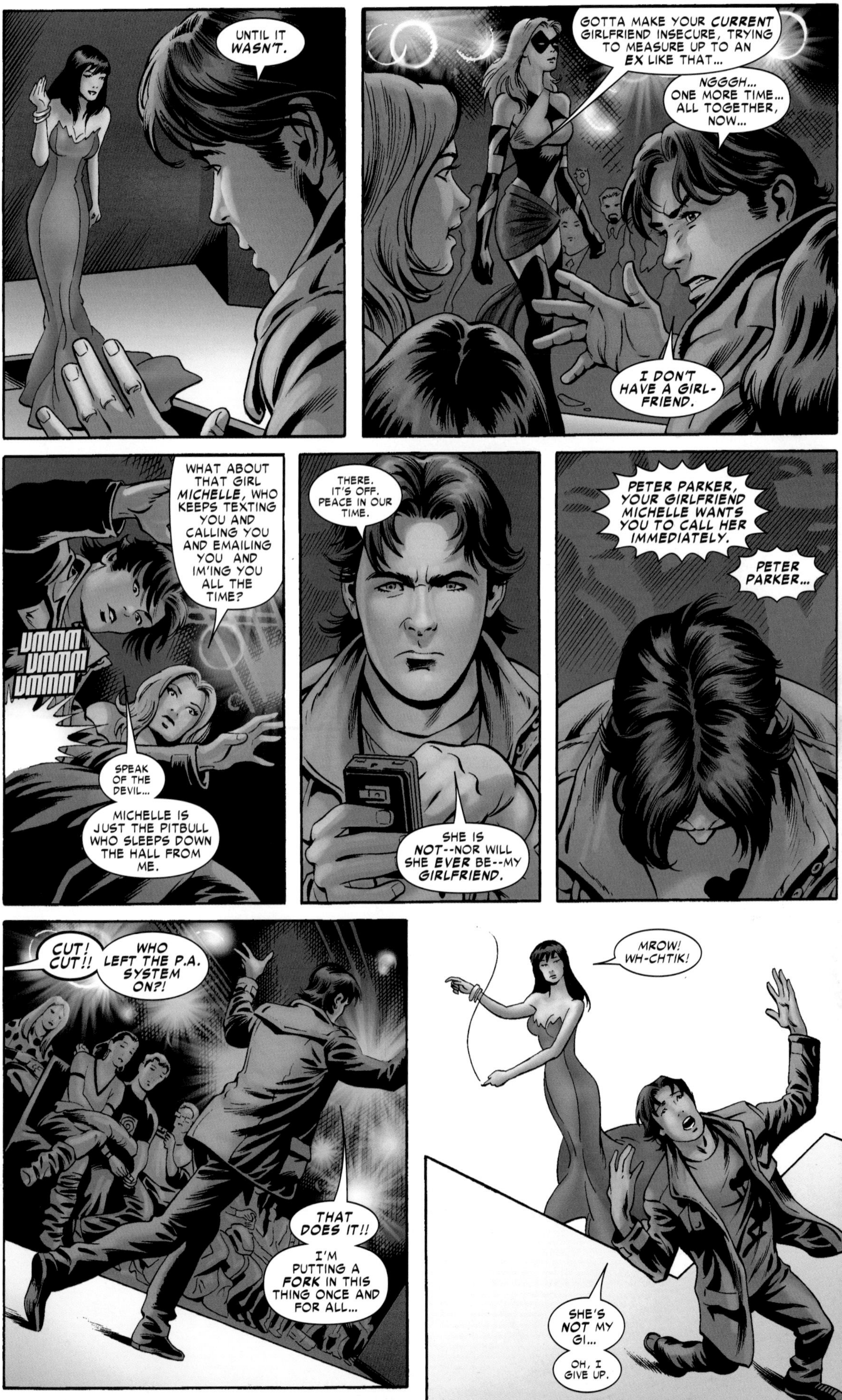
UNTIL IT WASN'T.
GOTTA MAKE YOUR CURRENT GIRLFRIEND INSECURE, TRYING TO MEASURE UP TO AN EX LIKE THAT...
NGGGH... ONE MORE TIME... ALL TOGETHER, NOW...
I DON'T HAVE A GIRL-FRIEND.
WHAT ABOUT THAT GIRL MICHELLE, WHO KEEPS TEXTING YOU AND CALLING YOU AND EMAILING YOU AND IM'ING YOU ALL THE TIME?
VMMM VMMM VMMM
SPEAK OF THE DEVIL...
MICHELLE IS JUST THE PITBULL WHO SLEEPS DOWN THE HALL FROM ME.
THERE. IT'S OFF. PEACE IN OUR TIME.
SHE IS NOT--NOR WILL SHE EVER BE--MY GIRLFRIEND.
PETER PARKER, YOUR GIRLFRIEND MICHELLE WANTS YOU TO CALL HER IMMEDIATELY.
PETER PARKER...
CUT! CUT!!
WHO LEFT THE P.A. SYSTEM ON?!
THAT DOES IT!!
I'M PUTTING A FORK IN THIS THING ONCE AND FOR ALL...
MROW! WH-CHTIK!
SHE'S NOT MY GI...
OH, I GIVE UP.

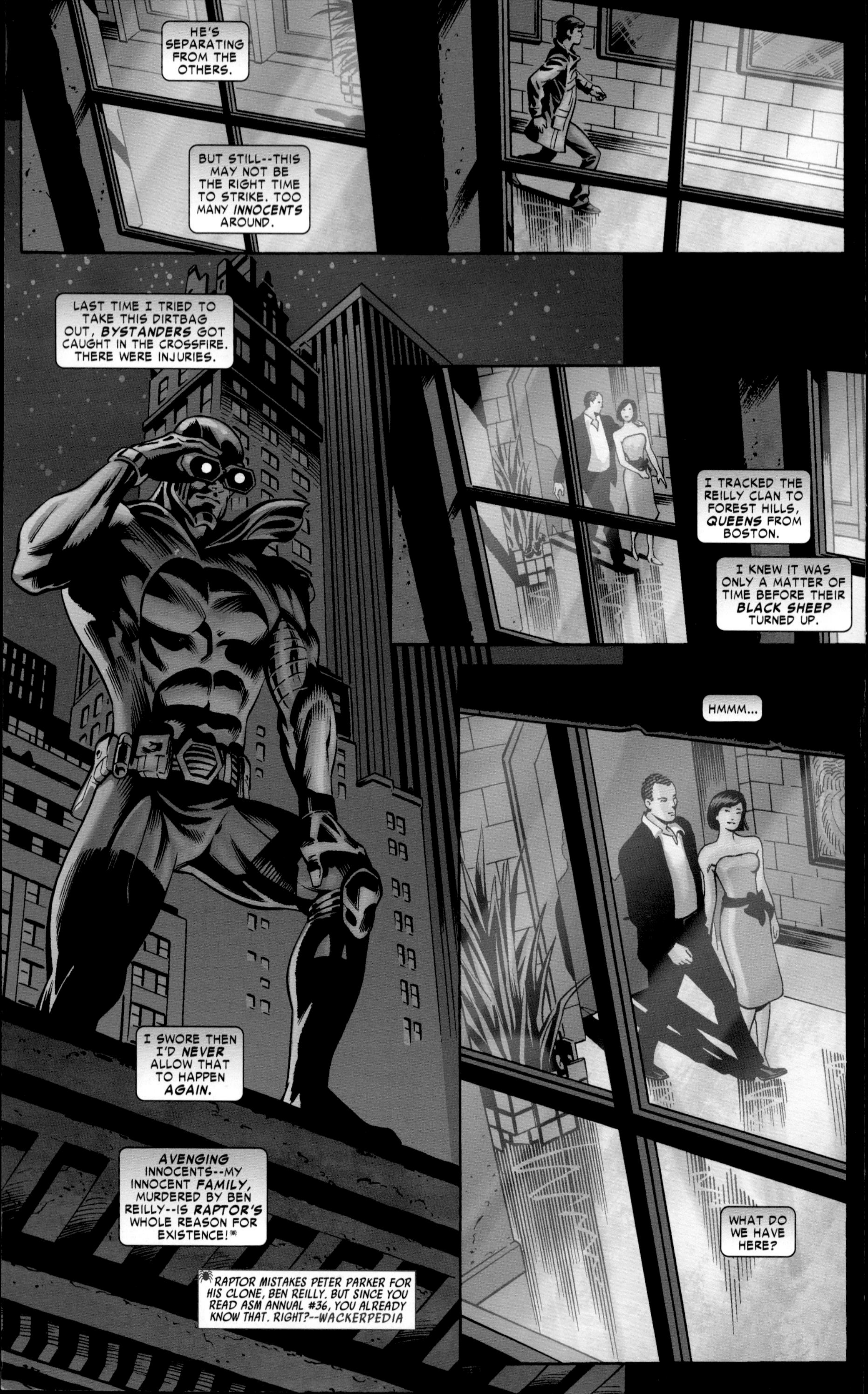
HE'S SEPARATING FROM THE OTHERS.
BUT STILL--THIS MAY NOT BE THE RIGHT TIME TO STRIKE. TOO MANY INNOCENTS AROUND.
LAST TIME I TRIED TO TAKE THIS DIRTBAG OUT, BYSTANDERS GOT CAUGHT IN THE CROSSFIRE. THERE WERE INJURIES.
I TRACKED THE REILLY CLAN TO FOREST HILLS, QUEENS FROM BOSTON.
I KNEW IT WAS ONLY A MATTER OF TIME BEFORE THEIR BLACK SHEEP TURNED UP.
HMMM...
I SWORE THEN I'D NEVER ALLOW THAT TO HAPPEN AGAIN.
AVENGING INNOCENTS--MY INNOCENT FAMILY, MURDERED BY BEN REILLY--IS RAPTOR'S WHOLE REASON FOR EXISTENCE!*
WHAT DO WE HAVE HERE?
*RAPTOR MISTAKES PETER PARKER FOR HIS CLONE, BEN REILLY. BUT SINCE YOU READ ASM ANNUAL #36, YOU ALREADY KNOW THAT. RIGHT?--WACKERPEDIA

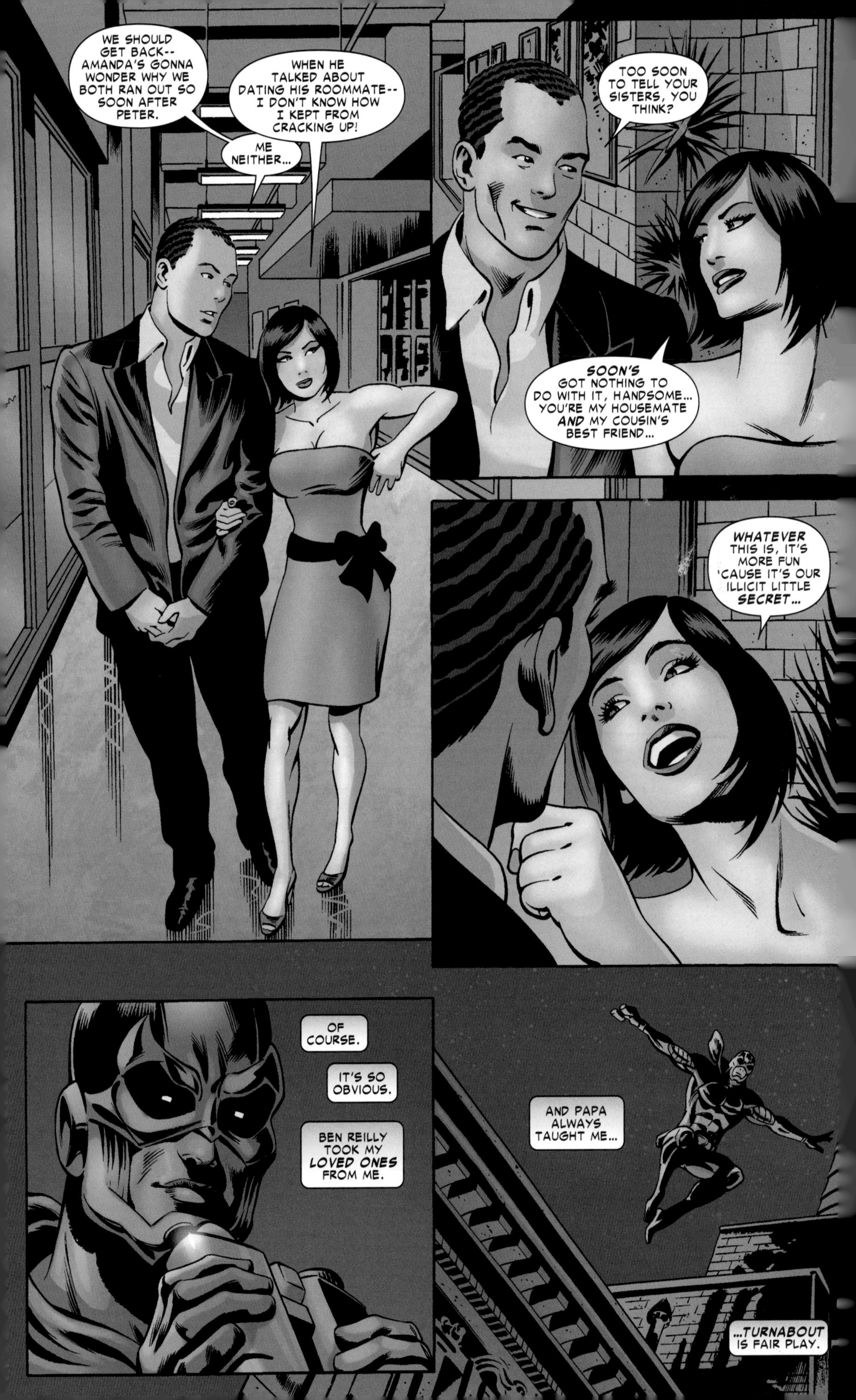
WE SHOULD GET BACK-- AMANDA'S GONNA WONDER WHY WE BOTH RAN OUT SO SOON AFTER PETER.
WHEN HE TALKED ABOUT DATING HIS ROOMMATE-- I DON'T KNOW HOW I KEPT FROM CRACKING UP!
ME NEITHER...
TOO SOON TO TELL YOUR SISTERS, YOU THINK?
SOON'S GOT NOTHING TO DO WITH IT, HANDSOME... YOU'RE MY HOUSEMATE AND MY COUSIN'S BEST FRIEND...
WHATEVER THIS IS, IT'S MORE FUN 'CAUSE IT'S OUR ILLICIT LITTLE SECRET...
OF COURSE.
IT'S SO OBVIOUS.
BEN REILLY TOOK MY LOVED ONES FROM ME.
AND PAPA ALWAYS TAUGHT ME...
...TURNABOUT IS FAIR PLAY.

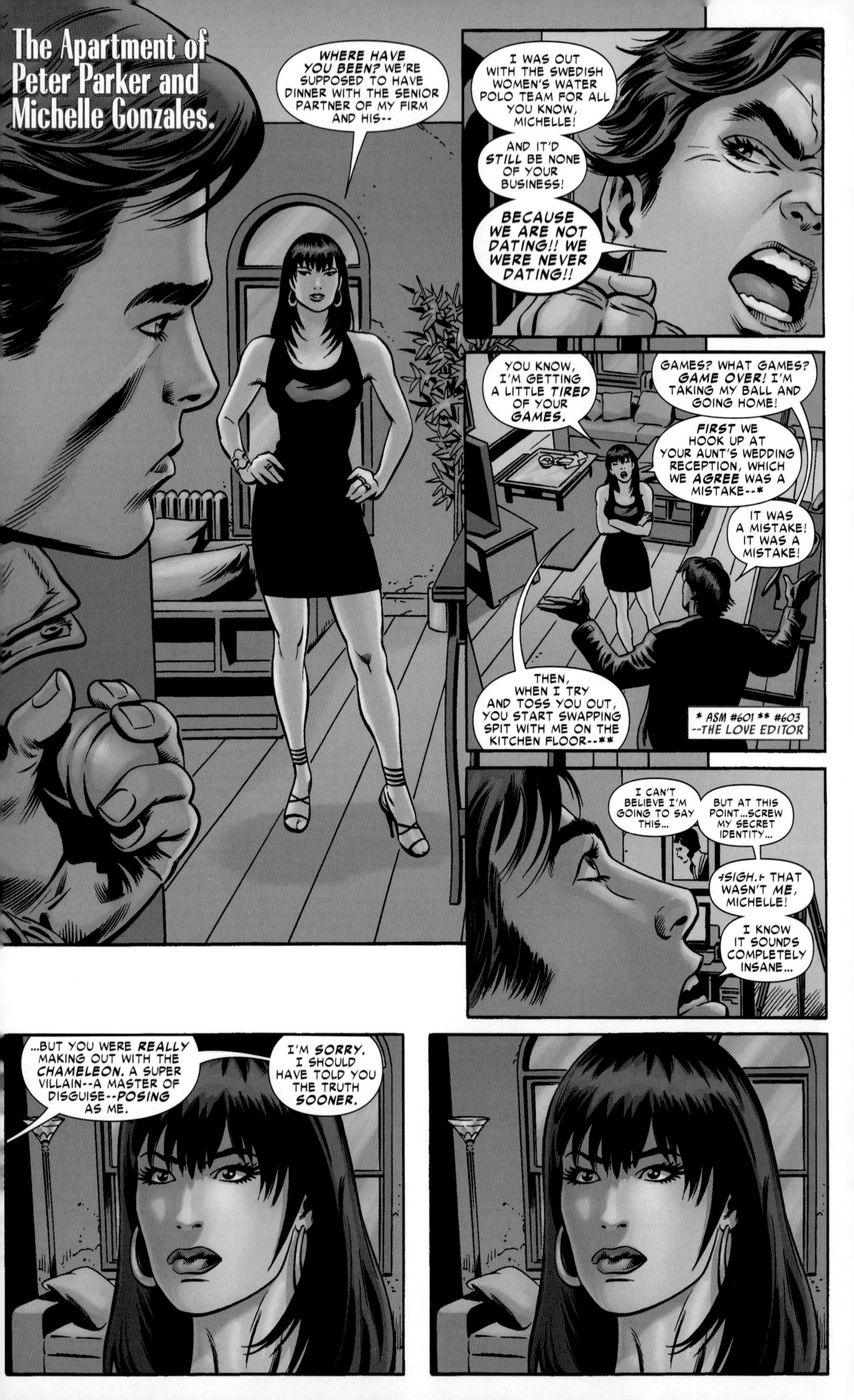
The Apartment of Peter Parker and Michelle Gonzales.
WHERE HAVE YOU BEEN? WE'RE SUPPOSED TO HAVE DINNER WITH THE SENIOR PARTNER OF MY FIRM AND HIS--
I WAS OUT WITH THE SWEDISH WOMEN'S WATER POLO TEAM FOR ALL YOU KNOW, MICHELLE!
AND IT'D STILL BE NONE OF YOUR BUSINESS!
BECAUSE WE ARE NOT DATING!! WE WERE NEVER DATING!!
YOU KNOW, I'M GETTING A LITTLE TIRED OF YOUR GAMES.
GAMES? WHAT GAMES? GAME OVER! I'M TAKING MY BALL AND GOING HOME!
FIRST WE HOOK UP AT YOUR AUNT'S WEDDING RECEPTION, WHICH WE AGREE WAS A MISTAKE--*
IT WAS A MISTAKE! IT WAS A MISTAKE!
THEN, WHEN I TRY AND TOSS YOU OUT, YOU START SWAPPING SPIT WITH ME ON THE KITCHEN FLOOR--**
* ASM #601 ** #603 --THE LOVE EDITOR
I CAN'T BELIEVE I'M GOING TO SAY THIS...
BUT AT THIS POINT...SCREW MY SECRET IDENTITY...
‡SIGH.‡ THAT WASN'T ME, MICHELLE!
I KNOW IT SOUNDS COMPLETELY INSANE...
...BUT YOU WERE REALLY MAKING OUT WITH THE CHAMELEON. A SUPER VILLAIN--A MASTER OF DISGUISE--POSING AS ME.
I'M SORRY. I SHOULD HAVE TOLD YOU THE TRUTH SOONER.

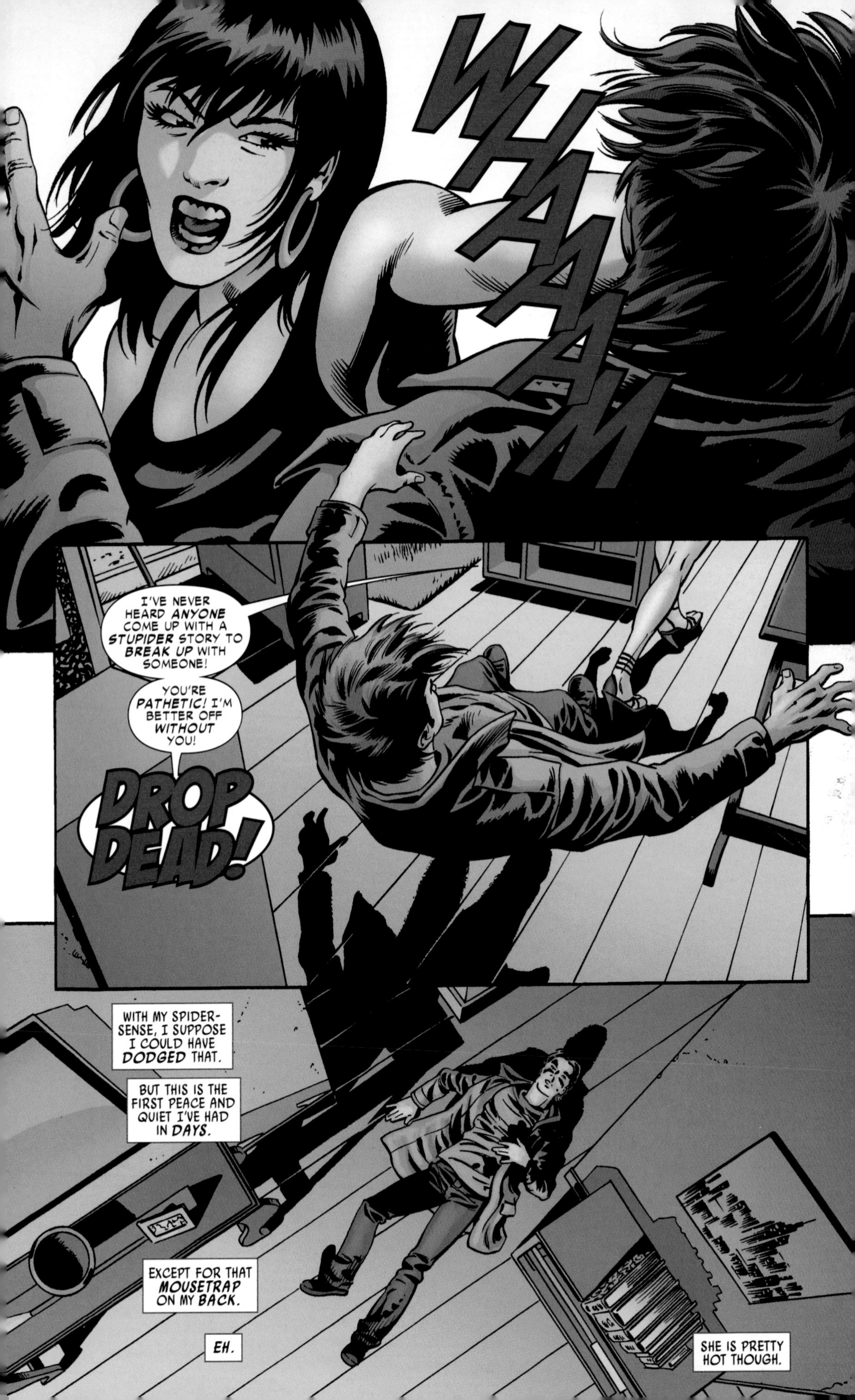
WHAAAM
I'VE NEVER HEARD ANYONE COME UP WITH A STUPIDER STORY TO BREAK UP WITH SOMEONE!
YOU'RE PATHETIC! I'M BETTER OFF WITHOUT YOU!
DROP DEAD!
WITH MY SPIDER-SENSE, I SUPPOSE I COULD HAVE DODGED THAT.
BUT THIS IS THE FIRST PEACE AND QUIET I'VE HAD IN DAYS.
EXCEPT FOR THAT MOUSETRAP ON MY BACK.
EH.
SHE IS PRETTY HOT THOUGH.

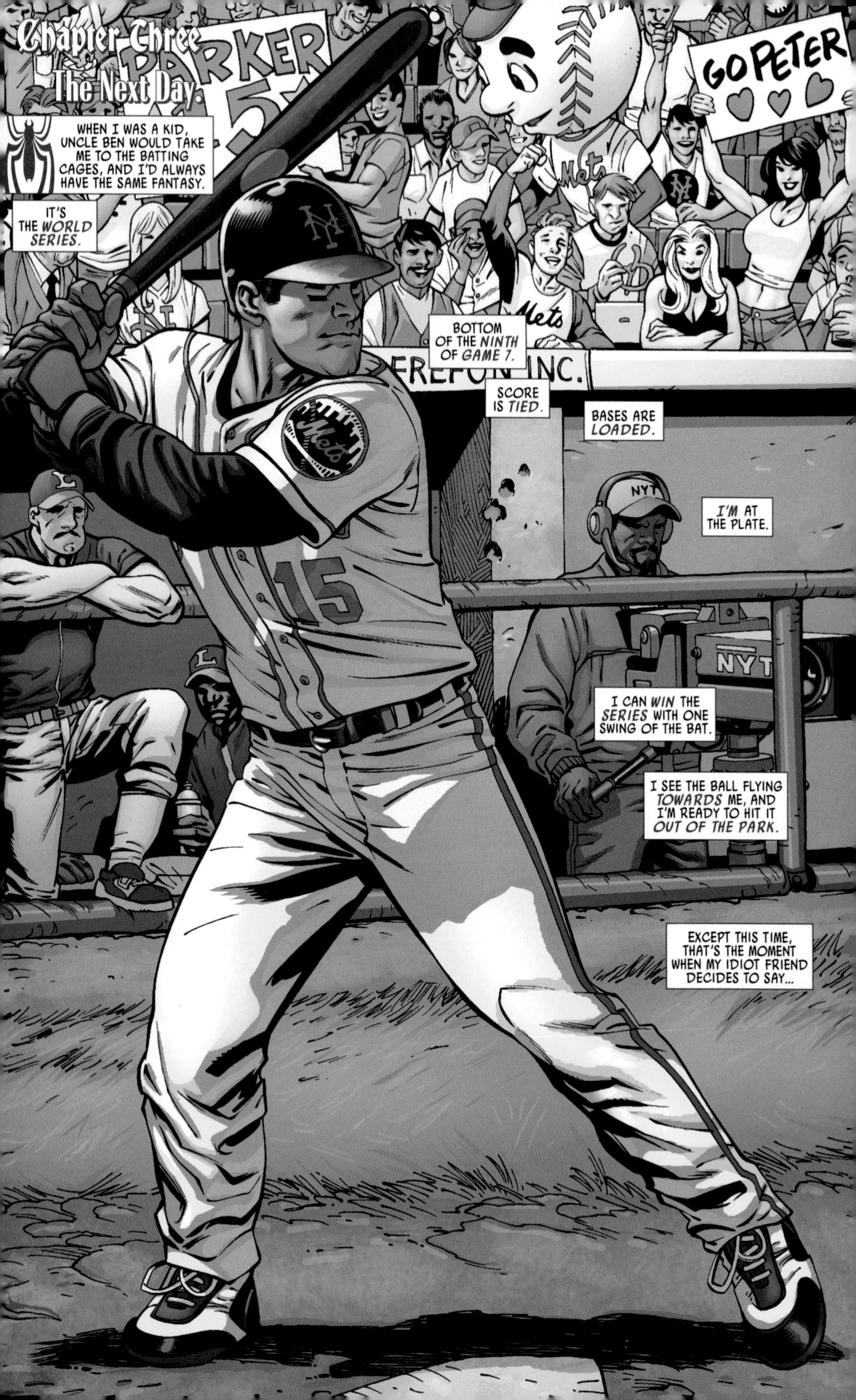
Chapter Three
The Next Day.
PARKER
GO PETER
WHEN I WAS A KID, UNCLE BEN WOULD TAKE ME TO THE BATTING CAGES, AND I'D ALWAYS HAVE THE SAME FANTASY.
IT'S THE WORLD SERIES.
BOTTOM OF THE NINTH OF GAME 7.
SCORE IS TIED.
BASES ARE LOADED.
I'M AT THE PLATE.
I CAN WIN THE SERIES WITH ONE SWING OF THE BAT.
I SEE THE BALL FLYING TOWARDS ME, AND I'M READY TO HIT IT OUT OF THE PARK.
EXCEPT THIS TIME, THAT'S THE MOMENT WHEN MY IDIOT FRIEND DECIDES TO SAY...

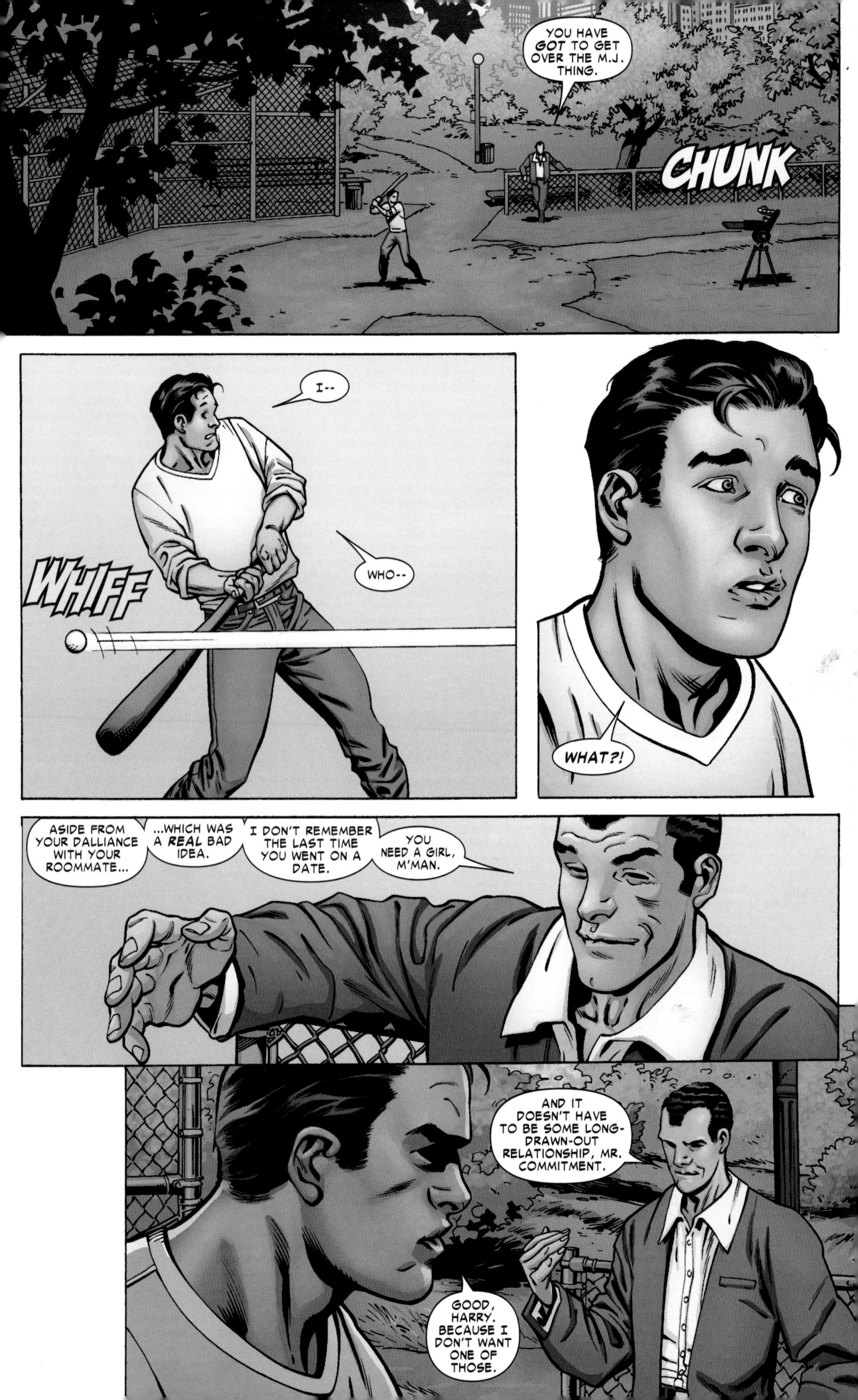
YOU HAVE GOT TO GET OVER THE M.J. THING.
CHUNK
I--
WHO--
WHIFF
WHAT?!
ASIDE FROM YOUR DALLIANCE WITH YOUR ROOMMATE...
...WHICH WAS A REAL BAD IDEA.
I DON'T REMEMBER THE LAST TIME YOU WENT ON A DATE.
YOU NEED A GIRL, M'MAN.
AND IT DOESN'T HAVE TO BE SOME LONG-DRAWN-OUT RELATIONSHIP, MR. COMMITMENT.
GOOD, HARRY. BECAUSE I DON'T WANT ONE OF THOSE.

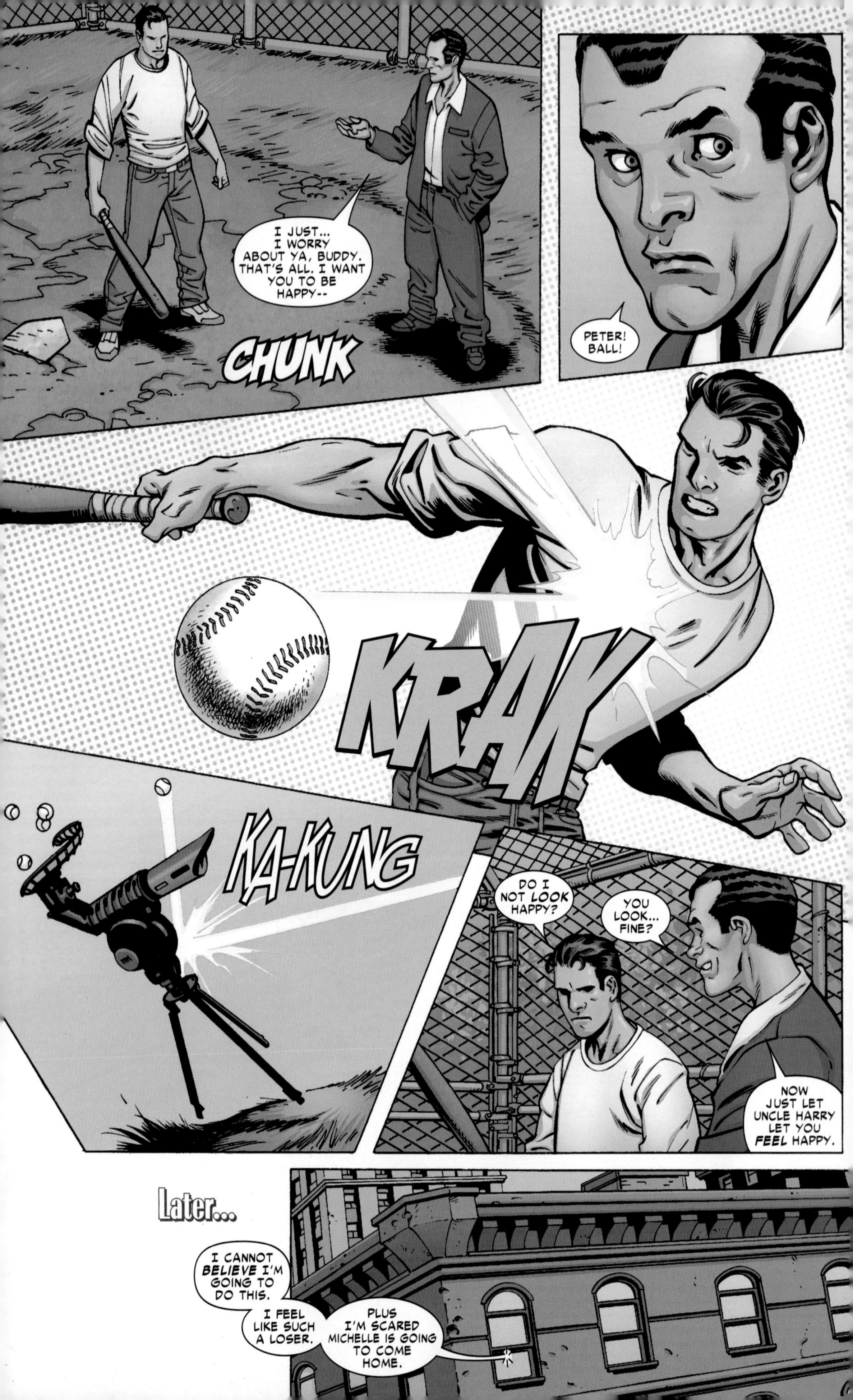
I JUST... I WORRY ABOUT YA, BUDDY. THAT'S ALL. I WANT YOU TO BE HAPPY--
CHUNK
PETER! BALL!
KRAK
KA-KUNG
DO I NOT LOOK HAPPY?
YOU LOOK... FINE?
NOW JUST LET UNCLE HARRY LET YOU FEEL HAPPY.
Later...
I CANNOT BELIEVE I'M GOING TO DO THIS.
I FEEL LIKE SUCH A LOSER.
PLUS I'M SCARED MICHELLE IS GOING TO COME HOME.

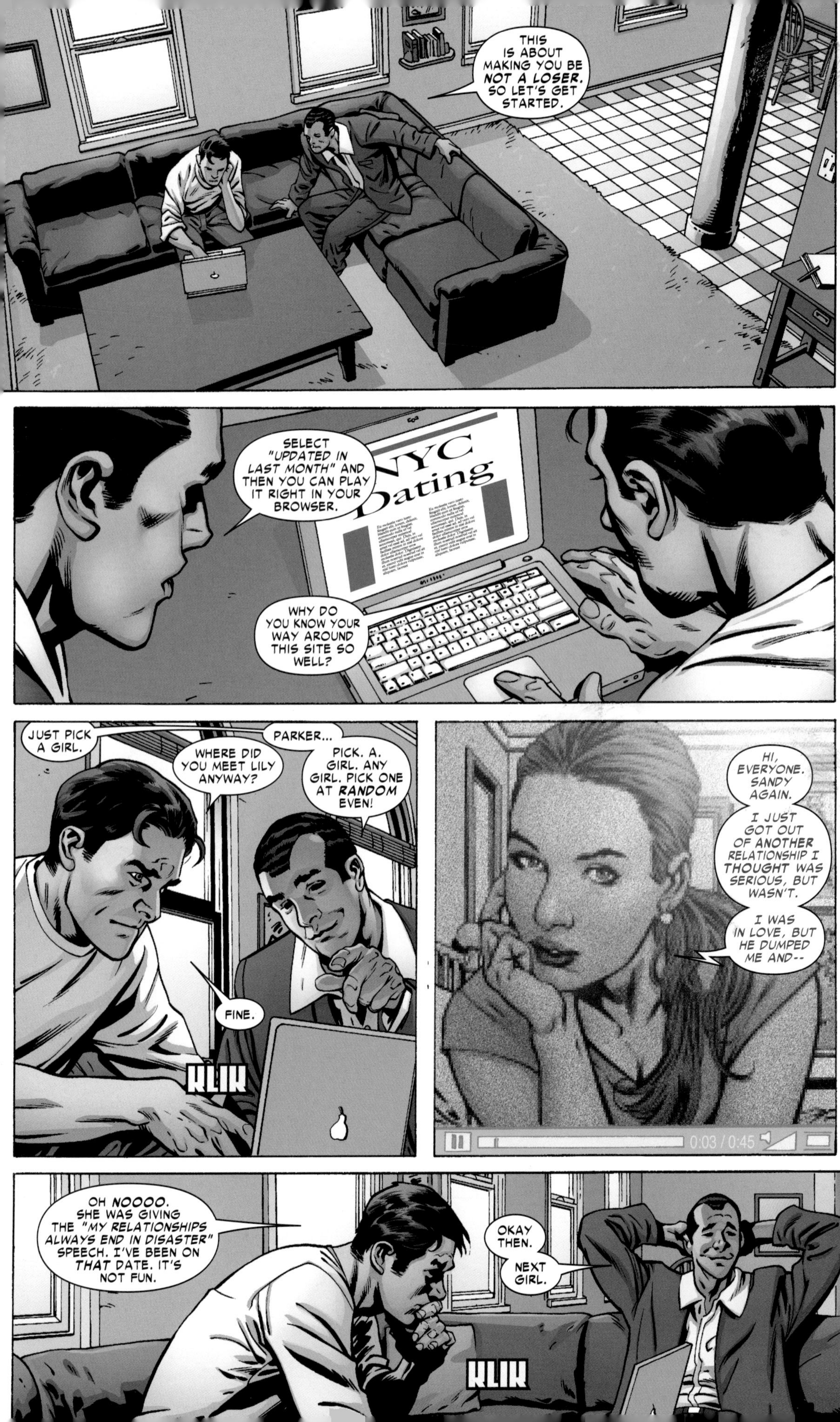
THIS IS ABOUT MAKING YOU BE NOT A LOSER. SO LET'S GET STARTED.
SELECT "UPDATED IN LAST MONTH" AND THEN YOU CAN PLAY IT RIGHT IN YOUR BROWSER.
NYC Dating
WHY DO YOU KNOW YOUR WAY AROUND THIS SITE SO WELL?
JUST PICK A GIRL.
PARKER...
WHERE DID YOU MEET LILY ANYWAY?
PICK. A. GIRL. ANY GIRL. PICK ONE AT RANDOM EVEN!
FINE.
KLIK
HI, EVERYONE. SANDY AGAIN.
I JUST GOT OUT OF ANOTHER RELATIONSHIP I THOUGHT WAS SERIOUS, BUT WASN'T.
I WAS IN LOVE, BUT HE DUMPED ME AND--
0:03 / 0:45
OH NOOOO. SHE WAS GIVING THE "MY RELATIONSHIPS ALWAYS END IN DISASTER" SPEECH. I'VE BEEN ON THAT DATE. IT'S NOT FUN.
OKAY THEN.
NEXT GIRL.
KLIK

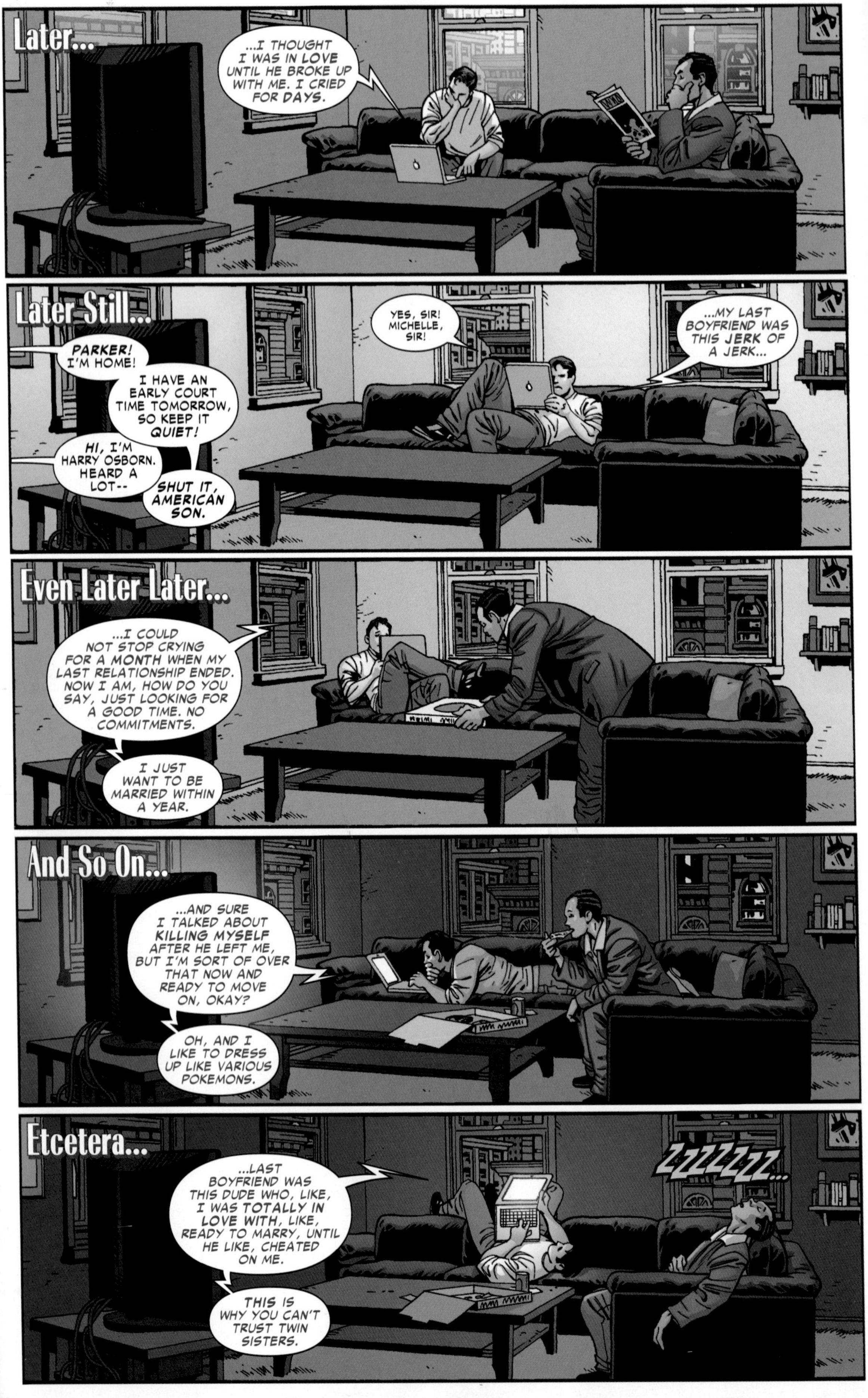
Later...
...I THOUGHT I WAS IN LOVE UNTIL HE BROKE UP WITH ME. I CRIED FOR DAYS.
Later Still...
PARKER! I'M HOME!
I HAVE AN EARLY COURT TIME TOMORROW, SO KEEP IT QUIET!
HI, I'M HARRY OSBORN. HEARD A LOT--
SHUT IT, AMERICAN SON.
YES, SIR! MICHELLE, SIR!
...MY LAST BOYFRIEND WAS THIS JERK OF A JERK...
Even Later Later...
...I COULD NOT STOP CRYING FOR A MONTH WHEN MY LAST RELATIONSHIP ENDED. NOW I AM, HOW DO YOU SAY, JUST LOOKING FOR A GOOD TIME. NO COMMITMENTS.
I JUST WANT TO BE MARRIED WITHIN A YEAR.
And So On...
...AND SURE I TALKED ABOUT KILLING MYSELF AFTER HE LEFT ME, BUT I'M SORT OF OVER THAT NOW AND READY TO MOVE ON, OKAY?
OH, AND I LIKE TO DRESS UP LIKE VARIOUS POKEMONS.
Etcetera...
...LAST BOYFRIEND WAS THIS DUDE WHO, LIKE, I WAS TOTALLY IN LOVE WITH, LIKE, READY TO MARRY, UNTIL HE LIKE, CHEATED ON ME.
THIS IS WHY YOU CAN'T TRUST TWIN SISTERS.
ZZZZZZZ...

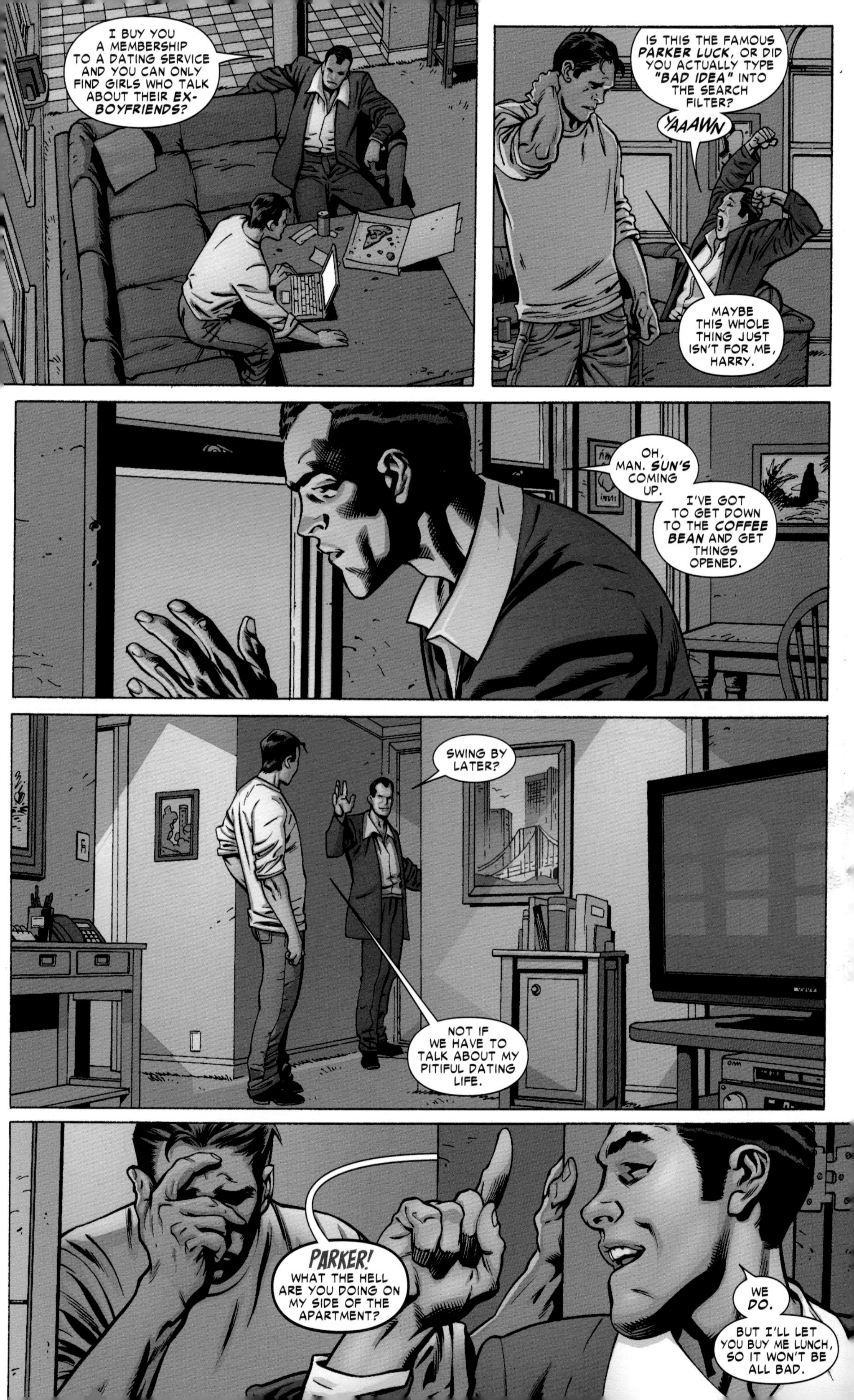
I BUY YOU A MEMBERSHIP TO A DATING SERVICE AND YOU CAN ONLY FIND GIRLS WHO TALK ABOUT THEIR EX-BOYFRIENDS?
IS THIS THE FAMOUS PARKER LUCK, OR DID YOU ACTUALLY TYPE "BAD IDEA" INTO THE SEARCH FILTER?
YAAAWN
MAYBE THIS WHOLE THING JUST ISN'T FOR ME, HARRY.
OH, MAN. SUN'S COMING UP.
I'VE GOT TO GET DOWN TO THE COFFEE BEAN AND GET THINGS OPENED.
SWING BY LATER?
NOT IF WE HAVE TO TALK ABOUT MY PITIFUL DATING LIFE.
PARKER! WHAT THE HELL ARE YOU DOING ON MY SIDE OF THE APARTMENT?
WE DO.
BUT I'LL LET YOU BUY ME LUNCH, SO IT WON'T BE ALL BAD.

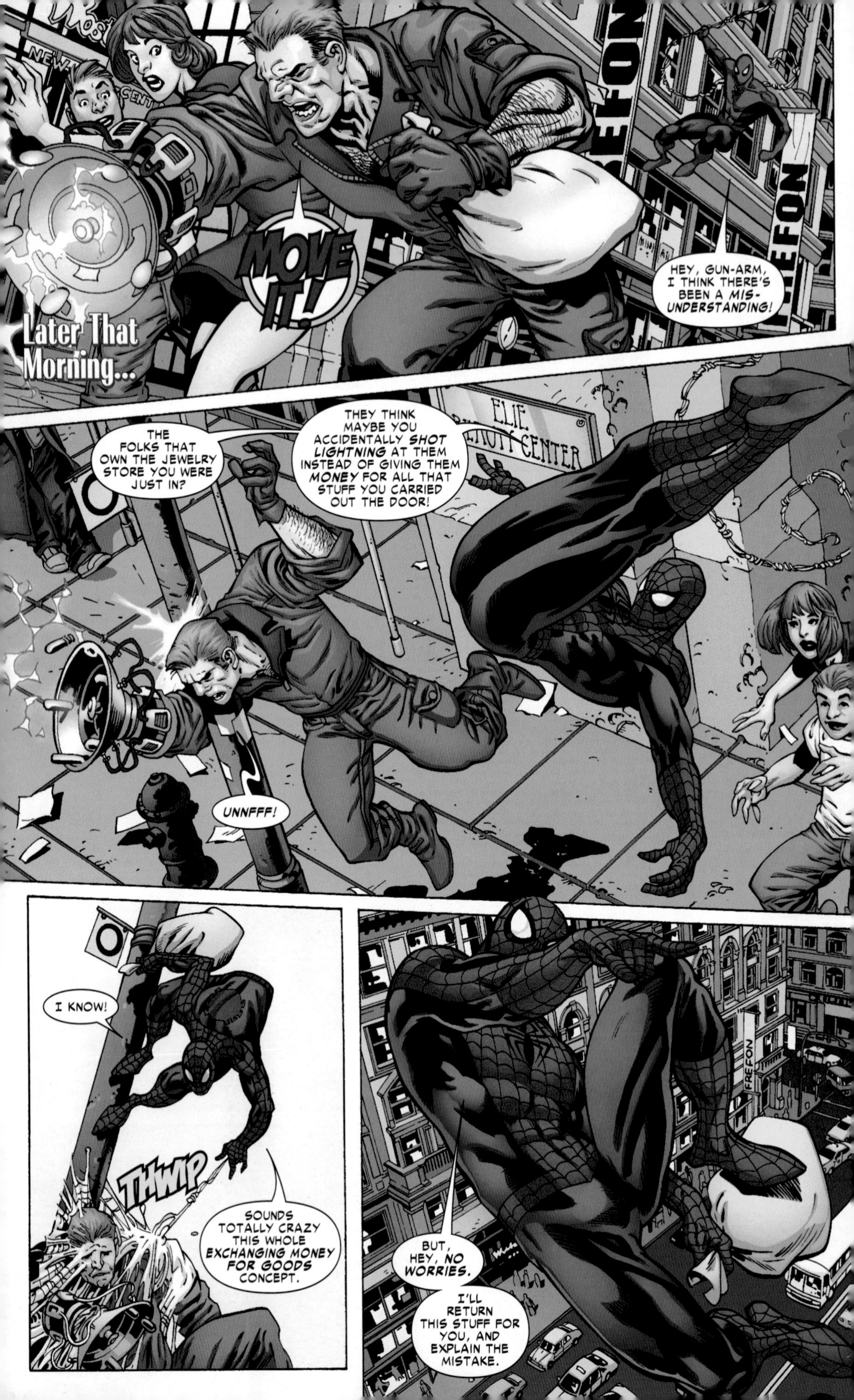
Later That Morning...
MOVE IT!
HEY, GUN-ARM, I THINK THERE'S BEEN A MIS-UNDERSTANDING!
THE FOLKS THAT OWN THE JEWELRY STORE YOU WERE JUST IN?
THEY THINK MAYBE YOU ACCIDENTALLY SHOT LIGHTNING AT THEM INSTEAD OF GIVING THEM MONEY FOR ALL THAT STUFF YOU CARRIED OUT THE DOOR!
UNNFFF!
I KNOW!
THWIP
SOUNDS TOTALLY CRAZY THIS WHOLE EXCHANGING MONEY FOR GOODS CONCEPT.
BUT, HEY, NO WORRIES.
I'LL RETURN THIS STUFF FOR YOU, AND EXPLAIN THE MISTAKE.

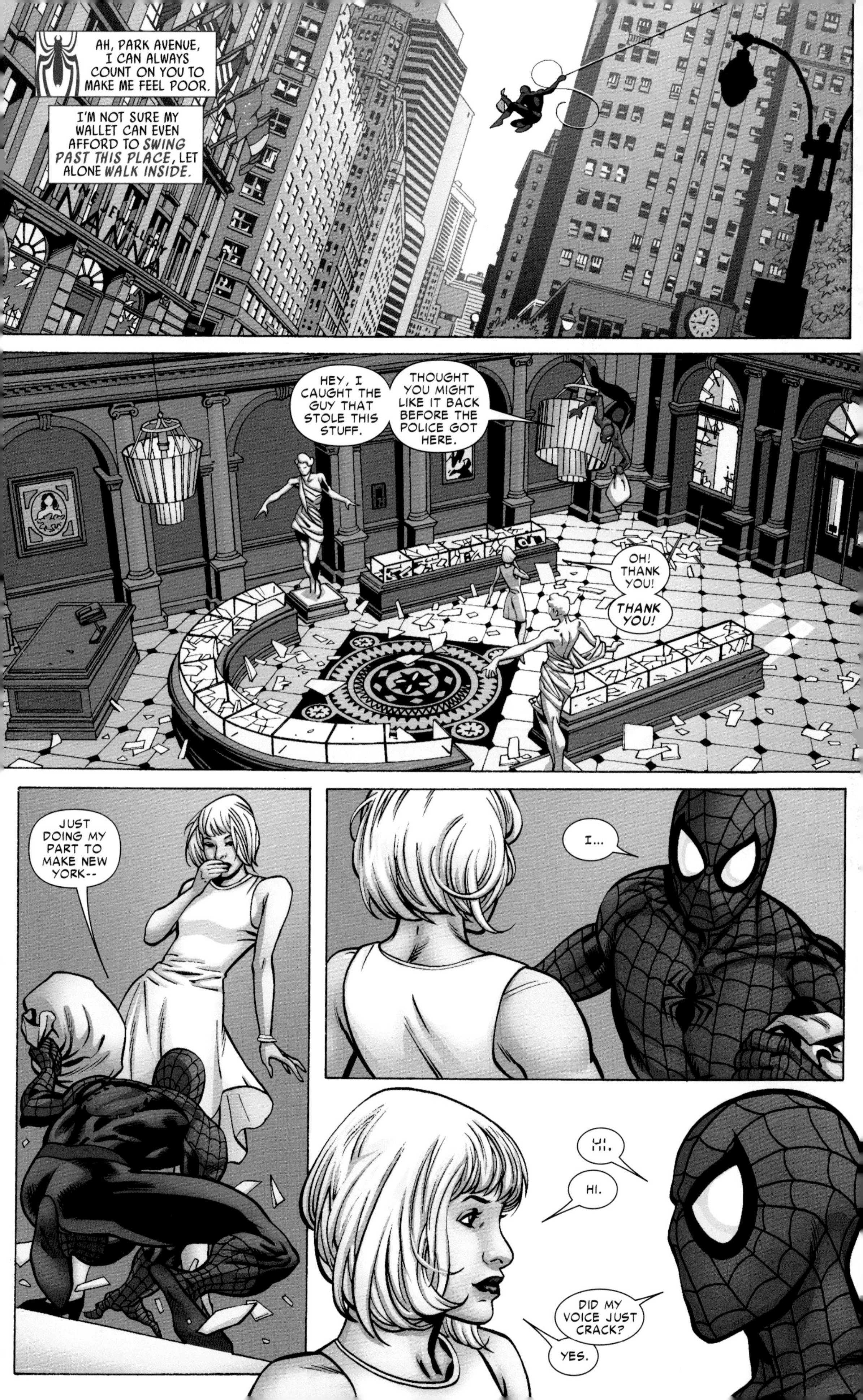
AH, PARK AVENUE, I CAN ALWAYS COUNT ON YOU TO MAKE ME FEEL POOR.
I'M NOT SURE MY WALLET CAN EVEN AFFORD TO *SWING PAST THIS PLACE*, LET ALONE *WALK INSIDE*.
HEY, I CAUGHT THE GUY THAT STOLE THIS STUFF.
THOUGHT YOU MIGHT LIKE IT BACK BEFORE THE POLICE GOT HERE.
OH! THANK YOU!
THANK YOU!
JUST DOING MY PART TO MAKE NEW YORK--
I...
HI.
HI.
DID MY VOICE JUST CRACK?
YES.

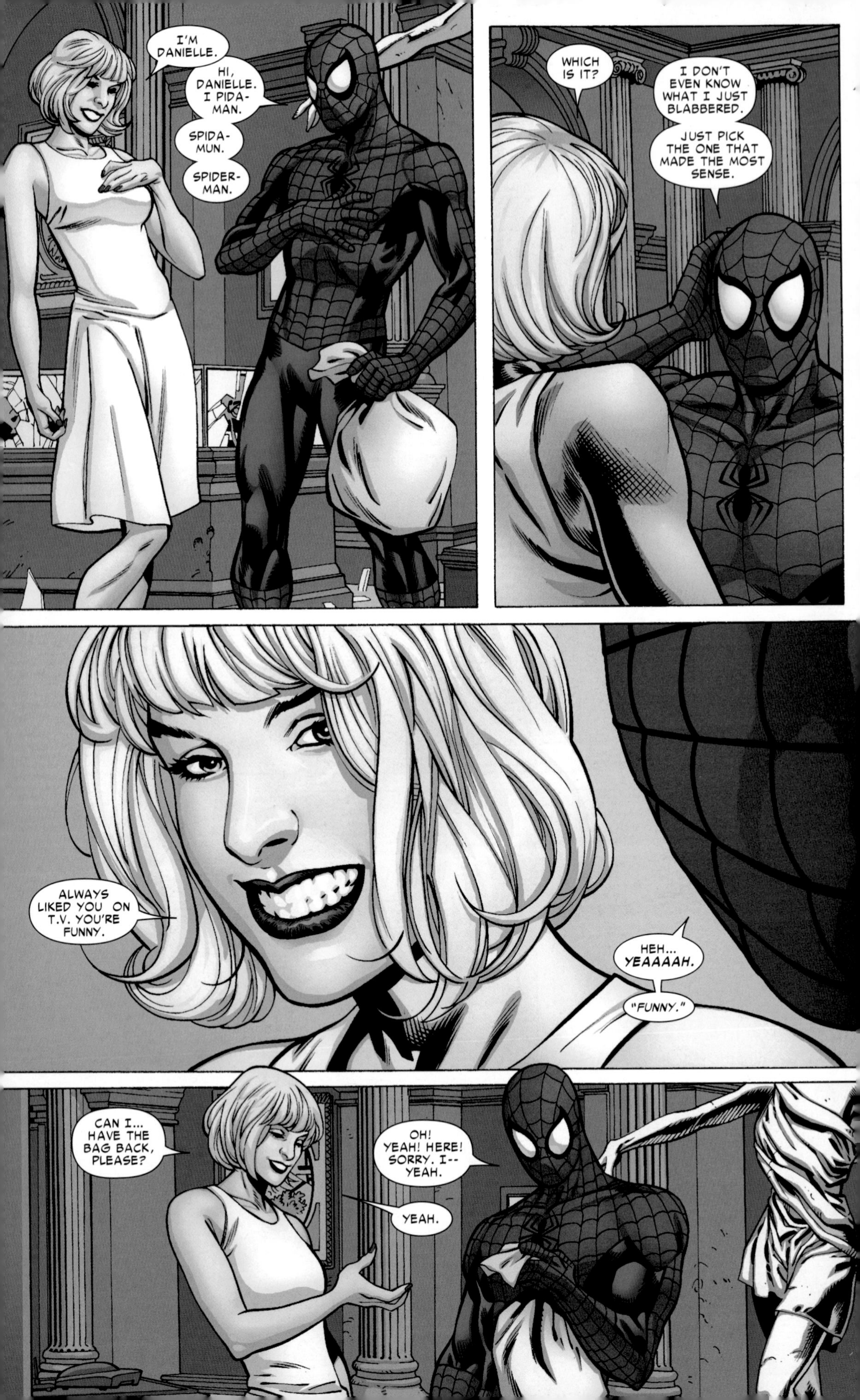
I'M DANIELLE.
HI, DANIELLE. I PIDA-MAN.
SPIDA-MUN.
SPIDER-MAN.
WHICH IS IT?
I DON'T EVEN KNOW WHAT I JUST BLABBERED.
JUST PICK THE ONE THAT MADE THE MOST SENSE.
ALWAYS LIKED YOU ON T.V. YOU'RE FUNNY.
HEH... YEAAAAH.
"FUNNY."
CAN I... HAVE THE BAG BACK, PLEASE?
OH! YEAH! HERE! SORRY. I-- YEAH.
YEAH.

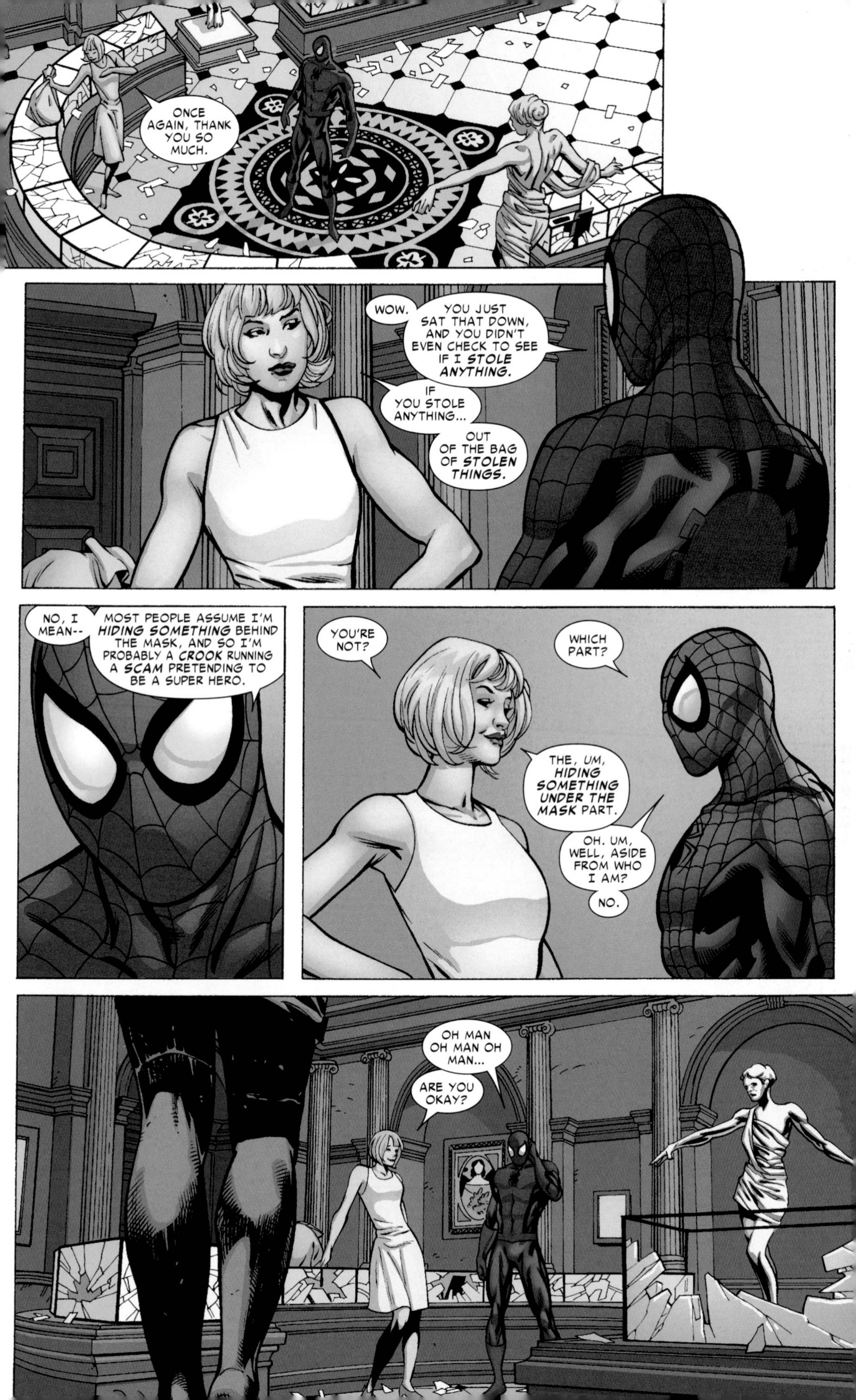
ONCE AGAIN, THANK YOU SO MUCH.
WOW.
YOU JUST SAT THAT DOWN, AND YOU DIDN'T EVEN CHECK TO SEE IF I STOLE ANYTHING.
IF YOU STOLE ANYTHING...
OUT OF THE BAG OF STOLEN THINGS.
NO, I MEAN--
MOST PEOPLE ASSUME I'M HIDING SOMETHING BEHIND THE MASK, AND SO I'M PROBABLY A CROOK RUNNING A SCAM PRETENDING TO BE A SUPER HERO.
YOU'RE NOT?
WHICH PART?
THE, UM, HIDING SOMETHING UNDER THE MASK PART.
OH. UM, WELL, ASIDE FROM WHO I AM?
NO.
OH MAN OH MAN OH MAN...
ARE YOU OKAY?

I'M TRYING REALLY HARD TO FIGURE SOMETHING OUT...

WHAT IS IT?

I OWE YOU BIG TIME FOR GETTING THIS STUFF BACK.

MAYBE I CAN HELP?

NO, IT WOULD BE SILLY--

YOU WANT TO KNOW HOW TO ASK ME TO HANG OUT AND NOT REVEAL YOUR SECRET IDENTITY?

I...

YEAH, ACTUALLY.

WELL, MAYBE WE COULD MEET SOMEWHERE TONIGHT?

WEE-OOOO WEE-OOOO

OH, HEY, THERE'S THE POLICE SIRENS.

I SHOULD PROBABLY SKEEDADDLE.

HOW ABOUT THE TOP OF THIS BUILDING? NINE O'CLOCK?

FINE JEWEL IN A W

I'LL BE THERE!

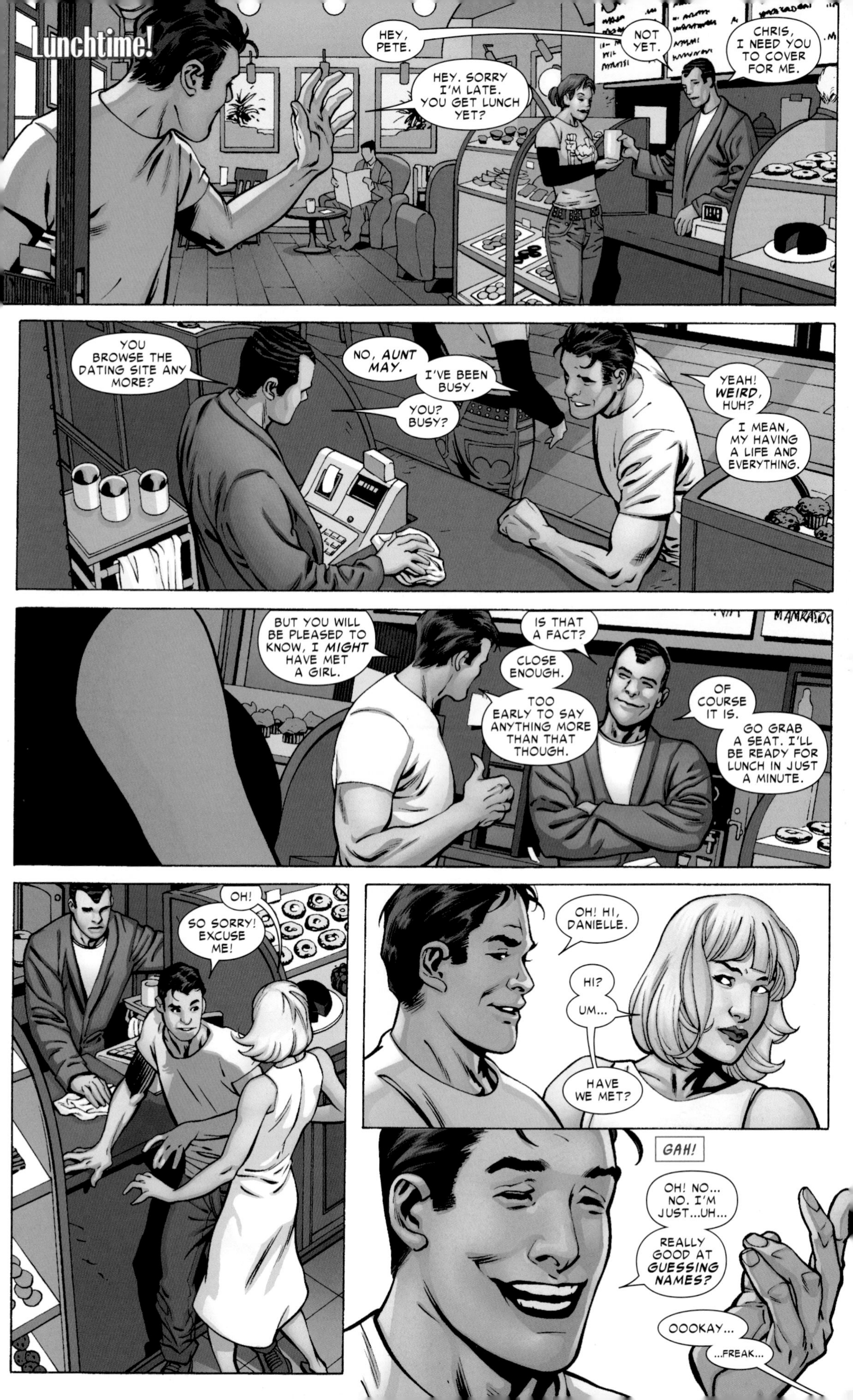
Lunchtime!
HEY, PETE.
HEY. SORRY I'M LATE. YOU GET LUNCH YET?
NOT YET.
CHRIS, I NEED YOU TO COVER FOR ME.
YOU BROWSE THE DATING SITE ANY MORE?
NO, AUNT MAY.
I'VE BEEN BUSY.
YOU? BUSY?
YEAH! WEIRD, HUH?
I MEAN, MY HAVING A LIFE AND EVERYTHING.
BUT YOU WILL BE PLEASED TO KNOW, I MIGHT HAVE MET A GIRL.
IS THAT A FACT?
CLOSE ENOUGH.
TOO EARLY TO SAY ANYTHING MORE THAN THAT THOUGH.
OF COURSE IT IS.
GO GRAB A SEAT. I'LL BE READY FOR LUNCH IN JUST A MINUTE.
OH!
SO SORRY! EXCUSE ME!
OH! HI, DANIELLE.
HI?
UM...
HAVE WE MET?
GAH!
OH! NO... NO. I'M JUST...UH...
REALLY GOOD AT GUESSING NAMES?
OOOKAY...
...FREAK...

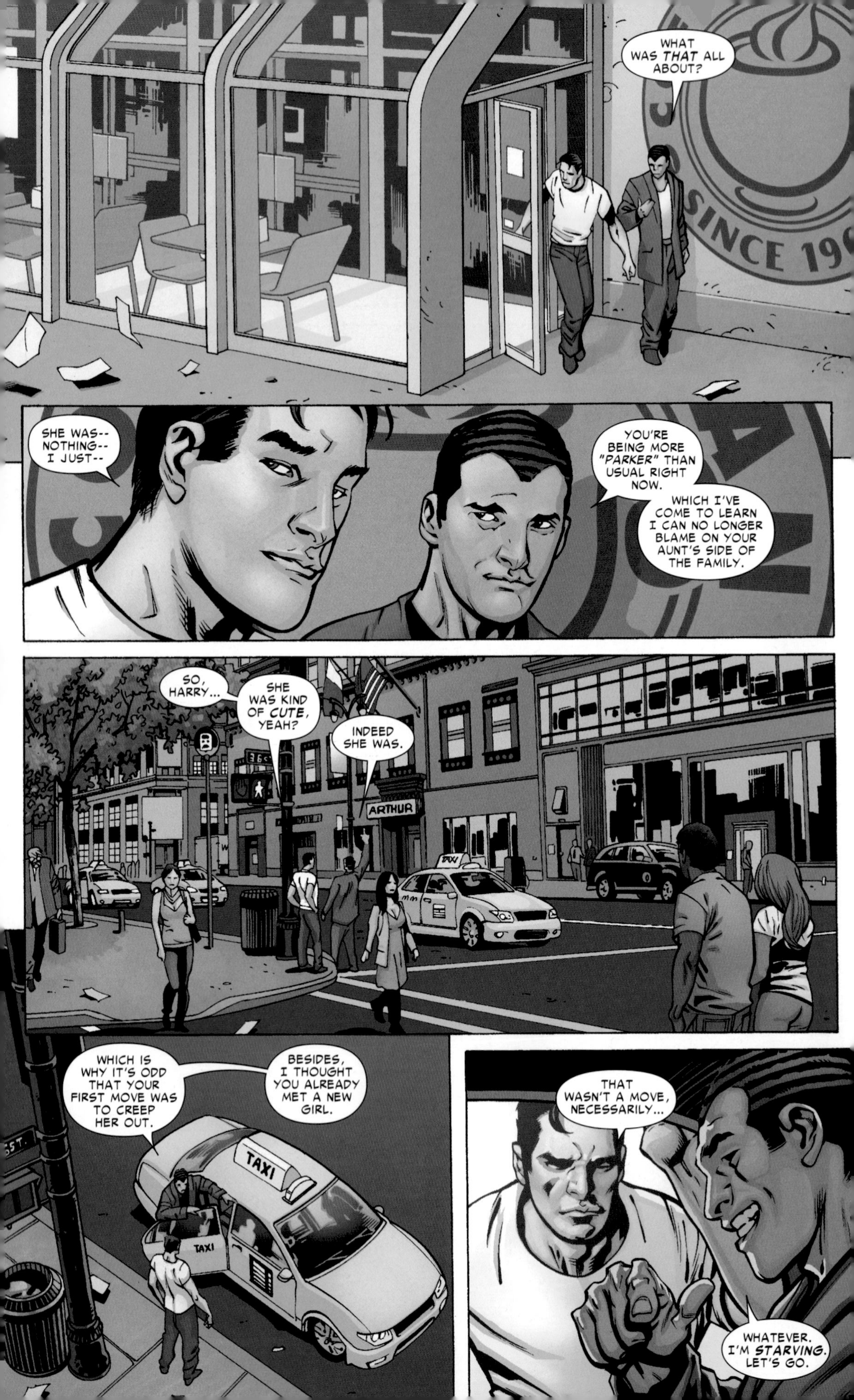
WHAT WAS THAT ALL ABOUT?
SINCE 19
SHE WAS-- NOTHING-- I JUST--
YOU'RE BEING MORE "PARKER" THAN USUAL RIGHT NOW.
WHICH I'VE COME TO LEARN I CAN NO LONGER BLAME ON YOUR AUNT'S SIDE OF THE FAMILY.
SO, HARRY...
SHE WAS KIND OF CUTE, YEAH?
INDEED SHE WAS.
ARTHUR
TAXI
WHICH IS WHY IT'S ODD THAT YOUR FIRST MOVE WAS TO CREEP HER OUT.
BESIDES, I THOUGHT YOU ALREADY MET A NEW GIRL.
TAXI
TAXI
THAT WASN'T A MOVE, NECESSARILY...
WHATEVER. I'M STARVING. LET'S GO.

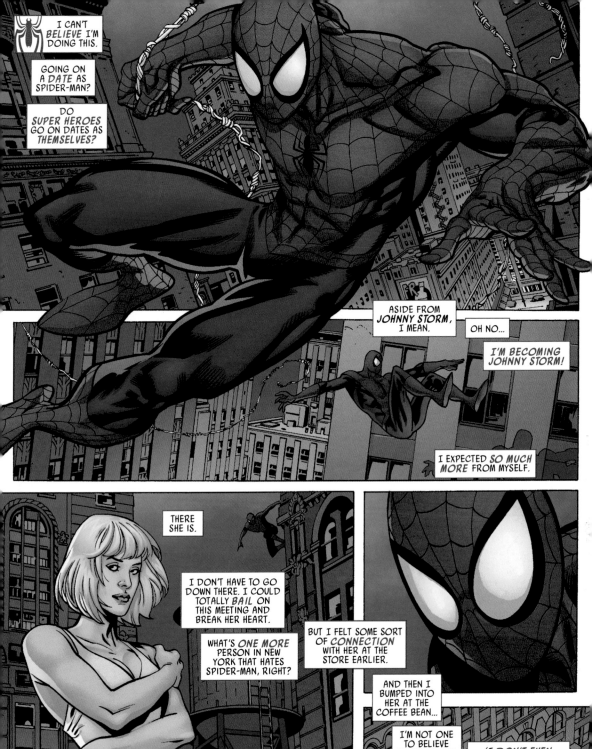

I CAN'T *BELIEVE* I'M DOING THIS.

GOING ON A *DATE* AS SPIDER-MAN?

DO *SUPER HEROES* GO ON DATES AS *THEMSELVES?*

ASIDE FROM *JOHNNY STORM*, I MEAN.

OH NO...

I'M BECOMING JOHNNY STORM!

I EXPECTED *SO MUCH MORE* FROM MYSELF.

THERE SHE IS.

I DON'T HAVE TO GO DOWN THERE. I COULD TOTALLY *BAIL* ON THIS MEETING AND BREAK HER HEART.

WHAT'S *ONE MORE* PERSON IN NEW YORK THAT HATES SPIDER-MAN, RIGHT?

BUT I FELT SOME SORT OF *CONNECTION* WITH HER AT THE STORE EARLIER.

AND THEN I BUMPED INTO HER AT THE COFFEE BEAN...

I'M NOT ONE TO BELIEVE IN *SIGNS* AND *PORTENTS*--

(I *DON'T EVEN KNOW* WHAT A *PORTENT* IS, NOW THAT I THINK ABOUT IT...)

OK, PARKER. STOP TALKING TO YOURSELF. GO DOWN THERE AND SAY--

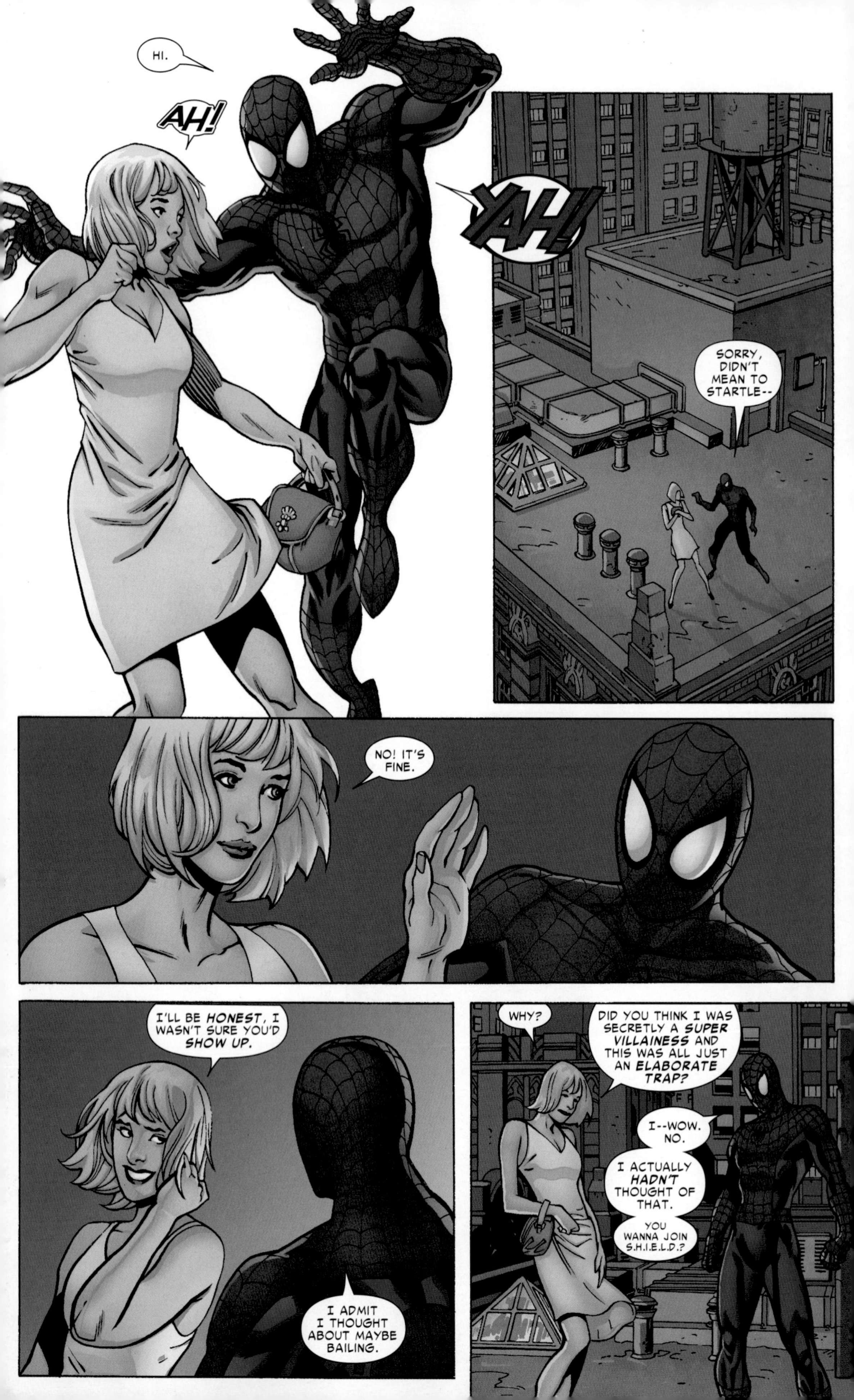
HI.
AH!
YAH!
SORRY, DIDN'T MEAN TO STARTLE--
NO! IT'S FINE.
I'LL BE HONEST, I WASN'T SURE YOU'D SHOW UP.
I ADMIT I THOUGHT ABOUT MAYBE BAILING.
WHY?
DID YOU THINK I WAS SECRETLY A SUPER VILLAINESS AND THIS WAS ALL JUST AN ELABORATE TRAP?
I--WOW. NO.
I ACTUALLY HADN'T THOUGHT OF THAT.
YOU WANNA JOIN S.H.I.E.L.D.?

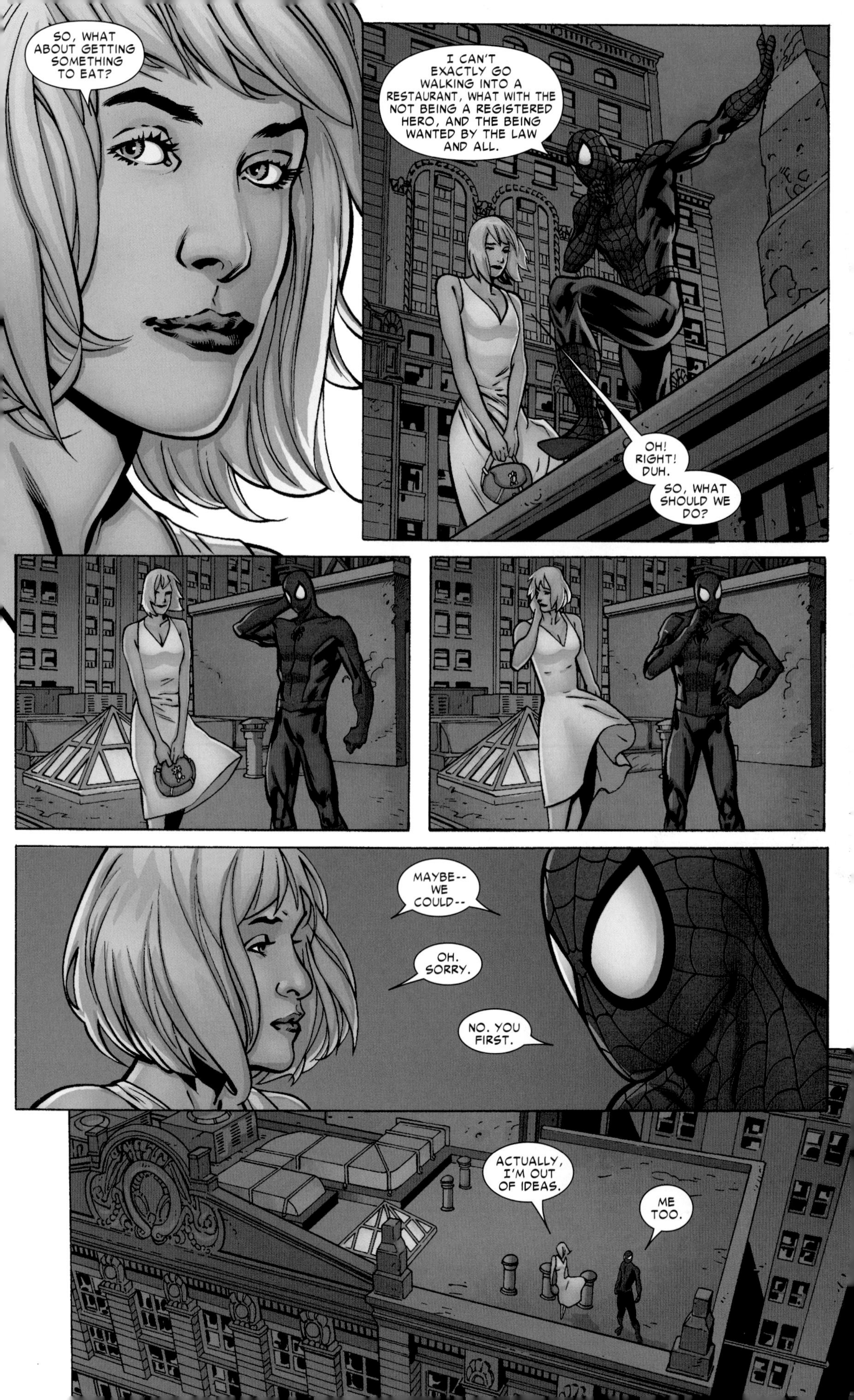
SO, WHAT ABOUT GETTING SOMETHING TO EAT?
I CAN'T EXACTLY GO WALKING INTO A RESTAURANT, WHAT WITH THE NOT BEING A REGISTERED HERO, AND THE BEING WANTED BY THE LAW AND ALL.
OH! RIGHT! DUH.
SO, WHAT SHOULD WE DO?
MAYBE-- WE COULD--
OH. SORRY.
NO. YOU FIRST.
ACTUALLY, I'M OUT OF IDEAS.
ME TOO.

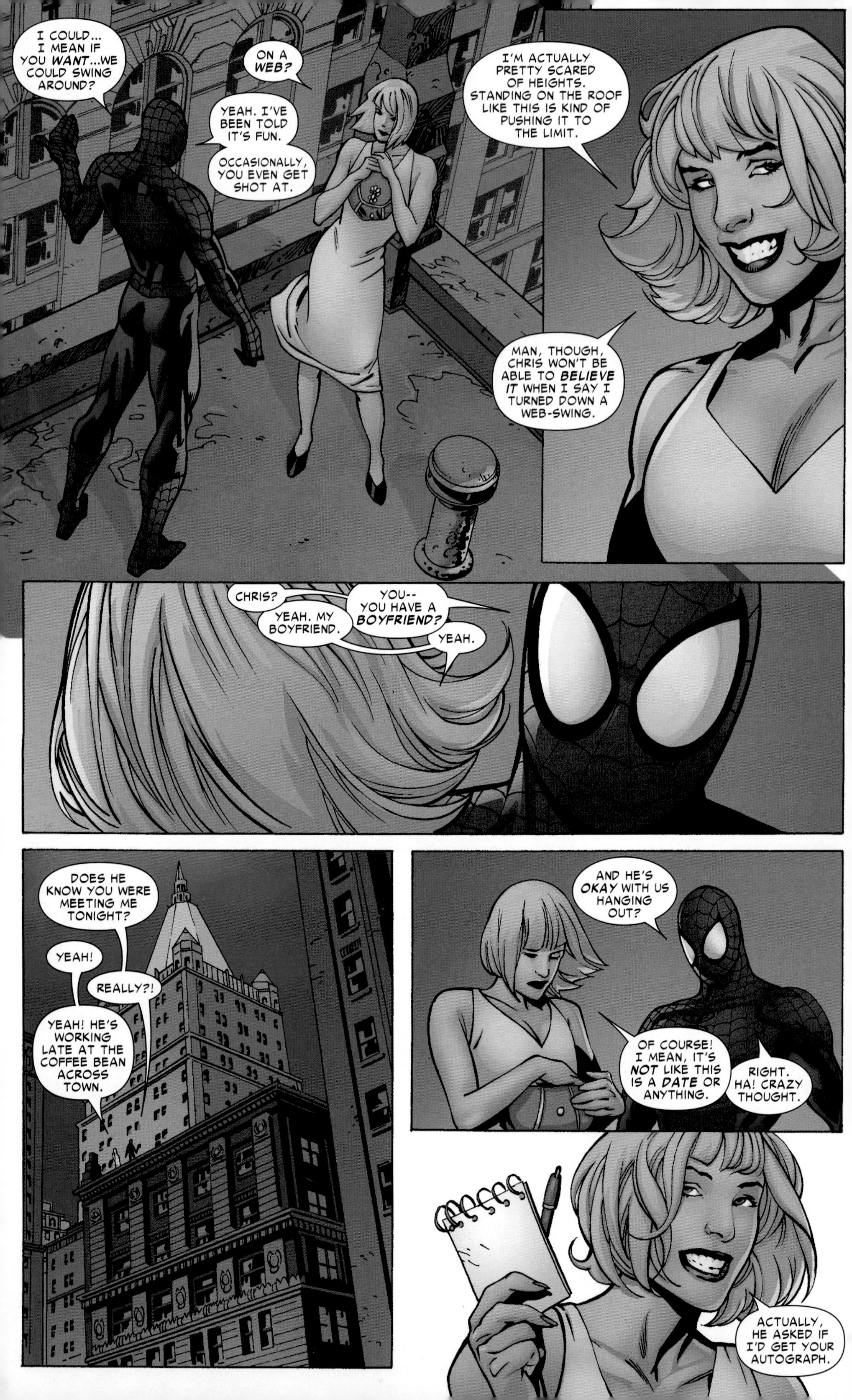
I COULD... I MEAN IF YOU *WANT*...WE COULD SWING AROUND?
ON A *WEB?*
YEAH. I'VE BEEN TOLD IT'S FUN.
OCCASIONALLY, YOU EVEN GET SHOT AT.
I'M ACTUALLY PRETTY SCARED OF HEIGHTS. STANDING ON THE ROOF LIKE THIS IS KIND OF PUSHING IT TO THE LIMIT.
MAN, THOUGH, CHRIS WON'T BE ABLE TO *BELIEVE IT* WHEN I SAY I TURNED DOWN A WEB-SWING.
CHRIS?
YEAH. MY BOYFRIEND.
YOU-- YOU HAVE A *BOYFRIEND?*
YEAH.
DOES HE KNOW YOU WERE MEETING ME TONIGHT?
YEAH!
REALLY?!
YEAH! HE'S WORKING LATE AT THE COFFEE BEAN ACROSS TOWN.
AND HE'S *OKAY* WITH US HANGING OUT?
OF COURSE! I MEAN, IT'S *NOT* LIKE THIS IS A *DATE* OR ANYTHING.
RIGHT. HA! CRAZY THOUGHT.
ACTUALLY, HE ASKED IF I'D GET YOUR AUTOGRAPH.

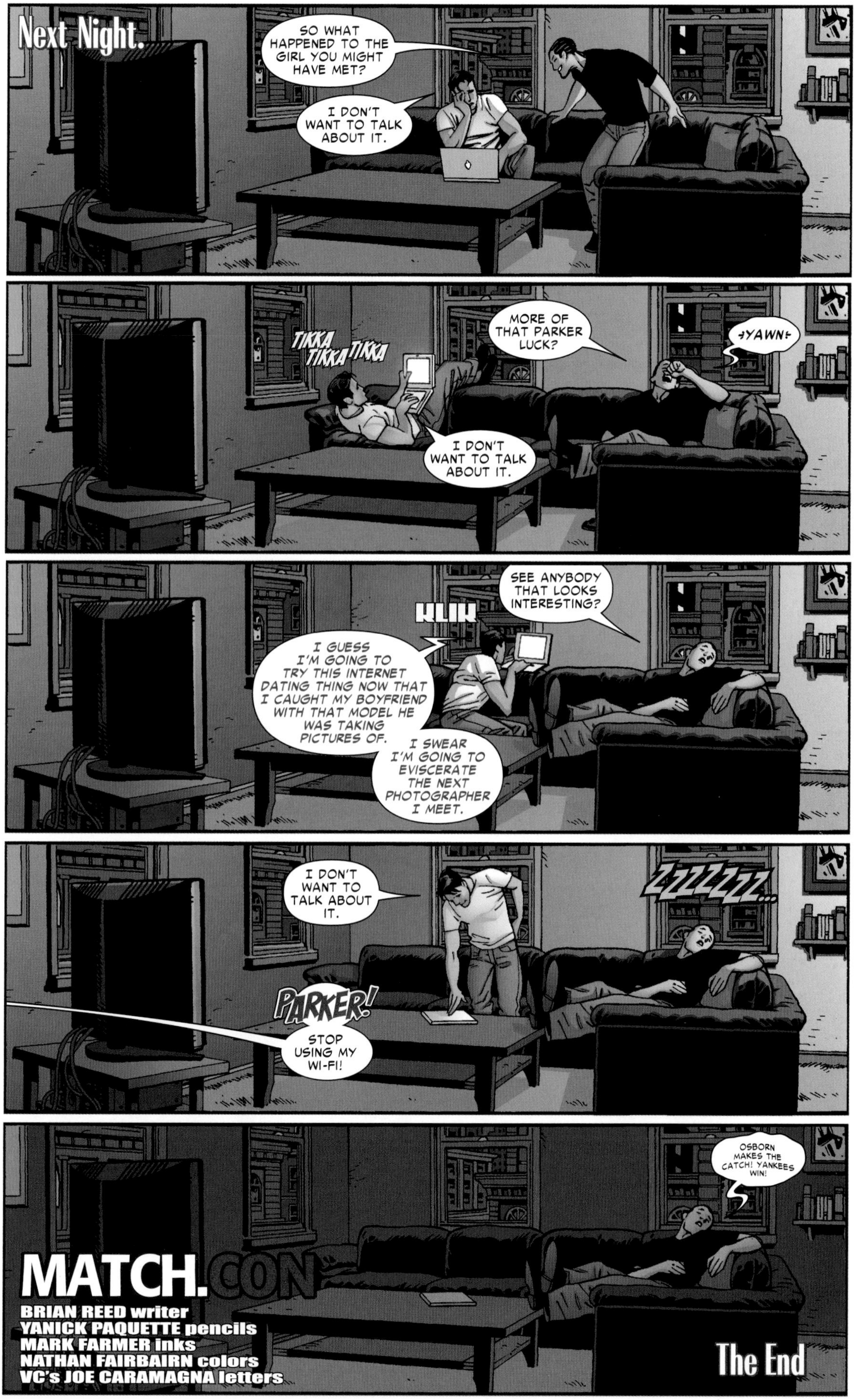
Next Night.
SO WHAT HAPPENED TO THE GIRL YOU MIGHT HAVE MET?
I DON'T WANT TO TALK ABOUT IT.
TIKKA TIKKA TIKKA
MORE OF THAT PARKER LUCK?
YAWN
I DON'T WANT TO TALK ABOUT IT.
SEE ANYBODY THAT LOOKS INTERESTING?
KLIK
I GUESS I'M GOING TO TRY THIS INTERNET DATING THING NOW THAT I CAUGHT MY BOYFRIEND WITH THAT MODEL HE WAS TAKING PICTURES OF.
I SWEAR I'M GOING TO EVISCERATE THE NEXT PHOTOGRAPHER I MEET.
I DON'T WANT TO TALK ABOUT IT.
ZZZZZZ...
PARKER!
STOP USING MY WI-FI!
OSBORN MAKES THE CATCH! YANKEES WIN!
MATCH.CON
BRIAN REED writer
YANICK PAQUETTE pencils
MARK FARMER inks
NATHAN FAIRBAIRN colors
VC's JOE CARAMAGNA letters
The End

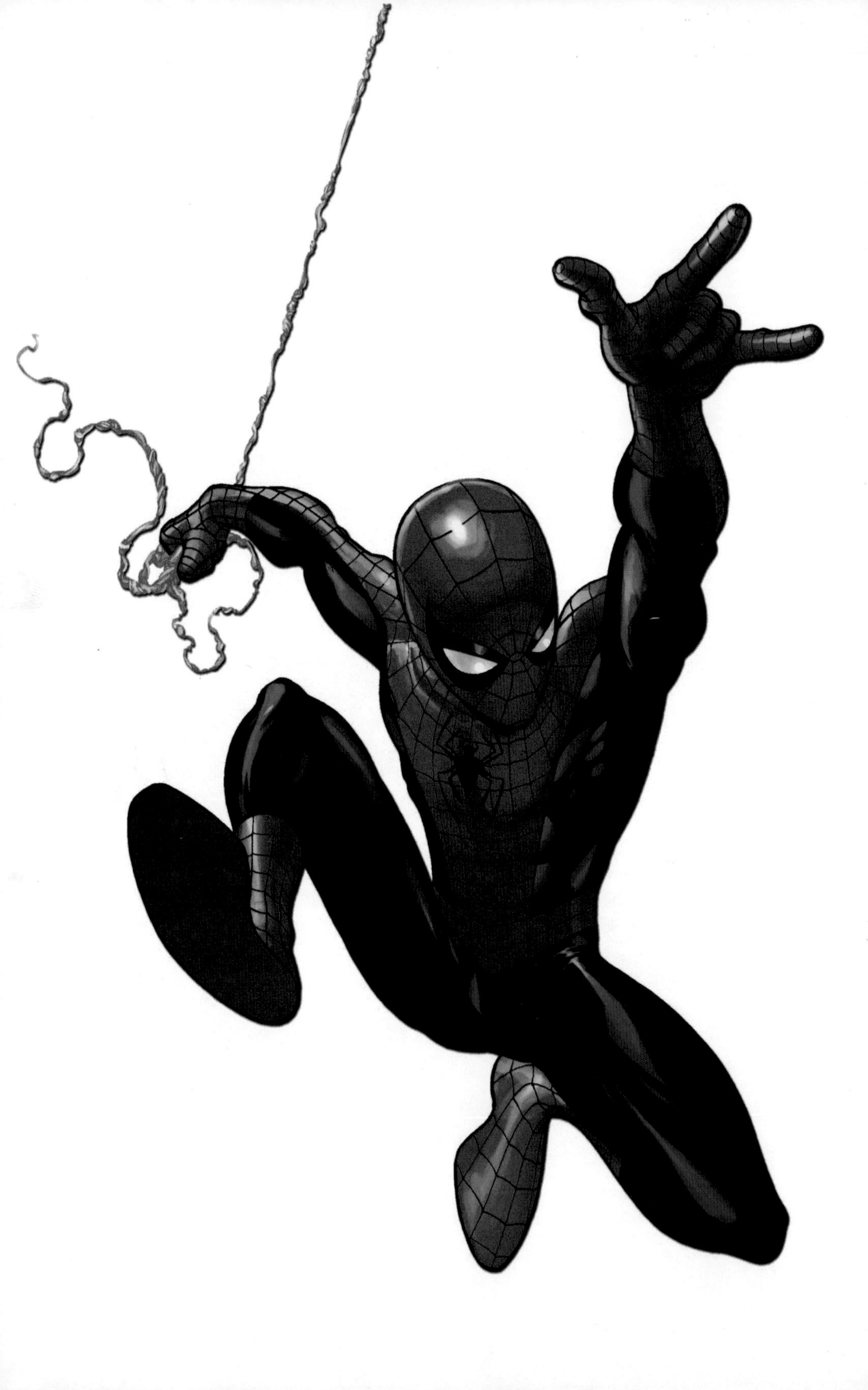

AMAZING SPIDER-MAN #602 70TH ANNIVERSARY FRAME VARIANT

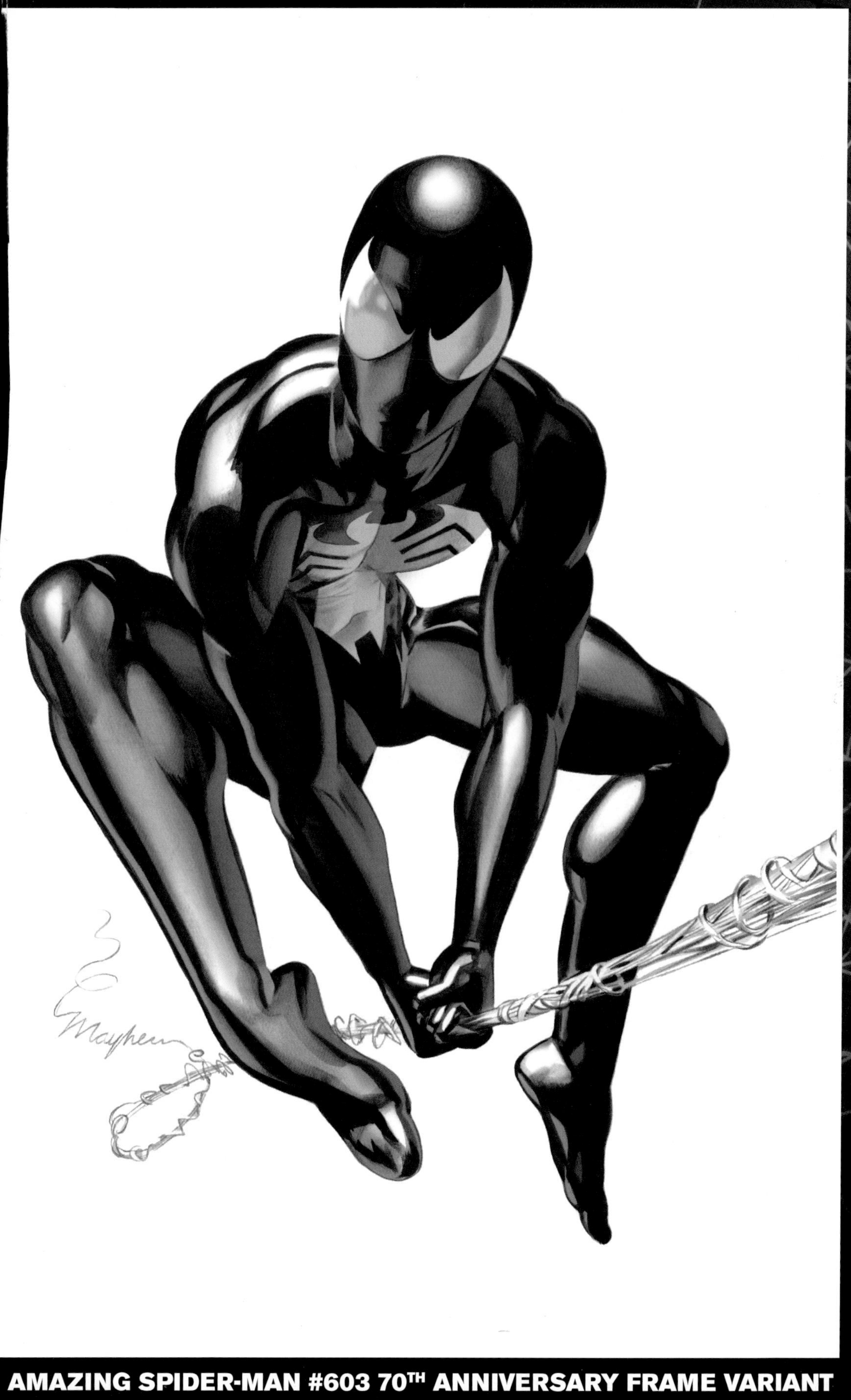

AMAZING SPIDER-MAN #603 70TH ANNIVERSARY FRAME VARIANT
BY MIKE MAYHEW

CHAMELEON

REAL NAME: Dmitri Anatoly Smerdyakov Kravinoff
ALIASES: Dr. Ashley Kafka, Dr. Turner, J. Jonah Jameson, Torpedo, Rick Jones, Dr. Henry Pym, Peter Parker, Captain George Stacy, Dr. Robert Bruce Banner, General Thaddeus Ross, Captain America, Kraven the Hunter, Spider-Man, Professor Newton, others
IDENTITY: Secret
OCCUPATION: Professional criminal, freelance spy; former crimelord, servant
CITIZENSHIP: Russia
PLACE OF BIRTH: Russia
KNOWN RELATIVES: Nikolai Kravinoff (father, deceased), Sonya Smerdyakov (mother, deceased), Sergei Kravinoff (Kraven the Hunter, half-brother, deceased), Vladimir Kravinoff (Grim Hunter), Nedrocci Tannengarden (nephews, deceased), Alyosha Kravinoff (Kraven the Hunter, nephew)
GROUP AFFILIATION: Formerly Exterminators, Sinister Twelve, Sinister Six
EDUCATION: Unrevealed
FIRST APPEARANCE: Amazing Spider-Man #1 (1963)

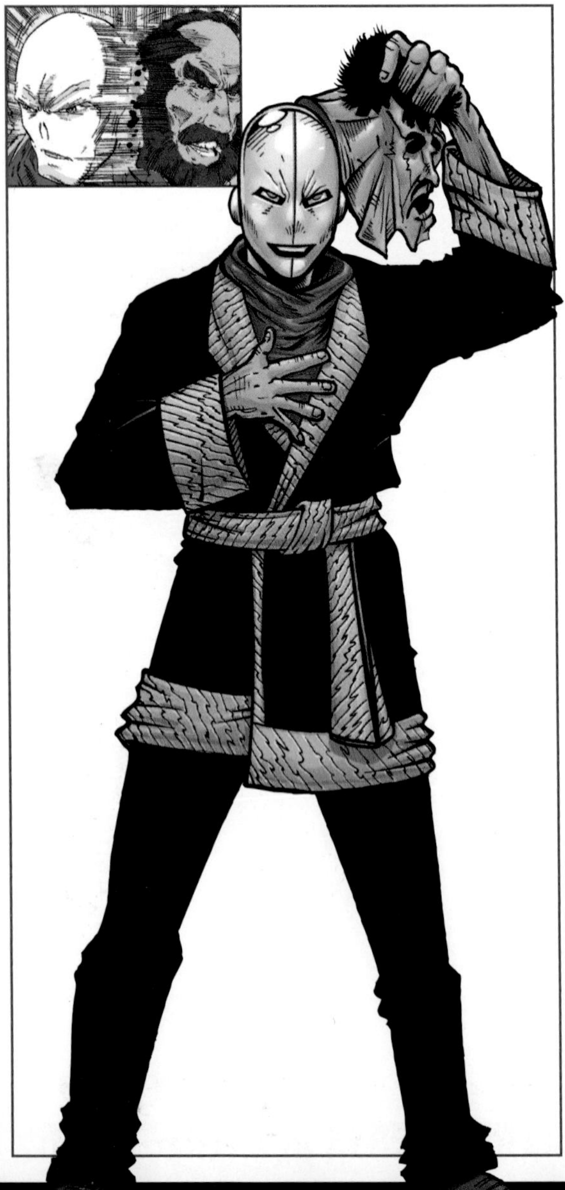

HISTORY: Dmitri Smerdyakov was the illegitimate son of the patriarch of the Russian Kravinoff family and a servant. His only friend growing up was Joe Cord, an American boy who once saved his life while his half-brother Sergei, the legitimate heir, and his father treated him with contempt and brutality. This scarred Dmitri so deeply that he repressed his very identity and came to believe he had been friends with Sergei instead. His loss of self led him to become a master of disguise and a Soviet spy. Initially without super-powers, the Chameleon relied on his skills and a mixture of costumes and make-up to conceal his identity. He wore a multi-pocket disguise vest in which he kept the materials he would need to mask himself at short notice.

In his first known appearance, Chameleon impersonated Professor Newton, a government scientist, to steal half of some missile defense plans. He then sent a message to Spider-Man (Peter Parker), electronically contacting him via his spider-sense, requesting a meeting and implying a profitable venture. Chameleon disguised himself as Spider-Man, though, and stole the second half of the plans, making his escape just as the real wall-crawler showed up. Spider-Man was at first framed for the theft but managed to bring Chameleon back to the police. Chameleon disguised himself as a police officer, scaring Spider-Man off by siccing the other cops on him. Spider-Man left the scene, thinking he had failed, not realizing that he had torn Chameleon's police uniform, allowing the cops to see the phony Spider-Man outfit underneath.

Chameleon was deported back to Russia, but returned soon after, having given up being a spy, and turned instead to a life of crime. Stymied again by the wall-crawler, Chameleon invited his half-brother, now known as Kraven the Hunter, to America to capture Spider-Man. The duo worked together, with Chameleon even dressing as Kraven to fool Spider-Man. Ultimately, though, both were defeated and deported by freighter where they bribed a sailor to set them loose in a lifeboat near Long Island. They came ashore right by Tony Stark's munitions factory and Kraven was quickly captured by Iron Man. Chameleon concealed his presence but decided to prove his superiority over Kraven by defeating the armored Avenger. Disguising himself as Captain America, Chameleon contacted Iron Man and convinced him that he was the real Cap and that the Cap at Avengers Mansion was really Chameleon. Iron Man and Cap fought it out until Giant-Man (Henry Pym) captured Chameleon and revealed the truth.

Chameleon quickly escaped prison and went to work for the Leader as his top lieutenant. The Leader sent him to New Mexico to learn the secrets of the Hulk. There, Chameleon impersonated General Thaddeus "Thunderbolt" Ross and Dr. Bruce Banner, stole a grenade-size gamma bomb and took Betty Ross as a hostage. Realizing he couldn't escape, Chameleon set off the bomb, which was smothered by the Hulk, dampening the blast. Though caught in the rubble, Chameleon survived and escaped, remaining in the Leader's employ until his boss' supposed death.

Chameleon next encountered Spider-Man after taking the place of Captain George Stacy who had been hired to protect a valuable art exhibit at the Midtown Museum. Peter Parker and Stacy's daughter Gwen were there and noticed that the Captain didn't seem to recognize them. After the exhibit was stolen and Stacy found drugged back at his apartment, Peter realized the Chameleon must have been involved. He persuaded Joe Robertson to plant a story in the Daily Bugle about a transfer of bonds and trapped Chameleon trying to steal them. Chameleon tried to escape through disguise but made the mistake of impersonating the one person Spider-Man knew to be a fake: Peter Parker.

The terrorist organization Hydra arranged for Chameleon's escape from prison so that he could impersonate Dr. Henry Pym and steal Pym's research combating their biological weapon Virus Nine. Pym, as Ant-Man, teamed with the Hulk and thwarted Chameleon, though it

Art by Sal Buscema with Todd McFarlane (inset)

appeared at the time that Chameleon had murdered Bruce Banner. Later, Chameleon impersonated Spider-Man, attempting to free his friend Joe Cord from the New York Men's Detention Center. Accidentally striking the Hulk with his car, Chameleon quickly disguised himself as Hulk's friend Rick Jones and convinced the green goliath to break Joe out of jail. However, in a battle with police, Joe protected Chameleon from gunfire and was killed.

Designing a new costume that could instantly duplicate any clothing, Chameleon went back to crime. He was pursued after a jewel heist by Torpedo (Brock Jones) and Daredevil. His quick-changes failed to help him since Daredevil tracked him by his heartbeat. His next costume innovation used a holographic belt that stored the appearances of people he came into contact with and allowed him to take on their look. In one encounter, he managed to convince people that Spider-Man had attacked an old lady, leaving the wall-crawler's newly restored reputation in tatters. Later he obtained further powers by using a serum that could let him change his appearance at will. This liquid actually allowed his skin to be flexible enough to shift its appearance into any disguise Chameleon desired. He tried to kidnap a top scientist but was again thwarted by Spider-Man.

Chameleon then set his sights on ruling the New York underworld. He kidnapped publisher J. Jonah Jameson, impersonating him him in a long-term bid to influence events through the Bugle, and formed an alliance with Hammerhead. The Kingpin of Crime was embroiled in a power struggle with the werewolf Lobo Brothers. Chameleon and Hammerhead tried to instigate a full-on gang war, from which they would pick up the pieces. Chameleon, posing as Jameson, injected Spider-Man with a potion that left him unconscious for several days. Recovering, Spider-Man went after Jameson and discovered he was the Chameleon all along. Hammerhead and Chameleon's plans continued as they ambushed the Lobo Brothers and Kingpin during peace talks. After carving up the city into territories they each agreed to control, their alliance collapsed and their influence waned.

Soon after, Chameleon took the guise of Dr. Turner and persuaded Spider-Man to subject himself to a machine that supposedly would analyze his spider-powers. The machine, designed by the Tinkerer, ended up temporarily removing the wall-crawler's abilities instead. After discussing it with Mary Jane, Spider-Man decided to have his powers removed permanently. Now powerless, Spider-Man was attacked by Tarantula (Luis Alvarez) and Scorpion and needed the Black Cat's help to survive. Changing his mind, Spider-Man searched for Dr. Turner, eventually realizing he was actually Chameleon, by which time his powers returned naturally.

The Chameleon's next big plan was set up by the Green Goblin (Harry Osborn) before his death. The Goblin persuaded Chameleon to create two robots that would appear to be Peter Parker's dead parents in an effort to get Peter to tell them who Spider-Man really was. The Goblin already knew Spider-Man's identity but wanted to mess with Peter's head so he convinced Chameleon that Parker, due to all the photos he had taken, was sure to know Spider-Man's identity. When Spider-Man discovered the fraud, he went crazy with rage and disappointment at losing his parents again. The Chameleon escaped to Kraven's old mansion while Spider-Man hunted him down. Faced with a more fearsome and vicious Spider-Man than ever before, Chameleon's repressed memories of his unhappy childhood with Sergei returned and he fell into a coma-like state.

The Chameleon was taken to Ravencroft Institute but escaped after assuming the identity of his doctor, Ashley Kafka. He kidnapped Spider-Man and unmasked him, finally understanding why Spider-Man had been so mad after discovering the robot parents. Chameleon imprisoned Peter and convinced him he was a writer named Herbert Smith who was incarcerated in an insane asylum. Chameleon then took on the role of Peter himself but was foiled by Mary Jane, armed with a baseball bat, who knew her husband too well to fall for the impersonation. Escaping, he was shot by his nephew Alyosha Kravinoff, who said there could only be one Kravinoff in the world. Chameleon again barely survived. Later, he arranged to meet Spider-Man on top of the Brooklyn Bridge, wanting to make up for his crimes. There, he tried to commit suicide by jumping. Spider-Man blamed himself for this apparent death but Chameleon somehow survived.

Chameleon was a new addition during a gathering of the Sinister Six, formed as part of an elaborate, yet ultimately failed plot to destroy Spider-Man and gain immeasurable wealth by destroying the world's monetary system. He was later recommitted to Ravencroft. Following a time he believed himself to be Sergei, Chameleon joined Norman Osborn's short-lived Sinister Twelve after Osborn coerced Spider-Man into liberating him from prison. Members of the Avengers and Fantastic Four rescued Spider-Man and defeated the Twelve. When Spider-Man publicly revealed his secret identity as part of the Superhuman Registration Act, Chameleon formed a team called the Exterminators who distracted Spider-Man at Liz Allan's home while he, disguised as Peter, targeted Aunt May.

May detected the guise and drugged the Chameleon with cookies laced with sleeping pills. Chameleon no longer knows Spider-Man's secret identity; a bargain Spider-Man made with the demon Mephisto eliminated all knowledge of Peter Parker's dual identity. After Spider-Man publicly revealed his secret identity as part of the Superhuman Registration Act, Chameleon formed a team called the Exterminators who distracted Spider-Man at Liz Allan's home while he, disguised as Peter, targeted Aunt May. May detected the guise and drugged the Chameleon with cookies laced with sleeping pills.

Art by Keith Pollard

Art by Steve Ditko   Art by Todd McFarlane

HEIGHT: Unrevealed   EYES: Brown
WEIGHT: Unrevealed   HAIR: Unrevealed

ABILITIES/ACCESSORIES: The Chameleon can instantly change his appearance and imitate others so convincingly that practically no one can tell the Chameleon and his victim apart. His natural talents are now augmented with a face-changing serum. The Chameleon often employs masks, a multi-pocket disguise vest, a special costume that instantly duplicates clothes and a holographic belt.

POWER GRID	1	2	3	4	5	6	7
INTELLIGENCE							
STRENGTH							
SPEED							
DURABILITY							
ENERGY PROJECTION							
FIGHTING SKILLS							

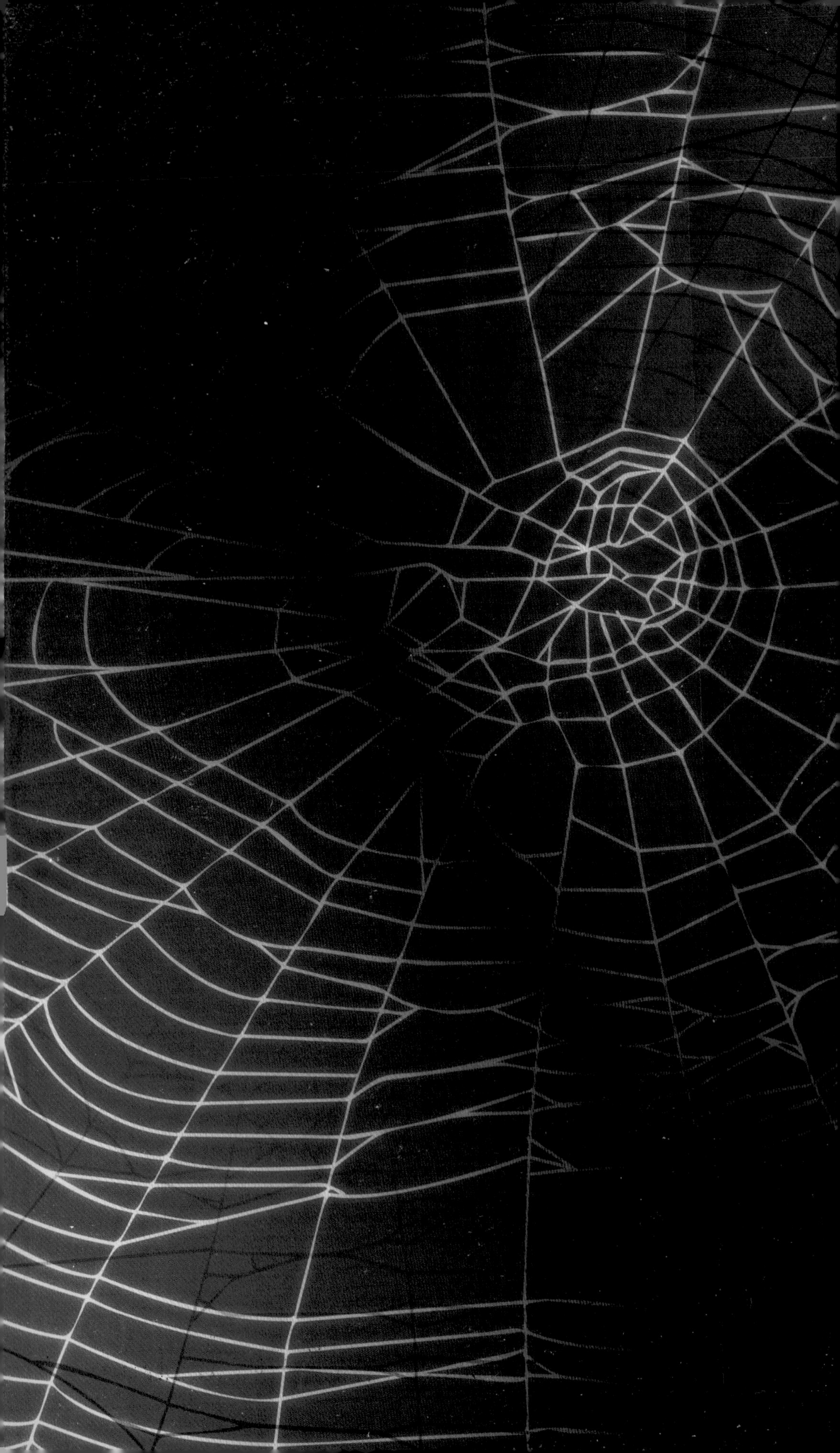